A Zillion Chess and Life Hacks

Maria Manakova

A Zillion Chess and Life Hacks
Author: Maria Manakova
Translated by Alexei Zakharov
Typesetting by Andrei Elkov
Photos in this book are provided by Yulia Manakova, Lev Makarshin, and Boris Dolmatovsky, as well as taken from the author's personal archive
Artwork, including front cover, by Maria Manakova using Midjourney
© Elk and Ruby, 2024
Follow us on Twitter/X: @ilan_ruby
www.elkandruby.com
ISBN 978-1-916839-11-3 (black and white paperback); 978-1-916839-12-0 (black and white hardback); 978-1-916839-37-3 (color hardback)

Contents

8

Index of Games

How it All Began

God knows why, but I somehow wound up as a chess player in my childhood. I learned the game at the age of four, and I did it by myself, just like Capablanca. I carefully watched my dad play with his friends, and then asked to play a game against him. He said, "But you don't even know the rules!" "I saw you play and figured it all out."

At the age of eight, I enrolled in a chess club, and I got a little bit crazy: I saw the whole world as a chess game, people and events looked to me like pieces and combinations played out between these pieces.

The smell of chess sets in the old Pioneers Palace on Stopani in Moscow, the pieces (varnished, known as "Grandmaster chess sets"), the ticking of the clock in the silence, the glare of mirrors in the playing halls – all this mesmerized me with its atmosphere, and I got stuck in this magical virtual world.

Back then, I didn't know that it would be for life.

In my childhood, I was a classical *Wunderkind*. One of those who go "wide" instead of "deep". Those who easily master anything we set our sights on, but after achieving a bit of success we drop it and search for something new. Nevertheless, after being touched by chess, I got seriously stuck on it for some reason. Perhaps because back then, there was not much competition in girls' tournaments, so I quickly started winning cups and medals. Besides, I was constantly surrounded by boys, traveled everywhere without my parents, played in endless tournaments and won... isn't that the perfect recipe for happiness?

Interestingly, despite having tons of talent, the fate of the *Wunderkinds* (i.e. us) is usually hard: only a few achieve real success in life. One reason, as I already mentioned, is a constant change of interests. But there's another, bigger reason – pathological laziness, a conviction that anything can be achieved without much work, simply by doing it. But completing projects – no, that's totally uninteresting. And while the *Wunderkinds* simply enjoy life for years, their peers work very hard and overtake them in all spheres where they shone brightly not so long ago.

The years go by, but I still "sing the summer away". If you are... actually... reading this book now, this means that, for the first time in my life, I did the impossible – I finally pulled myself together and *followed through* with my 10,000[th] project to the very end. And this is a true achievement, an even greater one than gaining the WGM title, which essentially happened by itself, without any special effort by me.

Maria Manakova in childhood.
Photo by L. Makarshin

Psychology

I have a researcher's mind — according to socionics (i.e. in Jungian terms), my psychotype is ENFP (bonus points if you know what that means). One of the characteristic features of that psychotype is an interest in psychology: the passion for studying people and social groups, physiognomy, gestalt and similar sorcery.

I've been reading psychology and neuroscience books since I was ten. At the age of 14, I attended the Young Psychologist School of Moscow State University (MSU); at 15, I made contact with certain people to obtain a pass to the Brain Institute of the Russian Academy of Sciences; and at 17, I lied about my age in a questionnaire to take part in a psychological training program for adults named "Prologue" (of course, they immediately saw through my ploy, but still allowed me to participate because they were charmed by my determination!). I finished school by writing a paper on biology — a paper on the human brain — and the subject of my thesis in the journalism school was manipulation and ways to combat it.

My mom wanted me to enroll in the MSU School of Psychology, but I always did what I, not others, wanted ("That's all because your dad and I never spanked you, but we should have!"). As I finished school, I got so deeply sucked into the chess world that psychology, among most other interests, played a distant second fiddle to it. Every day, my mom pestered me about higher education, and I once asked her, "Will you finally get off my back if I become a grandmaster?" She promised that she would. And so, I had to win the title. Still, my fascination with psychology stayed with me for my whole life. (I did obtain a higher education, too, but a bit later.)

Chess

Hosting a chess festival in 2011 at Luzhniki stadium. I'm playing against a chess computer with a robotic arm designed by Konstantin Kosteniuk, the father of Alexandra Kosteniuk. Photo by Y. Manakova

If I, as a grandmaster, was only interested in chess matters (such as, what's the strongest reply to ♖c8 on the 23rd move of the Cambridge Springs Variation of the Queen's Gambit), I would have become the world champion a long time ago. Among both sexes, you know. But I was always fascinated by something else — *non*-chess matters surrounding the game — while the moves themselves were rather secondary to me.

> *I don't believe in psychology. I believe in good moves.*
> — *Bobby Fischer*

And recently, I got thinking: why did this talented chess player face such trouble, why were my priorities so skewed? And then I realized. In addition to my fascination with psychology (and esoteric passions which I haven't yet mentioned), simple laziness was to blame. Yes, the same desire to enjoy myself that has played a defining role in my life.

I grew up on fairy tales and always wanted to find the genie in the lamp, the fairy godmother, or, at the very least, the golden fish, and have these friends grant all my wishes... or at least three... or one. Per week. I wanted to dig and dig, and then dig up a treasure – a magic key that could help me win tournaments without much effort, simply because I wanted to. A key which would work like this: I get into a proper mood before the game, and then I win easily.

Funnily enough, this happy-go-lucky approach *did* actually work while I was young: my energy supply was boundless, I felt like I could take on the whole world and win. I wouldn't touch chess at all for three months, then show up at some tournament completely unprepared and still score brilliantly because I was in the right frame of mind. I could eschew the tedious study of pawn endgames, which I hated; I didn't know them, but I instinctively avoided them in play because I was "in sync with my intuition".

However, when I got to forty, I realized that neither "self-improvement", nor the secrets of "psychological battles", nor the fiercest attitude at the board works without painstaking, well-structured chess prep. I am sure that the material I have put together for this book will be very useful in your chess journey, and not only, but it's still ancillary to the main ingredients – a passionate love for chess and serious, regular study.

A Zillion Hacks

My biggest advantage over Nepomniachtchi is
that I am better at chess
— Magnus Carlsen

Lately, my students and others have been asking me a lot: "How to eat properly before the game?", "How to get rid of unnecessary tension before the game?", "How to calm down after a loss?", "How to prepare, how to get into a proper mood, can you exert psychological influence on your opponent and how to 'repulse' their influence on you, is it normal to roam around during the game, or do you need to sit there without moving at all?" etc. etc. I answered all those questions individually, but then I felt that a book answering all of them at once would be highly useful! And recently, one "chess mom" told me, "I read that it's useful to eat protein before the game, do you agree?"

Really, I can't stand it anymore! So someone once scribbled or mumbled something about eating protein before the game, and now this phrase is passed from parent to parent like a precious diamond! But what about me?! Me?!!! I've been asking my coaches and grandmaster friends questions on these matters for years. And I didn't just write down their advice and learn it by heart, I actually applied it in my practice, and also "did my own research".

Therefore, I thought, the time has come to gather a collection of useful tips (lifehacks), where not only my students and their family, but all chess fans at large will find answers to these questions.

When I started to conduct my research for this book, I studied a huge number of tomes and online articles and saw that nobody else had thought of writing such a book. There were some individual tips in books, in social media, in magazines, on chess sites. I even found a book of short recommendations by an American chess journalist. But there was no fundamental work that encompassed *all* non-chess aspects of the struggle.

Furthermore, I don't just talk the talk, I walked the walk, too – from zero to the highest title there is, Grandmaster. Well, OK, I'm not the best GM there is, I'm actually "only" a WGM, but I honestly strived to reach the greatest heights of mastery! I'm still striving ☺. I know how the life of a professional player looks from the inside, not only from the tales of my chess-playing colleagues, but from my own career, too.

I have played at Olympiads, at both team and individual world and European championships, and I'm still an active player. I was a European champion and vice-champion in team tournaments. As an individual player, I won the

With Veselin Topalov at the 2016 candidates tournament, where I worked as a journalist

Moscow and Serbian women's championships, and also played in the Russian Women's Championship Superfinal.

I didn't reach the greatest heights in chess because my head was always full of thoughts about love, art, esoterica, some "research" and other things entirely unrelated to sport (I also always had trouble – catastrophic trouble – with self-discipline). I can't give you any deep analysis of an opening variation or complicated endgames – that would be desecration. But I *can* share some information on what happens beyond the board, which will help you both to achieve success in chess and develop as a person. I'll do the best I can.

I borrowed a lot of quotes and tips from various celebrities, chess players included. First of all, I simply like quotes – not all, of course, but non-standard, witty stuff – and, secondly, I simply won't be able to express an idea better than them.

But I would like you to know that there's nothing in the book that I haven't encountered personally, based on my own experience. Like a true scientist, I have studied every lifehack presented here, and I guarantee that *they work* (in some isolated cases, where the lifehacks haven't been properly tested, I warn the reader, in which case further research is necessary).

The book doesn't purport to be an academic work, because all the issues are covered in a popular format, without getting too deep. It's more like a compilation of tips and reminders that guide the readers, and they are welcome to study a particular subject academically should they have the desire.

This book is also intended for those people who are interested not so much in chess moves, but in the chess world and its inhabitants, because I discuss the latter's problems a lot, describe them and their life, and consider some real-life cases.

There are a few chess games and fragments in the book. In rare cases, I used them as examples. On the other hand, there's a lot of chess jargon in it. Don't be afraid, I'm sure it'll come in handy in case you ever find yourself in chess-playing company. Chess professionals speak that jargon exclusively, and you'll be able to pass as "one of the guys" rather than resembling a fish out of water. I'll explain the meaning of especially weird-looking terms.

Vanya

I had a student once, a teenaged boy named Vanya (Ivan). We worked together for several years, and he achieved superb results: he became a great IT specialist and enrolled in one of the best universities in Russia. Vanya was an ideal student for me: he didn't want to become a world champion, but enjoyed his chess progress. His parents didn't interfere with our lessons, only paid, he set his own schedule and loved chess loads. And he reflected on everything we did. He could ask, for instance, "Why do we need this subject matter, maybe let's instead improve this weakness of mine?", or "I need to take a rest from chess for a couple of weeks," or "Send as many endgame studies as possible..." All in all, he actively participated in his growth rather than being a silent and obedient consumer of services.

This is especially valuable for me because I'm that stupid kind of coach who cares more about my student's intellectual development and positive human qualities than actual chess progress. That's why I wave away anyone who tries to call me a "coach" and impose this role on me. I'm a teacher.

Of course I, like a true hereditary schoolmarm, managed to give Vanya various life lessons during our sessions as well. I consider my nurturing a contribution to his already great upbringing at least as important as my purely chess-related input.

Why did I tell you about Vanya? Let me explain. When I finally gathered all the material for my book, I needed to give a shape to this collection of words and values to... well, actually to make a book out of it. And I found this form: **the book as a lesson for Vanya**. I tell my student about the psychology of chess struggle, the psychophysical preparation for a tournament game, the principles of energy conservation and distribution, the mindfulness, the intuition, the ease and practicality of play, the fears and complexes that can rear their ugly head during a chess game, the qualities of a winner, and lots of other ideas. I also add some schoolmarm/life-coach tips, which are given in separate textboxes.

By the way, regarding those life-coach tips in textboxes. They were an easy fit for the book. We all know that chess is a microcosm of life, it radiates philosophy and mysticism. It was always a metaphor and model for war, life and even death, and everyone has been using chess symbols and meanings since time immemorial. So, I simply took a chess situation and then reframed it as a real life event:

chess → read: problem, task, goal
opening → beginning

endgame → end
game → work, process
time control (40th move) → deadline
move → step, choice, action
variation → a chain of actions
blunder → screw up
advantage → progress
lost position → dead end
and so on.

Thus, I created a collection of both chess and life tips: for personal and professional growth, solving problems, and achieving goals. Since all this life-coach stuff is likely not news to you, after all, there's nothing new under the sun, you may consider it simply a reminder as well.

Since this book is basically addressed to Vanya, I'll try to speak in a "youthful" tone as well. My observations show me that the young generation digests information better if it's presented in newspeak. Scrap the *Oxford English Dictionary* and *The Times* newspaper, they simply can't digest that kind of language. So... Keep Walking, as they say!: from now on, I'm gonna address you as though you're my teenage student and allow myself some unprintable liberties. I've censored myself as well as I could, honestly. But what's done is done.

Let's go!

This Book in a Nutshell

If you aren't sure about splashing the cash on my book and whether it's worth reading at all, I'll give you a brief summary.

First of all, it's a long-read. *TLDR*. Keep this in mind. Secondly, it's a real chess book. Moreover, it's a book on professional chess. Of course, you can read only the textboxes if you prefer. As I've already said, it's pure life-coaching advice there. Though, if I were you, I wouldn't buy the book just for that. But it's up to you.

The book is split into chapters according to the following principle: a chess player's problems *before* the game, *during* and *after* it.

BEFORE the game, a chess player should work up a winning mindset and a good mood, and maintain their fitness as well. You should avoid contact with toxic people, as well as going overboard with superstitions and other things that eat up your energy. The journey to the game and the last 5–10 minutes before the clock starts are especially important. A separate subject is developing leadership qualities in yourself. I'll also share my own way of preparing for opponents.

DURING the game, a player should manage their time, their mental state and the logical flow of the game. **Time trouble** is an evil, a malady, and you have to combat that malady – I'll tell you how. You should pay special attention to the last, most tense moves before the time control, especially the 40th move itself, and the first post-control moves, when your body relaxes and tries to go to sleep. I'll share tips on playing both in your own and your opponent's time trouble.

Concerning a **player's mental state**, it should generally be "Orange", or "Yellow" when the opponent is to move – this means that as soon as the player leaves home, they should be as aware and collected as possible (I'll also discuss Jeff Cooper's famous Color Code of Mental Awareness within this context). During the game, the **emotional state** can fluctuate because of unexpected moves by your opponent or your own ideas. I'll tell you what to do in such cases.

The player needs to **concentrate** and control their **energy** expenditure. It's important to know where and how to expend it. We'll discuss this as well.

I present the topic of the **unconscious** and the necessity of using it in decision making; I encourage the development of such character traits as **flexibility** and **tenacity** and also touch upon some **psychological problems**, such as premature relaxation or "intrusive thoughts" during the game.

Then I share lifehacks dealing with **conduct during the game**. I answer questions that to the best of my knowledge have never been adequately answered before, neither in print or online. Students always ask their coaches these questions, and their answers are usually based only on their own experience, which is sometimes rather scarce. The students will never learn any other answers anywhere, even though the subjects are very important and concern every chess player. For instance: should you run to the restroom during time trouble, or is it better to put up with your urge to go? Should you sit at the board while your opponent thinks, and, more generally, what should you do if they think for 30–40 minutes?! Should you write neatly or sloppily on your scoresheet? What's better to wear to a game? Should you engage in light **exercise** during the game? I'm getting a bit ahead of myself, but yes, you should, and I'll explain what kind of exercises you can do, and bring up the image of a chess player who unconsciously rubs his neck during a game, especially in a complicated position.

As I discuss managing the logical flow of the game itself, I'll give you advice on playing **pragmatically** and share some lifehacks from super-cool coaches I got to work with in the recent past. Instead of asking them about opening variations, I pestered them with questions about the **algorithm** of move choice. My friends later relayed me the words of one of my coaches: "Masha? We didn't even work on chess much, didn't analyze any positions, I never sent her my opening ideas. I just talked to her about chess." Well, back then I didn't know that I would write this book, but their tips have made it into the chapter about move choice.

The same topic of managing the logical flow of the game also encompasses an equally important theme of the draw: when to agree and when to offer one. How experienced players use their right to offer a draw as a cunning trick and how to deal with that trick.

Then we'll discuss handling **opponents**: over- and underestimating the person sitting opposite you, as well as how to combat the rather widespread disease of being overawed (or afraid) of famous and/or high-rated players.

I'll tell you about the **theatrical tricks** used by chess players – this is quite funny. Then, after some tips on following the **rules of chess** and demanding that your opponent follow them, we come to a discussion on **losses**. How to cope with one, and how to help a friend survive one, too. The last chapters are dedicated to **tournaments**: what kind of schedule should you keep, how to eat, how to fall sleep, how to combat bad luck, how to interact with journalists, whether to go to parties or discos. You'll learn how the great players relieve stress after the game.

In the final chapters, we'll discuss **cheating** and – oh horror! – various unfair tricks used by chess players, their coaches and tournament organizers. A toolkit of **dirty lifehacks**, so to say. Forewarned is forearmed!

I also should add another important point. As this is a book about how to achieve success, I need to explain what the word "success" means for me. Success does not equal popularity. I was once very popular, not a week passed without a media interview or photo shoot, but I quickly got fed up with all that hoopla. I almost physically felt how my public media image had separated from the real me and started a life on its own. I saw how desirable it was for people, how it was used by the media, how different it actually was for me, and how little spiritual value it had. I started to feel serious discomfort. And then I applied a hard brake on all that nonsense.

I remember one incident very well. A journalist from a well-known German magazine met me in a cafe for an interview. He asked the same questions I'd already heard from dozens of other journalists. He didn't even listen to the answers, quickly moving on to the next questions. At the end of the meeting, I finally figured out why I was here: the editors had tasked him with getting an "exclusive" interview with me, so as not to copy-paste interviews from other publications. They were interested in the FACT that they had interviewed me, not the actual CONTENT of the interview.
Dejected, I left the cafe, got back home and started crying because of that feeling that I had been "used and discarded". Afterwards, I told myself "That's enough!", stopped giving interviews and, obviously, lost the media's attention. This was a huge relief for me, and I've never regretted that decision.

That is not success. Success for me is self-actualization. Every person possesses certain talents, and it's important to express them. When this happens, the person becomes happy. And then – miraculously – they start attracting money as well. Yes, by the way, about money. I can't equate being rich (without happiness and self-actualization) with being successful.

Let me also tell you something about talent. Of course, talent is found not only in chess or creativity. Talent is everywhere, in everything. And everyone has their own talent, be that sport, or in a service industry, or deep sea diving, or piloting a plane, or vlogging, or caring for the infirm, or parenting, or even simply doing good things daily and making everyone around happy. Talent is doing what you love and being in your rightful place.

And God will ask: "You, who achieved nothing,
Why did you live? What meaning does your laughter have?"
"I soothed the slaves who were too tired to live."
And God will burst into tears.
(Igor Guberman)

Acknowledgements

Since I've been gathering this material for literally years, I can't, of course, remember exactly where I got what (I didn't even think about recording that before, because I had no plan to write a book). So, it's simply impossible to remember all the sources, sorry! Here's what I do remember:

Main sources:
1. My **coaches**, of course. I say BIG THANKS to all of them, and they'll understand why they were addressed.

I also want to remember my first chess teachers and coaches here: my dad, Boris Alexeevich Manakov, Viktor Konstantinovich Kott and Sergey Gertrudovich Grabuzov. They "uploaded" the essential knowledge and skills into me. After them, there was my late husband, Serbian grandmaster Miroslav Tosic, who gave me a very important lesson: "Forget about 'should', play as you want!" I owe my development as a chess player to these four. And the Serbian grandmaster Milos Pavlovic taught me my strongest weapon, 1.e4. He's great, too.

2. **Internet sources:**
chess-news and its chief editor Evgeny Surov
www.ruchess.ru and its chief editor Vladimir Barsky

3. **Books:**
Amatzia Avni, *The Grandmaster's Mind*, 2016.
Lev Psakhis, *Advanced Chess Tactics*, 2015.
Boris Gelfand, *Positional Decision Making in Chess*, 2016.
Mikhail Shereshevsky, *The Shereshevsky Method*, 2019.
Garry Kasparov, *How Life Imitates Chess*, 2007.
Reuben Fine, *The Psychology of the Chess Player*, 1967.
David Bronstein, *200 Open Games*, 1970.
Mark Dvoretsky, various books.
Rudolf Zagainov, various materials.
Lots of quotes from the chess classics.

4. I would especially like to thank the following people **for their ideas, thoughts and quotes:** Lev Psakhis, Boris Postovsky, Igor Kovalenko, Rashid Ziyatdinov, the late Alexander Nikitin, Yuri Gelman, Eduard Eilazyan, Artur Kogan, Alexey Dreev, Evgeny Bareev, Boris Gelfand, Alexander Morozevich,

Alexei Shirov, the late Yuri Averbakh, Igor Zaitsev, Roman Liberzon, the late Evgeny Sveshnikov, Alexander Indjic, Sergey Zhurov, Evgeny Dragomaretsky, Mikhail Prusikin and my student Vanya,

and **also** all the chess players, psychologists and sportspersons whose quotes I used in the book.

5. **Special thanks** to those who used persuasion, coercion, kind words, threats, blackmail, help, nagging, support, motivation, advice, tea with lemon, long talks or "that sacred word"...

...to finally force me to finish (and also start and continue) the book. These are:

Borislav Tosic, Igor Tsykunov, Moshe Slav, Sergey Voronkov, Eduard Eilazyan and Maxim Khantaev. Some of them will be rather surprised when they see themselves in this list. But I do know what stimulated me to continue!

6. I should probably add my sister Yulia Manakova and my friend Maria Kostyleva as well. They didn't know anything about me writing a book (I kept that a secret from almost everybody), but they still supported me even without the book.

My friends and acquaintances also supported my happy and productive state with their belief in me, heartwarming or useful talk, tips, intelligence, humor and good mood. All of them know whom I mean.

I love you all!

With Viktor Korchnoi, at a suicide chess tournament, Moscow, 2004

Before the Game

What a chess player needs before the game is above all a fresh mind, a good mood, and a healthy body. Then come a positive attitude and self-belief. Only five factors, but they are so hard to deliver! And their **balance** is so important!

For instance, as you prepare for the game, you want to recheck an important line just in case, and so you study it for three, four, even five hours in the morning, you're full of enthusiasm and raring to go. You think you should quickly and confidently win the game, but, alas, reality has other plans. Your mind is not fresh anymore because of all the chess work, and after you start playing, as early as the opening, you feel that your head is too heavy, and you can't clearly understand what's happening on the board. And so you lose.

This leads you to draw a certain conclusion, so the next day you go out for a prolonged walk to keep your mind fresh... but the wind is strong, you catch a cold, and so your nose is blocked during the next game and several more. You feel ill, your head refuses to work, and you lose to everyone and their dog.

Towards the end of the tournament, you seem to get better and decide to keep a closer eye on your health. You get up early, go running, go swimming, do exercises, but then you sit at the board and remember that you haven't looked at the Scandinavian (your opponent once played it). You start to worry, and... of course, obviously (!!!) your opponent plays the only opening you didn't prep. How can this be?! Did they somehow sense your fear?!

Thus, like in life, the ingredients aren't as important as their balance, use all in moderation.

And now let's discuss every factor separately.

Go to the game with a fresh mind and in a good mood

> Do important things in a good mood and with a clear, fresh mind

Boris Postovsky is the author of the "Fresh Mind Theory". The concept was likely coined much earlier, but he discussed it in the press a lot and advocated for it in practice, and so the theory was named in his honor.

The gist of the theory is this:

The most important thing for a tournament game is a fresh head and a good mood.

A good mood is a state when the hormone dopamine is rushing through your body. Interestingly enough, dopamine helps govern both happiness and motivation, the desire to act, to go towards the goal. Simply put, by improving your mood, you also increase your desire to win everything on Earth.

But it's not that simple to control your mood, you can't feel happy on demand. However, what you can do is keep your mind fresh.

A fresh mind. Chess players tend to forget about it a lot. A venturesome lot, they spend all their free time before the game on opening preparation. They simply cannot stop, assuring themselves that this line, no — that one and also this one — will deffo occur in the game, and you need to be prepared!

Nonsense! Every minute you spend on opening prep makes your mind more tired and fuzzier. Even physically, you feel that your head becomes heavier, as though someone stuffed a bunch of nails inside it. This, of course, does not mean that you shouldn't prepare at all. But there's a difference between "refreshing your memory" and "studying an opening". Researching lines, analyzing variations, coming up with novelties, finding cutting edge examples — you should have done all that at home. At the tournament, you simply check your notes and recall what you did at home.

Of course, I don't mean top-level matches here, where a full-blown "opening war" of coaching teams occurs, and the players must understand and memorize all the new variations in all lines — the fruit of their coaches' sleepless nights. We don't mean top-level play here, they've got their own atmosphere.

Ideally, the preparation must look like this:

In the evening before the game, you learn the draw. You study your opponent (you shouldn't spend your precious time on that on the game day), then choose an opening you want to play against them. In the morning, you refresh your memory with the lines.

Why is a fresh mind so important? Well, look. Even if you manage to "catch" your opponent with home preparation and get an extra pawn or a strategically won position (which is tantamount to a win on master or grandmaster level), you still need to actually win the game. Or, should I say, work with your head. And when your head is filled with hard morning work, and all you can think about is "how not to forget something" from your mess of lines, you lose the most important thing — ease and clarity of vision.

And so, the question is, **How to preserve a fresh mind before the game?**
1. Preparation time.

Do not prepare for more than three hours on a game day. Three hours is the absolute maximum! It would be better if you don't play a new opening. But if you do, play it from scratch, without any preparation at all. Otherwise, there's a danger that all the new lines you tried to cram into your head will turn into a mush, and you'll mix up the move order. If you want to study an opening in all its nuances, do it at home.

2. Mood.

You need to come to the game in a good mood. You can improve your mood with your favorite activities and some small fun.

You like sleeping until 2 p.m.? Sleep all you want, just don't come late to the game (of course, I'm talking about tournaments where rounds start at 4 or 5 p.m.). You like chatting incessantly, torturing everyone with your presence? Do your worst! Get down for breakfast — there'll be a lot of chess players. Buttonhole one of them and drag him or her "for a walk". You can usually catch some introvert who likes to listen more than to talk. They will enjoy the walk too, otherwise they would simply refuse the "torture".

Or maybe not. Such things do happen, too; afterwards, such poor souls usually come to the game in a bad mood, with their energy depleted, and lose without a peep. By the way, learn to refuse (this is a super-important skill!). If you know for sure that your companion will energetically "disembowel" you, say that you need to prepare — such an excuse is enough for any chess player to stop pestering you, it's the most tactful way to get rid of someone.

You like to lie in bed instead of going anywhere? Do that. For instance, Valentina Gunina would lie in her room before games at the European Championship in Slovenia and simply work on some embroidery. Embroidery, man! She confidently won that championship. You like taking hot tubs? That's actually a no-no, it doesn't help anybody. Even though... what if you become the first chess player ever whose head gets clearer after hot water? Might as well try.

Swimming on the game day is not recommended, but some grandmasters do like to take a dip in a river or sea early in the morning, before breakfast. And I achieved my best result at the European Team Championship in Turkey where I went into the sea before every game. But still, I did it before lunch. I also take a hot shower 10 minutes before I go to play — it invigorates me. This seems incredible, but I do get great results! Therefore, let's leave it in, too.

Exercise... Avoid strenuous exercise, but some light exercise (a run, therapeutic gymnastics, dancing) benefits many players. Walks in fresh air benefit basically everyone. But not everyone wants to take a walk before the game – in this case, if you feel too lazy, it's better to simply lie down like a vegetable in the garden and accumulate energy. It's better to walk to the games, this helps to regulate your breathing.

So, keep in mind: you need to spend your time before the game in a way that ensures a good mood and a fresh mind.

3. Sleep and Food

You'll need a lot of energy for the game. Five or six hours of play, with almost half of that time spent in total concentration, is no laughing matter! And in time trouble, a chess player may lose as many calories as a sprinter during a race. Where can you get them?

You can obtain energy through correct conduct *before* the game. This consists of sleeping, eating and the aforementioned favorite pastime.

Still, there are caveats: you should do the things that make you happy but help you concentrate energy rather than spend it. Taking a sauna, for instance, is a fun activity, but it saps your energy. Sex is recommended for women during tournaments, but not recommended for men, just like in any sport. Although some male sportsmen claim that they need sex in order to perform well. So try, experiment, study your own body. Information sheets for medications call for weighing risks and rewards. Let's weigh them: if your happy mood after an intimate encounter compensates your energy loss, then why not? You have an energy surplus. Let's leave it at that.

Sleep

I'll share an incredible discovery with you: you need to sleep at night. But if you do have some more pleasant plans than sleeping at night, go for it (well, of course, it doesn't mean that you should analyze opening variations all night long). But bear in mind: you can only last a few rounds in such a happy, sleepless, anti-healthy state. Then it will catch up with you. And if it doesn't catch up with you during the tournament, it sure as Hell will later. So I don't recommend rampant debauchery more than once or twice per tournament. But can I really stop you?..

It's not for nothing that all prominent coaches in all sports, not only chess, enforce a strict training regimen for their pupils – there are positive sides to it as well (I personally don't like strict schedules, but I do admit that they have a positive effect).

By the way, if you get all lovey-dovey during the tournament, keep in mind that it's not necessary to sacrifice your results for love. There's always the so-called "last night" – the night after the official closing ceremony of the tournament. Everyone goes home the next day, the actual play is over, the tournament has ended, everyone is relaxed, people have been sizing each other up, some of them do fall madly in love, everyone wants to prolong that sweet moment... And the real fun begins! Some begin their revelry the night before the last round, when they see that they have no chance of getting a prize. While the young guns simply revel during the entire tournament: chess? What chess?!

Still, you need to remain professional and give your 100% at the tournament. Well, stats show that you get the best results in this way (I invented these stats on the spot, just so you know).

Sleeping Before Games

When I was younger, I usually lost after an afternoon nap. I take a nap a hundred times, I lose a hundred times. But lately, my body has started falling asleep on its own accord, and so I have had to convince myself that this is normal. I sleep. I sleep like a log. And I have to win after that. So, it depends on what you tell yourself. Tell yourself that sleep doesn't affect your play, or affects it positively, and it will happen.

At any rate, you should remember that your mind must be fresh, so if you did take a nap, you'll need some time to freshen up — with a short walk, a shower or a cup of strong tea.

Most often, I just lie down for a time before the game, and then I "shut down" for a couple of minutes. This is a good technique, by the way. You lie down for half an hour, then take a nap for a couple of minutes. You feel raring to go afterwards.

Don't forget to set your alarm. Otherwise, something similar to what happened to us at an Indonesian tournament will happen: we ran around the hotel, knocking on our friends' doors to wake them up. (Indonesia is located in the Southern Hemisphere, and everything is reversed there — including the waking and sleeping hours. And there's no Polar Star either, which shocked me.)

If you don't want to fall asleep before the game, you need to establish a daily routine without naps two weeks before the tournament. Simply go to sleep only during the night.

Food

In the old days, they recommended vegetables and fruits, and then Kasparov with his meat appeared (he said in an interview that he ate meat before the game), making many chess players believe that it was necessary to consume animal protein prior to play. They are very insistent on that when you talk to them and can even get all wound up about it.

The latest opinion of professionals is that you must simply eat like you ate at home. You don't "have to" eat a certain food. What you must not do is overeat.

The best thing is a hearty breakfast, and then a light lunch before the game. If you eat too much, you'll become sleepy, your head will stop being fresh, and we must remember at all times that **a fresh mind is everything, our Alpha and Omega**.

4. Interactions

Humans are social animals, and they have to interact constantly with their own kind. But we know that there are two kinds of interaction: those that restore energy and those that sap it. Avoid the people who sap your energy. How can you identify them?

If you feel depleted and tired after talking to a person, your body signals to you that it didn't like this interaction. You shouldn't skedaddle at the first sight of them, but try to avoid long interactions with them. The presence of a coach or a family member at a tournament is good in this regard: they act like a shield, saving you from the dilemma: how to avoid feeling lonely *and* not fall victim to an energy vampire.

If Gayane [Mrs. Botvinnik] couldn't accompany me to a tournament, she gave me helpful advice: "Do not distract yourself with anything on the game day, ignore everything. Take a cue from Galina Ulanova [one of the greatest ballerinas of the 20th century]: on the performance day, she never speaks with anyone in the morning. Remember that humans only have one nervous system."
— Mikhail Botvinnik

Be positive, and you'll attract success

> Positivity begets success

This is the main selling point of all life coaches and their bestselling books on self-actualization and achieving success. Luck comes only to those who are positive, they say. This wave of positivity has become *positively* overflowing lately: it has engulfed the internet, commercials, the media... I so wanted to hide in a hole, to tell everyone to buzz off and just be myself. Horrible events in the world recently have somewhat toned down the positive vibe, and so we can examine it objectively, without much emotion.

The idea of positivity is very useful for sportspeople. Chess coaches have their own terms to describe it. Boris Postovsky talks about a "good mood", and Artur Kogan refers to it as "the *Ooh-La-La* state". The term *Ooh-La-La* encompasses not only the player's state during the game, but also moves that should be charged with that feeling. "And then, I made an *Ooh-La-La* move and won the game 10 moves later..." You should maintain the *Ooh-La-La* state even if you played like a total patzer in the opening and your position is beyond hopeless. In this case, you still have a chance to survive somehow. Otherwise, there are no chances at all.

Why does this work? Why do they say that you shouldn't even sit at the board if you don't have boldness?

In addition to dopamine, which I already mentioned, there's another important consideration. If you truly believe in your success, your unconscious kicks in. And the unconscious is capable of miracles. Your body starts seeking ways to win by itself, provoking your opponent into making mistakes.

> ***Be an optimist. Believing in victory means searching for a winning algorithm. It means believing that it exists even if it might not. The winning algorithm is the one that makes your opponent commit a forced error.***
> *— Igor Kovalenko*

Moreover, from a purely psychological point of view, the state of a "happy madman" deals a huge blow to your opponent. It disarms and paralyzes them — who can attack the holy fool? Harming holy fools is a great sin in all cultures and religions. That's the way it is, it's in our genes.

Well, and now let's talk seriously. Even if you lost while being cheerful and believing in your victory until the very end — is it really bad? You spent time well: made your brains work for five hours in a happy mood, which is good for your health. This is better than suffering. OK, OK, now I'm completely serious. Just be yourself, forget everything you just read about positivity. If you don't want to be positive, don't. Be a Stoned Fox or whatever. Staying in harmony with yourself is all that matters.

Prepare for battle

> You cannot half-ass an important task
> You need to have an intention to achieve the planned result

> *I don't play chess — I fight in chess.*
> *— Alexander Alekhine*

When someone gets really fascinated with chess and puts a lot of effort into their game, they, if possessing certain other qualities, progress to a new, higher level. They aren't an amateur anymore, they are a professional player. Chess isn't a sweet game with wooden pieces for them. It's now a sport, or, as Fischer used to say, "a total war". A real fight against angry and hungry people. And these people will tear their opponent apart if the latter doesn't prepare.

Preparation in the sport of chess is divided into three categories: psychological, physical and analytical.

→ Psychological Preparation
You are sure that you'll crush anybody, and that's that. Well, maybe not *every*body, but at least your opponent for today. And preferably everybody. Yes, it's an illusion, maybe even a delusion, but it works, I checked. If you can't prepare yourself for the game, you shouldn't sit at the board. Better go sightseeing – this will be time well spent, at least. Your "incredible chess talent", "genius" and "unbridled strength" won't help you without a decent mood, don't even think about it.

An important detail. If you're very emotional and have an inferiority complex when playing against famous and highly-rated players, it's better to prepare to play for a draw against them, not for a win. But play for a bare-king kind of draw, not for a perpetual check or move repetition. Such a mindset gives you a chance to win. I'll explain below why it works like that.

→ Physical Preparation
Your body is healthy: it can move easily, there are no pains and no strains anywhere. Your mind is fresh, you slept well, ate something light but filling, and the energy flow within your body is free, like a baby's.
That's the ideal.
And now I'll tell you how it really works (perhaps you'd really want to reconsider your decision to become a chess player). Regular game stress, mobilization and concentration of your entire body and mind are so great that they can cause both mental and physical problems. Add the necessity to sit for a prolonged amount of time in an uncomfortable, bent pose (both during play and analysis at home), and you can definitely say that there's no such thing as a completely healthy chess player. Thus, other sports and taking care of your body become all the more important.

All chess players without exception suffer from various forms of spine curvature.

Most of them have psychosomatic issues: during tournaments, they suffer from a lack of sleep and digestive troubles, and they often run to the toilet during games, because of indigestion or simply nerves.

Many drink alcohol or even become full-blown alcoholics. Thankfully, there have been far fewer of those in recent decades.

If someone calls themselves a chess player and they are neatly groomed, don't have restless legs and speak clearly, they are obviously an impostor.
— Ashot Nadanian

All these men showed considerable emotional disturbance. Morphy's illness was, of course, the most profound, and he gave up chess sooner than any of the others. Steinitz and Alekhine both had harmless megalomanic ideas towards the end of their lives. Capablanca suffered from extreme tension. (Morphy, Alekhine and Capablanca all died of sudden "strokes" between the ages of forty-five and fifty-five, which may well be related to the enormous tension under which they lived.)
— Reuben Fine

Brilliant talent — but a psycho.
— Daniil Dubov on Alireza Firouzja

Do you get it? Do some sport, movement is life, all that. The later generations of chess players make me happy with their attitude towards a healthy lifestyle: in older times, it was only important for the "chess elite", but now people en masse do understand its importance.

→ Analytical Preparation
You have masterfully convinced yourself that you are ready to play. There are no openings that you are afraid of. You know all the traps, and all the weird choices such as the Latvian Gambit or the Elephant Gambit. You have analyzed your last 10-move crushing loss and drawn appropriate conclusions. And you are sure that you remember how not to lose like that again. You know the key endgame positions, you know how to checkmate with a bishop and a knight, you'll easily outplay a rook with a queen, and you'll definitely figure out that complicated middlegame. So, your preparation is totally airtight. You are ready, and you are intimidating in your readiness.
Clearly, half of what I listed are just your fantasies that have no basis in reality, but the main thing is, *of course*, your self-belief. And now let's discuss psychological preparation more thoroughly.

Psychological Preparation for the Game

It's better to get pumped up for a fight at home. But some chess players seem to get going and become really fierce during the game. I think that they are driven by the very sight of their opponent (I am not, in case you wondered). On the other hand, ex-world champion Anna Ushenina (and not only her, Alexandra Goryachkina and some other players are notorious for it, too) stares at her future victim hypnotically before the start of the game, and the victim's bewilderment... what? Perhaps this bewilderment awakens Anna's bloodlust and maniacal "killer instinct". I don't know, I haven't asked her.

> *"How did you deal with Kasparov's withering stare during games?"*
> *"Well, this is annoying, because he first makes good moves, and then uses all those other methods of pressure. His moves were what made Kasparov dangerous. If he grimaced and made bad moves, we would have simply laughed at him. In our day and age, the importance of psychology is probably somewhat overestimated."*
> *— Viswanathan Anand*

Everyone tries to get psyched up right before the game, but still, the main mood-setting happens in your room on the playing day, several hours before the start. Players try to work up a desire to destroy their opponent, a feeling of superiority, a sense of their own importance. Of course, it's not that they suddenly come up with something along the lines of "I'm gonna go and destroy that twerp," or "I'm a Napoleon, and he's the trembling creature who has no right," or "I am the Strongest."

No, of course not. All these feelings and thoughts have long become a part of the chess player's nature. Now they're just preparing for the game, raring to go like a war horse, filled with desire to plunge into battle and taste some chess adrenaline.

By the way, take note: a normal, healthy person would be seriously worried by such "feelings" or "thoughts", and psychiatrists would even consider them symptoms that warrant a diagnosis. But they are completely necessary for a professional chess player to do their job. Well screw it, let's go on.

We really have to win? At any price?

> Your goal should be ingrained in you. But don't forget that you should move towards it with ease. Any internal tension only pushes you farther away. That's why mystics warn us: "The more you want to achieve you goal, the farther away you get from it."

Before moving on, let's discuss the question that every chess player and coach answers differently: should you set a goal to win the game or, on the contrary, not think about the result at all?

I always think, and I think how to win. Others like chess less than me and let themselves relax.
— Bobby Fischer

You should not strive to win! This is a surefire way to a loss. For some reason, in the vast majority of cases, people only think about the result: I must win, I must! Who said that you must? This thought — "I must!" — weighs you down and shackles you. You should chase this thought away! But how should you replace it? With simple things — play good chess, make good moves.
— Alexey Dreev

So, two big chess players (to put it bluntly) advise completely opposite things. Whom to believe? Should you think of winning at all costs, or should you forget about the result and simply try to make good moves? And why would the same coach during the same tournament recommend one thing at first, and then a completely opposite thing later?

Here's what I think. Dreev's tip is a more therapeutic one. Sometimes a player gets so overwhelmed by his desire to win that he simply can't play well. This is a common malady. And Dreev's radical quotes might come in handy here.

Many grandmasters know about that. Here's what **Boris Gelfand** said:

As a rule, I never ask myself what result I want to get. That might harm my play. I simply look for the strongest move.
— Boris Gelfand

The same thing applies to whole tournaments as well. An excessive desire to win first place, or to get a good result, often becomes a burden for players. Many have experienced that. Serbian GM Aleksandar Indjic once told me, "You should make yourself believe that it doesn't matter what result you get at the tournament. But this belief should be sincere, without self-deception."

But that is, should I say, a grandmaster-specific problem. As long as you haven't reached their level, you have to want to win, to sit at the board with the desire to win. So make this goal a necessity, a part of you. In fact, only people who develop that quality within themselves reach master titles.

Watch the **non**-professional chess players, those who play the roles of extras (and sponsors) at open tournaments. They are essentially amateurs, regardless of their title or rating. They love chess, and they play concurrently with their job or studies. A tournament is a feast for their body and soul. They don't have a goal to reach the chess heights (they actually think they do, but there's a difference between dreaming and setting a goal).

Look how relaxed their bodies are, how laid-back they appear when they get to the game, how unconcentrated they are, how picturesquely they move their pieces, how they walk about and chat during games...

Compare two halls of the Olympiad: the one where top contenders play – Azerbaijan, Armenia, India, Ukraine, Russia, United States, China – and the one where teams such as Burundi, Zimbabwe, New Zealand, Trinidad and Tobago and other amazing countries play. The "leader hall" is so electrified that you can literally plug in a generator and provide energy for a large city. The second hall looks more like a carnival: people run around, chat, laugh, hug each other, many are wearing national costumes and fancy hats, feathers, and palms with hanging fruit. Some four hours later, this difference becomes even more marked. The "leader hall" is still full, most of the games are still on except for a few quick draws. The second hall is almost empty! Everyone has already finished and is relaxing in their hotel or hanging loose at the bar.

That's why I advise my pupils to visit big tournaments and simply watch the players – they see how professional players act and can select good role models. Thus, I give you the following answer: Dreev's tip works for those who have already won master and grandmaster titles. You are already "professional killers", you don't just want to win. Your desire is so strong that it paralyzes you, depriving you of any creative chakras.

However, it's useful even for you to remember the will to win sometimes. Because life is a lengthy experience, and almost all professional players go through periods of reduced ambitions (because of age, a wiser attitude to life, love, marriage, birth of kids, other pursuits). And it sometimes happens that when a chess player returns to the board, they need to think hard to remember why they sat down at that table, what they need from it.

All others, non-professionals, should always listen to Fischer. Do not be an extra, be a protagonist, a winner. Dictate the play. Let others fear and respect you.

HE WHO WANTS IT MORE WINS.

Remember this rule and let it serve as your guiding star.

But there's a small caveat. It's incredibly hard to work up a winning mood for one tournament – you can't do that through sheer willpower. Sadly, it only works when your whole lifestyle revolves around chess, when your every day is focused solely on what is now your "fam". You can't be a "part-time professional". Therefore, if you do win a tournament despite not working on chess seriously, consider yourself incredibly lucky. Such things do happen. Indeed, it is always the case with me ☺.

So, in the following situations, the desire to win at all cost may be harmful:

→ When your desire to win **paralyzes your creative chakras** (I already mentioned this above).

→ When you have already **lost three games in a row**. Don't even think about immediately hitting back. You need to score a draw.

→ When you face a strong opponent and you know that you often play some **"active" anti-positional nonsense** against strong players. Play solidly, try not to lose, and the win will come.

Or it won't.

How pros get in the mood

> Important events in your life require the right mood. Some use images, music and atmosphere to get "in the zone", others require "magic words", a meaning that might motivate you. Choose what you like most and use it.

Chess pros, like warriors, always prepare to win, and every professional player has their own set of working methods. Here they are:

1.   An experienced coach or mentor who has worked with their pupil for a long time and knows them well. The coach knows when and what to say, how to avoid harm, what "magic word" will work today.

2.   If you come to a tournament alone, you'll have to pump yourself up on your own.

There are two groups of people: those with a "type 1" signal system and those with "type 2". People with the "type 2" signal system are better stimulated by an **idea**, a "magic word". It's easier for them to perceive the world through signs and symbols. People with the "type 1" signal system charge themselves up with **images**: listening to music, looking at paintings, or watching movies. It's known that Kasparov liked to listen to Vladimir Vysotsky's song "Koni Priveredlivye" ("Fussy Horses") before a game; I usually listen to rock music. I have heard tips from all sorts of players: you should listen to whatever music you like. But still, it's better to avoid relaxing music or romantic classics. You need to *psych yourself up.*

By the way, people in creative professions often psych themselves up by quarreling with those around them. I am prone to that, too. Before an important performance (as an actor, singer or TV interviewee), I turn into a vixen, and you should stay out of my way. Creative people usually have friends and loved ones who are understanding and forgiving after such outbursts.

For those with "type 2" signal systems, there are good videos available online. It's enough to search for "motivational video", and you'll find slogans such as "We are the champions!", "I am the first!", "I am the best!"

Sometimes it's useful to phone a motivator. I remember losing an important game in the penultimate round of the Russian Higher League in Voronezh, and I desperately needed to win in the last round to qualify for the Superfinal. I was so thoroughly dejected and hysterical that I had no chance to win. I called my good friend, a popular rabbi and talented psychologist. He spent a whole hour calming me down and motivating me. This spontaneous therapy session got coupled with a line in the Panov Attack that Evgeny Sveshnikov taught me, and — voila! — a quick and easy win!

Of course, every person has some elements from both "type 1" and "type 2" signal systems. But sometimes you need to simplify things to explain them. Psychology is a science, and it dissects people like a scalpel: these people belong to one group, and those to another.

By the way, let me say this once and we won't repeat it — I'm counting on your own intelligence. When a psychological article gets published online, it immediately attracts comments such as "Crap", "Bullshit", "What was the author smoking?", "How can you generalize like that?!", etc. etc. As I just noted, psychology is a science (even though not everybody agrees with that). Like any other science, it dissects, systematizes, classifies and names things. Were I to write something like, "Well, this is not about everybody, this is exaggerated, sorry if I offended anybody..." after every other sentence, it would be pulp fiction, not science. So, let's agree: I will explain trends and ideas to you, and you will treat them as trends and ideas, not as attacks or attempts to "offend everybody". Are we agreed? Thanks.

3.   Sometimes, after preparation for the day's game (or even instead of preparation, I have done that, too), you can play through some games of a player who inspires you.

For instance, I performed brilliantly in several tournaments in a row after playing through Garry Kasparov's games. It's possible that I catastrophically lacked confidence, aggression, readiness to take risks and bluff at the time.

Let's digress for a bit. Why did I lack all that? Where did it disappear to if I always had it? Here's where, and it's important: when you play in tournaments often or work deeply on strategy and endgames, you might forget the most important goal – to checkmate the enemy king. You lose sight of that goal sometimes, and instead of looking at the king, you get bogged down with weak squares, maneuvering, backward pawns and passive pieces, and you simply overlook an opportunity to attack when it presents itself. Kasparov's games helped me remember that above all, I need to attack the king. And they also got me pumped up. I should also add that my playing style in general is very aggressive. Always forward, to battle, towards the king, into complications, into rough waters.

With Kasparov's famous coach, Alexander Nikitin, Moscow, 2012. Nikitin was my friend and mentor, I adored him

The Goal

Not too long ago, I conducted an experiment. At the insistent recommendation of a coach — well, to be precise, he wasn't even a coach, he was a scientist who liked chess a lot — I had to think of myself as "I'm the strongest chess player! The cleverest! The most talented! I play chess better than anybody!" as I woke up in the morning. "First thing in the morning" was the strict condition. This scientist called me daily and asked if I was doing what he asked.

Uh, well, that's how it ended: I couldn't stand this stupid pretense for more than two weeks. I don't even know how I managed to last that long. I don't like untruths. So, I quit the experiment.

But directly before the game, you *can* engage in such "self-hypnosis" and try to believe that you are the best. I know people who benefit greatly from such an approach (as it turned out, I do not).

And there's more. For some, it's useful, in addition to general psychological mantras such as "I am the champion! I am the strongest! I, I, I! I am this and that!", to use some chess-specific motivational urgings. If you remember these phrases before the game, they'll help you to find the necessary combative mood. You can even write them down and look at them before the game. Paper does not cost you anything and weighs nothing, and you can carry it with you to tournaments.

Here are the phrases:
Sit at the board to win, not "to avoid losing"
Get ready to create problems for your opponent, not to solve yours
Crush your opponent
Dominate
Distance yourself from your opponent's behavior, maintain your own rhythm and mood

Let's look at these instructions in detail.

Sit at the board to win, not "to avoid losing"

> As you move towards your goal, cast aside the destructive thoughts of failure that slow you down

Do not even mention defeat in my presence. I cannot think about that.
— Bobby Fischer

The principle is simple: I am going to dictate the course of the game, not bend to my opponent's will.

Friedrich Nietzsche divided people into two categories: those who control life and events and create worlds, and those who follow the crowd and conform to circumstances. Masters and slaves. The former differ from the latter in one crucial quality, and this quality is willpower. Philosophers, psychologists and anthropologists have long argued over whether this quality is inborn. However, at any rate, willpower is like a muscle, and you can build up that "muscle". Maybe sometime I'll tell you how it's done.

There's no such thing as "I can't". If one could, others can too. If no-one could, be the first!
— Bruce Lee

Get ready to create problems for your opponent, not to solve yours

There may be obstacles in your way, but you should not fear them in advance or assign them too much importance in general. And you should navigate them without slowing down much. You solve your problem and then continue, as though you simply squashed a mosquito on the wall.

When I quit chess for the umpteenth time and then made another comeback, Magnus Carlsen was already a legend. I said, "Let me look at this highly praised world champion, what's so special about him? Why is he the absolute head honcho? His games don't seem too beautiful..." And so I thoroughly studied a random game of his, and his play struck me to the very depths of my soul.

Oops. I wanted to show the position that amazed me here, but I lost it. At any rate, it's not that important. I'll tell you the essence.

Carlsen's position was much worse, but he still had some defensive resources. For instance, he was able to get his king away from danger, or interpose from the attack, or close the position, or offer a piece trade... But from all of these depths, Carlsen fishes out a move that both defends his position and threatens to mount a counter-attack and dominate immediately. And then I figured it out: Carlsen is great because he is charged from head to toe with the desire to dominate, to create problems for his opponent, to play only to win. I don't know if anyone else from modern chess can equal him in that regard.

Crush your opponent

> Psyche yourself up for certain victory

Success most often comes to aggressive, self-confident chess players.
– Mark Dvoretsky

The desire to win, to be aggressive – this is the mentality I like.
– Hikaru Nakamura

I loved it when black was helpless.
– Gad Rechlis

Most elite players have a "killer instinct", otherwise they wouldn't be able to reach such heights.
– Alexander Morozevich

After I crushed them all, one after another, my superiority became evident.
– Jose Raul Capablanca

I like to make them squirm.
– Bobby Fischer

And now let's look at what Reuben Fine wrote in his famous book *The Psychology of the Chess Player.*

On Wilhelm Steinitz:
In Steinitz again the intellectualized aggression is brought out above all other qualities. He fought on the chess board, he fought in the chess columns, he argued endlessly with his friends.

On Alexander Alekhine:
Alexander Alekhine was the sadist of the chess world... Chess to him was primarily a weapon of aggression, a way of destroying the rivals he could not defeat in any other way...

Once he had a man down he wanted to destroy him; what he tried in real life with Capablanca he carried out in symbolic form on the chessboard.

At the same time, especially towards the end, Alekhine showed a marked weakness in defense play. Psychologically the reason is clear: he projected his own sadistic urges to the opponent, and feared the utter annihilation that he would like to have inflicted.

On Howard Staunton:
Aggression, organization and narcissism are the obvious threads which run through Staunton's life.

On Adolf Anderssen:
It is clear enough what role chess played in the placid life of a bachelor school teacher; it was his major libidinal outlet... He found all the players agreeable, the organizers courteous, the arrangements satisfactory. Everything else in life for him was secure and well-regulated; it was only in chess that he could really let himself go.

I don't want to upset you...

But I'll have too: without aggression, the most you can hope to achieve in chess is the FIDE Master title. Sorry, you won't go any further. If you're a kind, peaceful person, you should know your limits. And this limit is the FIDE Master title. That's all.

Wait, that's not all. If, on the other hand, you're a pathologically egocentric person, who bends your closest people, your farthest people and your mid-ranged people to your will, you've got a great chance of becoming not only a grandmaster, but even a world champion.

> **A good person will never become a world champion.**
> **— Mikhail Botvinnik**

Dominate

> Always try to look confident, dignified in your actions and thoughts. Dignity is a quality of kings

> *Self-confidence and the ability to convey this confidence to your opponent are the most important conditions for high-level achievements.*
> *— Magnus Carlsen*

There are some chess players who are awfully annoying to play against. Their behavior is so blatantly dominant that it is almost rude. Their opponents, if they are not experienced enough, often get confused and fall apart from the very first moves – their minds simply stop working. Like in an aphorism I once heard from Alexander Roshal: "He was born, lived and died without ever gaining consciousness." They come, play the game, lose after great play by both sides, and go home without understanding what really happened.

Such "rude players" are so dominating that they completely suppress the opponent's will to resist. They play rapidly, as though without thinking. They make moves confidently, and the moves themselves are charged with confidence. They largely don't linger at the board, they constantly roam around, watching basically every game but their own. They feel great, all their moves reflect their certainty of winning, and winning quickly. And they treat you as a second-class player who hasn't resigned yet for some unknown reason.

Of course, if such a model worked all the time, everyone would use it. This means that it has downsides as well, and they are serious.

As a rule, such players are rather shallow. They don't study their position deeply, they bluff often. At the start of my career, I always got confused when I played against such opponents, but gradually, a well-trained internal dialogue came to my rescue: **"Punish the scoundrel! Calm your nerves, treat all unexpected moves as bluffs, ignore the fast play and cocksure attitude. Play quickly too, but not lightning-fast like them. And the most important thing!!! – don't get into time trouble!"** Why is it so important? Because these clowns seem to hypnotize you, push you into time trouble and then quickly finish you off.

By the way, avoiding time trouble against such opponents is an important lifehack unto itself. Sorry, I have got a bit ahead of myself here – we'll talk about time trouble later.

Still, I would like to accentuate the upsides, not downsides of such dominant monsters' behavior. And I want you to master these upsides yourself.

Their domination consists of the following factors: 1) an uncompromising combative mood before and during the game; 2) an optimistic, joyful attitude and confidence in the eventual win; 3) fast and confident play; 4) the moves themselves, charged with constant threats and aggressive ideas.

Now let's list where they are lacking: in deep study of the position and work at the board.

With such an arsenal at your disposal, you will be unbeatable!

In games against inexperienced opponents, you might try this fierce playing style yourself, but don't go overboard with it, because it will be hard to reorganize your play later, when facing experienced players.

Another situation where it helps to be openly dominant is when you see that your opponent clearly lacks energy at the start of the game (because of illness, low self-confidence or some other reason). In this case, you can try to press them from the very beginning, going for a complicated opening and choosing the most aggressive continuations.

By the way, take note. I say "choose an opening", "choose a style", "change your tactics", etc. This means that you should possess a rich arsenal: from knowing many diverse opening structures to being able and ready to play in different styles. This is serious chess homework. Work on creating your own "weapons and armor".

Distance yourself from your opponent's behavior, maintain your own rhythm and mood

> Do not be an obedient brainless sheep, think with your own head, make independent decisions, do not let others herd you

What's the difference between a leader and a loser? (Nietzsche's "master" and "slave".) A leader is a successful person who is sure of themselves and ready to take the lead, who goes about life in their own rhythm, shows their individuality, sets the trends. Leaders either become entrepreneurs or go into liberal professions.

A loser is not sure of themselves, full of fears and anxiety, hobbles after the leader, prefers not to take responsibility but to deflect it onto others, or waits until everything "resolves itself", always presenting themselves as a victim. A loser is a hired employee for life. They accept the rules set by leaders and readjust their nature in accordance with these rules.

A child tends to follow their parents or teachers, it's completely normal. A fully-formed, strong person must be able to say, "Thank you, sensei, now I'm continuing on my own," but this doesn't happen. School and parents who are also losers turn them into a great voiceless employee, a serf, a cog in the big social mechanism...

OK, I have shared all this life-coach voodoo with you for one purpose: just so you know that only people with a leader's psychology can make it big in chess. They show their leadership nature both in achieving long-term goals in tournaments and in every game.

A ten year-old pupil asks me how to avoid being swept up by your opponent's mood and playing tempo, their emotions and behavior. Read your books, kids: a century ago, Capablanca already recommended "not to play quickly if your opponent plays quickly". But the pupil asked not *what* to do, but *how* to do it.

And it's not that simple, dear Mr Capa. The player with the stronger will simply forces the other to follow their play and their tempo, and this other player becomes almost hypnotized by their leadership energy and self-assuredness. But a meeting between two chess professionals is a battle between two energies with leadership qualities, where one of them eventually prevails.

Why does this happen? Well, for instance, one of the players is ill-prepared for the game or for the tournament, or they don't feel well – their psychological state is suboptimal, and this will be sure to affect their moves.

So, how to avoid being "swept up"? Let's adopt social psychologist Daniel Wegner's Ironic Process Theory. Let me remind you of its gist. How to stop thinking about some item, for example, a white monkey? (He actually referred to a polar bear, though there is a legend involving Nasreddin Hodja and a monkey.) If you constantly remind yourself, "Do not think about a white monkey, do not think about a white monkey," this means that you are basically thinking about a white monkey all the time. But if you start thinking about, say, a giraffe, you'll automatically forget about the monkey.

It's the same here. If you keep thinking "how to avoid being swept up by your opponent's will", we will surely get swept up. You should think about yourself: how to play confidently, happily and powerfully. But do not forget to train your willpower, concentration and time management at home. Basically, to win at chess, we develop our leadership qualities *outside* of chess, and vice versa: to develop leadership qualities, we *play* chess. A mutually beneficial exchange between chess and real life. Such things happen often.

Let's sum it up: in every encounter, you should force your game upon the opponent, dominate, play in accordance with your own mood. Be bold, self-confident, optimistic, tough and concentrated.

Remember!

> You made a mistake, analyzed it and concluded that you shouldn't repeat it? Why then do you want to go down that road again? Stop and think: are you ready to face similar consequences again? You do? Then go for it!

In addition to motivational reminders that we have just studied, there are other activities that will help you become fiercer and more assertive. For instance, it won't hurt to remember the mistakes that you make regularly at tournaments yet swear never to repeat. But then they happen again, and all of your solemn vows simply evaporate. Nothing of them remains.

So, I recommend you to play a trick called "Remember!" Remember, dammit, your most common mistakes that make you fail at tournaments. Set aside two minutes before you start the game to remember key points:

Remember! – How surprised you are at the end of every tournament: "Why are there so few rounds?! Just three or four more games, and I would have surely taken first place. Such a fool I was for giving away points in the early rounds." It's helpful to consider that – it's not too late to change something now.

Remember! – Why do you play chess? Do you have a goal, or do you just like to push wood? The latter answer (no goal) is much more popular and healthy than the former (I have a goal). What can be better than a person who plays strictly for fun? But if you have decided to become a professional, then fun should play second fiddle. The most important thing is the result. And you should think about it regularly. Pour more fuel on the fire.

Remember! – Analysis of your tournament placing. For instance: will a draw ensure first prize? Or maybe you need to win on demand to avoid elimination? Or you need to get a norm? Or you still have some chance to win a prize?

Modern chess professionals are characterized by their pragmatism and calculating nature. Of course, you can jump in with both feet because you only live once, but in this case, you may as well go to a casino rather than a chess tournament. In our times, common sense rules.

In an open tournament in Greece, I once got to my last round game, and my opponent arrived 58 minutes late (barely making the 1-hour limit). He didn't extend his hand to me and behaved rather rudely. After about 15 moves, he got a worse position and offered a draw. I, of course, told him to get lost[1], and soundly defeated him. After the game, his friends ran up to him and started patting him on his back and laughing, and he also sheepishly laughed with them. What happened? I didn't know, but they did: it turns out that I only needed a draw to get a full IM norm, so the guy decided to have a blast. He was completely sure that I was keeping watch over my results carefully and would be delighted with a draw the moment he offered it. But I had been swimming in the sea, enjoying walks, partying and didn't care about the norm at all. Well... why am I recounting all this? Ah, yes. Don't do that. It's unprofessional. Admittedly, this sometimes does help relieve nervous tension before an important game, but we'll discuss that a bit later.

Learn to be a champion

> If you go into battle, do not settle for background roles – be first

---

[1]   OK, I politely refused

There are no "second places" in chess, only first. All the "second places" are
alike, you can't tell them apart. But there's only one who is first.
— Alexey Dreev

A chess player can either be a champion or not. A huge number of chess players have won titles without ever winning a big tournament, taking second or third places at best. Hurray, I got my norm. Hurray, I got my prize. Hurray, I'm great...

I remember the words of WGM Galina Strutinskaya, a prominent chess player and official. Years ago, I asked her about my chances of succeeding in chess. She said, "Well, did you ever win a strong tournament? Yes, you did. Therefore, you have a champion's character, and you do have chances."

Setbacks on the way to first place usually happen in the last rounds because of internal fears and complexes: a fear of success, or, on the contrary, a fear of losing, excessive nervous tension, premature happiness (and, consequently, relaxation), an inability to finish what you started, a lack of self-belief, etc. etc. And so, the player gains second prizes, and people say that he "lacks a champion's character".

Sometimes, the nervous tension becomes so strong that the player's common sense simply turns off. Such things have happened to me as well, this is my lifetime diagnosis. But the most infamous example occurred long ago, in 1964.

The Women's Candidates Tournament was on. The winner was to qualify for a world championship match against Nona Gaprindashvili. If first place were to be shared, a play-off match would be played — although nobody knew where or when.

The legendary Serbian Milunka Lazarevic crushed everyone in the tournament. Back then, she was one of the strongest woman players in the world, and she was in her best form in that tournament. She got one point ahead of all her main competitors, and she had to face the American player Gisela Kahn Gresser, who had nothing to play for, in the last round.

Gresser came to Lazarevic's hotel room the day before their game and offered her a draw. This draw would have been enough for Milunka to qualify for the world championship match and most probably win it too, as she was an extremely strong player at the time, probably even better than Gaprindashvili.

But then something inexplicable yet highly instructive happened. Milunka refused the American player's offer and, of course, got a big fat zero instead (see the chapter on Caissa's laws). Alla Kushnir and Tatiana Zatulovskaya managed to catch up with her. When she finally grasped the magnitude of her mistake, the blow to her confidence was so enormous that Lazarevic only took second place in the triangular play-off. The chess goddess Caissa does not forgive such liberties. Success is enjoyed by those players who apply common sense.

When I interviewed her, she explained her actions as follows: "For me, chess was always a chivalrous game, not a place for haggling, and I couldn't let it down! I couldn't agree to a draw without playing!" That was her public answer. Maybe she truly believed that. But it was clear how painful that matter was for her.

Some chess historians explained her actions by suggesting that she wasn't allowed to agree to a draw with the American player by the Yugoslav secret police (this happened during Tito's reign). I don't believe in this version. The secret police and the Yugoslav government would have benefited much more had Milunka won the world championship.

Give your 100%

> Do everything you do with full commitment, give it everything you've got, plunge into the abyss as though it's the last moment of your life – regardless of whether it's craft, art, love or self-improvement

Initiative always belongs to the player who is ready to kill himself for it.
– Boris Spassky

Please don't go overboard, though. Otherwise, you'll overexert yourself so much that your physiological processes shut off (remember Dreev's quote).

Giving everything you've got is essentially the only factor you can truly control. You may not know the opening, the best plan in the middlegame, the important endgame positions – but you can improve all of that by studying. However, the ability to dedicate yourself fully to a cause is controlled by you and only you. This is the first characteristic of professionalism – not only in chess.

What constitutes the chess player's "100%"?
– Preparation for the game
– Time management
– Fully focusing on the game.

That's all. If you fail with anything from this list, then you feel even sadder after losing. Because these were the only things that you could truly control. As they say, always try to do good, because you don't even need to try to do bad.

Even if I have lost, I come home with my head held high, because I know that I gave my 100% (and maybe even a bit more).
– Radoslaw Wojtaszek

If "fully focusing on the game" seems too abstract for you, I'll explain: it means diligently calculating lines, not getting distracted, not talking yourself into decisions, pouring all your energy into play. In other words, don't half-ass it.

I can explain it with an example of my own that I remember very well.

Game 1
M. Vujcic – M. Manakova
Serbian Women's Championship, Bajina Basta, 2022

Black to move

This game had gone very well. I specifically went for this position because it accorded me a large advantage. I intended to play 19... ♖ac8 and calculated the line: 19...♖ac8 20.♗c3 ♖c4, and now my opponent can either protect the knight with 21.a3 or retreat with 21.♘d3. And then I thought that my rook's position was quite loose and dangerous. Hell no, I thought, everything is hanging in this line, it just looks... wrong.

This "wrong" – assessing positions with intuition – may be your saving grace, but also may be a trap. It's a trap if you're too lazy to sit for a bit and diligently calculate the lines. Pull yourself together and get to work.

I didn't fully calculate the ♖c8-c4 idea, did not analyze the "loose rook" position deeply, trusted my feelings and made a different move, **19...a5?!**, which... squandered the advantage. The great move 19...♖ac8! would have given me a huge, decisive advantage.

There followed: **20.♗c3 axb4 21.♗xd4 ♛b5 22.♚d2!** The position was equal. I still tried to find some chances for another ten or so moves, and then we agreed to a **draw**.

The "Forty Good Moves" formula

A great method for achieving a goal is dividing it into stages and tasking yourself with completing each stage competently. Then you progress to the next stage, and the next... Dividing the whole path into stages helps you avoid anxiety about the "difficulty" of reaching the goal, to take things a bit more lightly. The goal seems more achievable this way, and you won't be paralyzed by fear and will be able to give your 100%.

I have only one task: come to the game and make 40 good moves. No excuses such as "I feel unwell", "I'm not in the mood" etc. work.
— Aleksandar Indjic

Such an approach is useful for internal self-organization and motivation.

And here's another conversation with Indjic, as I remember it:

"The need for inspiration in play? What are you talking about? What inspiration? You simply need to come and do your job professionally. When you call a plumber, you don't need him to be inspired, you simply need him to fix your plumbing."

"But what if you're feeling awful? Will you be able to play?"

"When I feel awful, I simply reduce the water flow," (continuing the analogy with plumbers), "I try to play solidly. But, of course, if I get a chance, I will bite my opponent's hand off."

Manage your luck

Luck favors bold, self-confident, flexible and open people. If you aren't like that, try to fake it, and "the rest is technique", as chess players say. This might not work, but at least you tried.

Chess is a game that is based on precise calculation and requires luck, luck and more luck!
— Savielly Tartakower

A good player is always lucky.
— Jose Raul Capablanca

He is lucky, and you are not? His opponents blunder in the opening, and you suffer for six hours in every game? He wins the tournament, and you barely cling to the last prize of Euro 50? Why is it so unfair? And in general: why are some people lucky in life, while others aren't? Can you summon luck? Can you control it?

Modern life coaches say yes, you can. They even insist that luck is actually a **skill**. But you can only develop it if you have certain other qualities, which can be developed as well.

What qualities do you need? What do these guys say?

Luck, some say, can be caught if your thinking is "fluid" and "open". If a person is as stubborn as a mule and deaf to anything new, to any ideas that can overturn their worldview, they likely won't become Fortune's darling.

And, of course, you need courage. To "open up" your thinking in the first place. And self-belief.

That's all. Sounds easy, right?

Ah, wait, there's more. They also say that luck favors happy, easygoing, healthy, hot and pretty people. That's the soup mix. People who have it possess the necessary confidence that attracts luck like a magnet.

And if you're a deeply insecure nerd, then the gods of self-improvement recommend that you fake it, pretend that you're a confident macho. People will be attracted by this fake confidence – they'll want to talk to you, to deal with you... and this, in turn, will give you true confidence, and you won't have to pretend anymore. Something like that.

So, the algorithm is as follows:
1. You pretend to be confident, even if you hate yourself with every fiber in your body and think that everything you do sucks.
2. This fake confidence attracts people.
3. You start to believe that you are a genuinely worthy guy.
4. You believe that luck will surely come now.
5. Luck does come.
6. You give everyone Scholar's mates and Légal mates and are first to finish your games in every round.

But, you might ask, sometimes a person gets lucky, even though, in your opinion, they are "nothing" and not self-confident at all. Where's the fairness in that?

The world is unfair. Life is pain. Bear it.

Don't create a system of excuses

> Where there's two, there's three, where there's ten, there's twenty, where there's a hundred, there's a hundred and one — forget this nonsense. You're a human (and that's fantastic!), and only you can decide where you can break the "pattern" that you invented in the first place.

All chess players suffer from setbacks. *And God saw that it was good.* Generally, setbacks should help a person grow and move forward. But there are people who turn their setbacks and failures into complexes. For instance, you convince yourself that you simply cannot play well in the last rounds. Or in the first ones. Or two games per day. Or win on demand. Or convert your advantage. Or, say, you constantly lose decisive games.

This is simply excuses, it's in your head. A tendency to play poorly in the first, the last or decisive games may exist, but it's nothing serious, and only you can turn this tendency into an entire system, a system of excuses, and believe it like gospel. For instance, I have lost in the last rounds of a hundred tournaments, therefore, I'm bound to lose the 101st, too. Actually, dear, you lost the first five games in this "series" because your nerves were shot to Hell, or because you were simply weaker than your opponents on those days, and you lost the other 95 games because you made yourself believe that you were bound by a system that cannot be overcome: you can't help but lose in the last rounds.

If you recognize yourself in this description, here are some tips from me.

First. Understand that it was your own feverish brain that created this system that you believe in wholeheartedly — and that it has no basis in reality.

Second. Look for the root cause. Ask yourself *why* you lose in the last rounds, what's the true reason for your problem. Sometimes, the reason can be incredibly simple. For instance, the final round is always played early. You are used to waking up at noon, but here, you have to get up at 9 a.m.. Your daily routine is screwed up, and you're sleepy for the whole game. Perhaps it will be useful to get up at 8 rather than 9, and go for a walk in that extra hour to regain your usual form? Yes, you'll suffer from a horrible lack of sleep, yes, it's awful, but maybe you'll feel better after a walk? It's just an example.

Third. After you calmly analyze the true reasons for your losses, the system of excuses will fall apart on its own. You aren't a slave to your convictions anymore, you proceed as a free person ☺.

And some general recommendations for specific cases:
– To win on demand, you need to want it badly.
– To play calmly in decisive games, you need to choose solid openings and avoid time trouble.
– To convert your advantage, you have to thwart your opponent's plans and avoid thinking that you won't be able to convert the advantage. A tip from GM Roman Ovechkin. I complained to him once that wins come much harder to me these days, because aggressiveness decreases exponentially with age. Here's what he answered: "Yes, to win a won position, you definitely need aggression. But if you lack aggression, you should treat every position like a puzzle. You just sit and solve puzzles."

And the last advice. Try convincing yourself of the opposite. Something like, "I have changed as a person lately, therefore now I'm very skillful in converting my advantage." (Or in winning on demand, or now I'm playing decisive games like a god.) You didn't know when this change would finally happen in you, and so, it did happen just recently. Go to the game and win it.

Member of the Yugoslav national team, European championship silver medalists, Batumi, 1999. Also in the photo are Borislav Ivkov, Alisa Maric, Natasa Bojkovic and Ivan Markovic

Demons

The fear demon

You're not the center of the universe. No, actually: every person is a center of the universe. Everyone has the same feelings as you, everyone has their own fate, concerns, anxieties, fears, joys and sorrows. When a person says something, the sentence is born inside of them and is absolutely determined by their life up to then, and even genetics. It's the same with actions. But all people, without exception, want to be happy. Deep acceptance of other people with all their quirks helps develop an important quality — wisdom.

There is no surer method to encourage your enemy than to seem to fear him.
— James Fenimore Cooper

Named must your fear be before banish it you can.
— Yoda

Do you fear your opponent? Sure that you will lose to them? Here's a magic formula that will help you get rid of this feeling:

Everyone fears everyone

And a bonus one:
RELAX YOUR BOOTY!

Alas, I learned these magic formulas too late. Like many others, I thought that the whole world revolved around me, that I was the sole center of the universe, that I was the only one who experienced good and bad feelings. But then I suddenly learned that other players can be anxious too, that they also fear me (oh, such a sweet feeling!).

Your opponent is as human as you are: they can pretend to be calm, but there's actually a storm brewing inside them. An upset stomach, an entire collection of lucky charms, point counting, long preparation, consultation with the coach... If they are 300 points above you, don't believe your eyes if they seem calm to you. They are simply more experienced and skilled in faking their emotions. They may even feel worse than you: a draw is not a satisfactory result for them, therefore, their task is much harder.

So, memorize this magic phrase and remember it every time you feel fear.

Let's repeat again: *everyone fears everyone.*

The worry demon

> Being worried before an important task isn't simply normal — it's even positive. It shows that you actually care, and that you will be really invested in the task. This is adrenaline, it's your friend. If there's too much adrenaline, and it paralyzes you or pushes you in the wrong direction, burn it with exercise. If this doesn't help, study yourself closely: you may have ascribed too great an importance to the task.

Everyone is nervous before a performance, not only you. And this is good: it means that you do care, that you're not a vegetable. But sometimes chess players get so nervous that their arms and legs tremble, and their heads are totally empty. In such cases, they can even play 1.d4 instead of 1.e4, despite the latter being what they prepared at home. Or push the clock on the neighboring board instead of their own. They can't do anything right, their brain is turned off. Sometimes, to hide their worry, these poor souls play lightning-fast in the opening, and when they finally come to their senses, they look at the work of their hands with horror.

Something like that happened to me at an Olympiad, together with my opponent. By the way, there are two kinds of people when it comes to worrying: the first kind become catatonic when they worry, they are completely paralyzed, they can't think straight. People of the second kind begin to scramble for something to do, rush purposelessly and can't think straight either. My opponent, like me, belonged to the second kind: we hid our worry with erratic actions. In our case – with chess moves. When we finally came to our senses after this "nervous attack", we had already made about 12 moves, the position was completely incomprehensible, but only then did we start to play properly.

One of my students, a grown man, described his problem rather vividly. He asked what to do with adrenaline during the game, and complained that he had a similar problem with ducks. Yes, the actual ducks that fly and quack.

He's a hunter, and he often draws parallels between chess and hunting. He says, "Here I see the ducks, I hide and wait for them to take off, and I start shaking so much that... it's just impossible to hit a flying bird in such a state! And if your hands are shaking at the board, it's not that much of a problem (you can still grab the correct piece and somehow put it onto the correct square), but if you try to shoot in such a state, you will certainly miss. And my student often misses his quarry because he cannot control himself.

Of course, it's much better to watch your opponent shake nervously rather than be driven mad by your own worries. But the thing is, nobody can avoid worry, even you. Almost all chess players have experienced this. You simply need to understand what to do, how to work with it.

Let's see what Boris Postovsky says on the topic. His advice is directed less to players and more to their coaches:

You need to calm the pupil down, so that they go to the game in a good mood, understanding that they are being treated well, and they are off to do their favorite thing, and there's a hard, serious struggle ahead... First of all, walks are important, and certain conversations during those walks, too. It's often important to remind the anxious player of a brilliant win of theirs: "See how you crushed him?" This will reduce their worry. I also think that it would be good to sit with them half an hour before the game and drink some tea with lemon. The most important thing is to calm them down, make them less worried. And it's important for the player to understand that the result is not a tragedy, that they have to enjoy the game. What are we playing for, anyway? Perhaps none of them will become

a professional chess player, and thank God — the fate of a chess professional is
very difficult. As well as in any other sport. This is a really tough job, and a tough
career. But, as Botvinnik used to say, if you can't live without it (like Ivanchuk
or Shirov), then it's normal.

But what should you do if you come to the tournament without a coach?
Who can help you? Who can share that cuppa with you and hold heart-to-
heart talks? Moreover, it's all, *all* rather simple and obvious: "playing for your
enjoyment", "not a tragedy", "hard work"... But how to calm down?!
    Here's how.
1. Repeat all these platitudes about enjoyment and not caring about the
    result. Process is everything!
    If this didn't work, go to 2.
2. A cuppa with cookies, your favorite music, meditation (if you know how
    to meditate. If you don't, learn how), a pleasant walk, and life is great!
    If this didn't work either, go to 3.
3. Burn the adrenaline with exercise. You are so worried because there's
    too much adrenaline in your system. Too much adrenaline blocks the
    thinking process. And I'm sorry to say, but it's hard to win a game without
    thinking.
    In the old days, dudes usually worked off stress by chopping wood, now they
usually hit the gym. Actors do some push-ups or squats, walk in circles around
the theater or squabble with their colleagues before going on stage. Actors
and entertainers also have another lifehack: if you're in public, and it's too
embarrassing to do squats and too late to pick a fight with somebody, then you
can rub your earlobes or squeeze one of your hands hard with the other — this
also seems to help.
    It's tough for chess players to overcome anxiety before a classical game: of
course, you'll come around eventually, but there'll be more than enough time
to commit so many mistakes that your position will be unsalvageable. It's a bit
simpler with blitz and rapid: this is a kind of "exercise" in and of itself. Your
hand is in constant motion, your body is in constant motion, and this burns
adrenaline. You get back to your senses after a few moves.
    My body discovered its own way of burning adrenaline — turning up late. I
chronically arrive late everywhere — for planes, for trains, let alone for chess
games! Disheveled, tousled, I run to the board (or onto the plane), and I fear
nothing afterwards. I got there just in time for take-off.
    But you should not follow my lead. The body is late, but the mind fights
against that. Because being late is rude and unprofessional. I am sincerely
ashamed. But I repeat this conduct again and again.
    If doing all of the above does not work, go to 4.

4. Your fear has disproportionally over-exaggerated the event or situation (your upcoming game, the tournament result, your opponent's strength). Or, as Vadim Zeland would say, you have assigned **too much importance** to this event.

Such a situation often occurs in children's tournaments. Parents instill the feeling that this tournament (meaning: *every* tournament *ever*) is incredibly important. They treat all the results with utmost seriousness, and sometimes they even hit the kid if they lose (I have seen this with my own eyes) or abuse them psychologically instead of physically, which is just as bad.

If, on the other hand, the pressure about the importance of the event is not external, but internal to you, then this is actually a serious psychological problem, and you can't simply get rid of it. Try, perhaps, reading Zeland's *Reality Transurfing*, or even seeing a psychologist. For instance, neuro-linguistic programming practitioners have a number of techniques to combat fears and pseudo-importance: you could imagine that your opponent is a cartoon creature. Or if you ascribe too much importance to an event rather than a person, then try to visualize it as being smaller, and black-and-white... Read about it, it's at least interesting.

If even this doesn't help, go to 5.

5. If you have actually reached *this* point, then I've run out of ideas to help you.

What should you do if the adrenaline rush comes unexpectedly during the game, rather than before it? We'll discuss this in the chapter on emotions.

The computer demon

> Be careful with technology: excessive immersion in the virtual space makes the brain sluggish, deprives it of freshness, and lowers the objectivity of evaluation of events and of yourself. In working with technology, you need to have an "external controller", and you need to learn to play the role of this "external controller" yourself.

Turn off the computer already, dammit! Get back to reality! You shouldn't prepare for more than two hours (three if you're a grandmaster) before the game!

Remember: with every minute of preparation, you lose a bit of freshness of your mind. It's like Balzac's magical skin: the more you have of one, the less you have of the other. The more you prepare, the less strength you will have over the board. You should have prepared at home, and here, you must only refresh your memory.

The superstition demon

Superstition is a nasty, dark, harmful phenomenon, but it's not easy to get rid of, because it inhabits the most ancient part of our brain, its very core. Its roots go back to Adam and Eve (or the apes, if you like). But humans didn't develop their cerebral cortex over millennia for nothing – this part of the brain controls rational thinking. If you get superstitious thoughts, get your mind involved, it should help you.

My opponent prayed before the game. I haven't seen anything like that in my career before. However, it seems that his numerous gods were busy.
– Mikhail Prusikin

The most common explanation of superstitions is weakness of the human mind. Like, somebody can't cope, and so he asks supernatural forces for support. But you can't say that sportspeople are weak people. I think there's some other thing in play.

I remember Anatoly Karpov once saying (not the exact quote, I'm speaking from memory): "Chess players cannot help but be superstitious. Like pilots or people of other professions where your fate depends on a single moment."

Indeed, superstitions most often come up in people's mind in emergencies (there's a popular meme about a well-known airline, "There are no atheists aboard our planes!"). Therefore, many sportspeople, just like people who engage in extreme activities, have their own mascots and amulets. They can protect you, help you win. But, of course, they only help if you treat them well, regularly wipe the dust from them and don't forget to take them when you go to competitions, putting them into the prettiest and most expensive box.

Here are some quotes from the materials of sports psychologist Rudolf Zagainov.

"Are you superstitious?"

"Before the match, I try to repeat exactly what I did when our team performed well. The clothes should be the same as on that happy day. However, I feel I should do away with superstitions. They are getting on my nerves too much."
– Roman Berezovsky, former international goalkeeper

"I must admit: I've got a Kind God, a small ivory figurine I received as a gift in Magadan. I have taken it everywhere for the last two years, guarding over me

when asleep at night and waiting for me to return from the ski track during the day."
— Yelena Valbe, multiple cross-country skiing world champion

"For some time now, I haven't been paying much attention to all those calendars, horoscopes or whatnot. Humans should be above such things."
"So, you did have superstitions before?"
"I did, but I don't need them now. I think that I'm on my way to perfection now."
— Ludmila Galkina, track and field world champion

I knew a woman grandmaster who appeared completely normal. Well, for a certain definition of "normal"... She's a WGM, and is it possible to call a person who has devoted their life to chess normal?... But still, she looks normal. Yet she was completely obsessed with superstitions. Her entire mind was fixated on the problem: how to repeat the exact conditions of the day when she won, and how to avoid repeating the actions she took when she lost. Literally. "I walked to the playing hall on the left side of the street, then I took a turn to buy some chewing gum. I threw the wrapper into a certain trash can. I wore jeans, a pink sweater and underwear with blue polka dots. I bought pasta with two meatballs for lunch, but left one meatball unfinished... And I won that game. Therefore, I should repeat everything tomorrow — down to the last detail, the polka dots and the unfinished meatball." There was even a rumor that she insisted that the captains of the women's Olympiad teams call up only certain players to the squad, justifying it with their good form, even though the actual reason was different: she scored better results on her board in the presence of those other players. You should never change anything if you play well.

Well, this is a pathological case, but I must admit that I sometimes was overly superstitious, too. And here's how I managed to overcome it:

I have a useful skill — instead of fighting "evil", I make it "work for me". How to use the madness of superstition for your benefit? Here's how: this is a **great indicator** of your playing form! The more your mind clings to various silly things, the more nervous, unsure and irrational you are. If you're in good form, you simply come to the tournament to win it.

What should you do if your belief in superstitions becomes excessive?

First of all: even *before* the tournament, in everyday life, develop your self-belief and the ability to take responsibility. At the end of the day, superstitions are directly connected with the idea of responsibility. My observations show that those people who are used to making decisions for themselves and others are much less superstitious in general. Those who aren't as skilled in decision-making are prone to shifting responsibility to God, forces of nature, spirits or objects. The ability to take responsibility can be trained – there are many methods and lifehacks in books and videos. Most of them are next to useless of course, just staid phrases that calm you down and motivate you for a bit, but are forgotten the very next day. The only lifehack that actually worked for me was devised by a well-known psychologist, Mikhail Labkovsky.

Labkovsky has lots of followers, mostly female, but he has a vocal hatedom as well. Let me explain my views on this. I don't have "likes" and "dislikes". I have nothing in common with him. But if I see an interesting thought or idea expressed by a person, I take it, say thank you and go on my way.

He gives a practical tip: try training small things. For instance, you cannot make a decision in some small affair – say, should you throw away your old tattered jeans or keep them? Do it, make a decision! And, what's most important, follow through with it. Even if you make a mistake, even if you lose everything, even if you throw away your jeans and then, two days later, some Hollywood producer contacts you and says he wants to buy your jeans as a prop for a million bucks, just forgive yourself – you've been training! After a while, your head is going to start working faster and more confidently, and your decisions will become more independent, clearer and better.

Let's repeat: this should be *your* decision, and you should *follow through* with it. Don't look back, as you're used to doing, at the opinions of the people closest to you: that is their opinion, not yours, and they are different people, to put it mildly. Don't let yourself be swayed by your family and friends, no matter how insistent they are. You may listen to them with an open mind, so that your view of the problem becomes wider. But only for that. Public opinion should not concern you either – it can condition you to go with the flow, and you'll never learn to go against it. After a while, you'll start to enjoy making independent decisions, then it will give you a great rush, and then it will become a skill and a character trait.

But even if none of the above applies to you, and you are already the master of your life, a good leader who is able to make independent decisions, you're still not totally safe from getting stuck on omens and superstitions during tournaments. Because you're a wacky chess player, whose "fate" fully depends on that Karpovian "moment". You will still be dependent on supernatural forces because there's nothing more important in life than winning a chess game. Still, more psychologically mature people are less prone to superstition.

And now, to the lifehacks.

1. Getting stuck on the "omens" is a symptom of your nervous, irrational condition. Pull yourself together!

2. OK, you're not in good form. Choose *one* superstition (for instance, listening to a certain song before the game) and forget about all the others. Because if you believe in too many omens and symbols, you might as well end up in the nuthouse. The most popular "lucky item" is a pen, but don't choose one – organizers often forbid players from using their own pens as an anti-cheating measure at important international competitions. If you do have an obsession with pens, then choose a pen that you are going to use for years (tell yourself that you're going to keep it forever) and bring it to all tournaments where it's allowed. Never use a different pen, unless you need to drastically change the course of the tournament. In this case, it's similar to plunging into an ice hole (we'll discuss this further in the chapter on tournaments).

3. Challenge yourself: play a round without any omens or mascots. Taste the freedom, feel the rush!

4. Challenge yourself again: give opposite meanings to omens. For instance, I convinced myself in my childhood that if I accidentally knocked over my king (this is considered a bad premonition), I would definitely win the game. And this actually works, folks!

5. And the most important advice. Superstition is an energy eater. If you feel it approaching, fend it off with everything you can, do not let it take deep root in you.

The sweater that I wore when I became world champion? I threw it away. What I was supposed to do, keep it for my whole life?
– Ruslan Ponomariov

Chess players have their own religion

A certain justice exists in the world.
The commandments, conscience, retribution, honor, kindness, love – it's all about that. You also know about this justice, but sometimes you pretend that you don't.

I have interviewed a number of famous players about their superstitions. And here's an interesting thing. They don't obsess about "small things" such as lucky pens or jackets, as amateurs do. They only have one superstition – Caissa, the goddess of chess. (By the way, religious people like to juxtapose religion and superstition. According to them, superstition is bad, it's idolatry, whereas religion, on the other hand, saves a person from vain beliefs in minor things, giving him one big belief in one big God. Well, maybe chess players believe in Caissa because she is their goddess, and chess is their religion?)

Caissa

Your relationship with a chess goddess is not simple, just like with any other woman. There are things that annoy and offend her *(well, that is out of order!!!)*, and there are other things that she can even punish you for. Let's call them Caissa's Laws for short.

Caissa's Laws

These laws are known to all professional players, who try to follow them to the best of their abilities. I'll tell you about them using some examples.

Example 1

Maxime Vachier-Lagrave told journalists that he would qualify for the Candidates Tournament for sure and... of course he didn't. Caissa's law: **"When you say that you will win a tournament ahead of time, you usually lose."**

Example 2

A very ill Mikhail Tal symbolically participated in a round-robin tournament, everyone prearranged draws with him. Some guy, who had one of the lowest ratings, thought that he could easily beat the ailing Tal. Being able to tell everyone "hey guys, I beat Tal!" is so cool, isn't it? Of course, the guy lost, and not "just" lost! Tal destroyed him in his signature crushing style! Caissa's law: **"Do not be an asshole!"**

Example 3

You do something dirty to your opponent to win the game. You may win this game, but you will definitely lose all the others. And I noticed that some people like that eventually quit chess altogether. Caissa's law... probably the same one as in the previous example.

Example 4

You're scheduled to play a weak opponent. And so you start to openly disparage them. Like, he's a weakling, a sucker, isn't worth my attention, I'll beat him with my hand tied behind my back, there's nothing to discuss about the game! Caissa's law: **"If you are dismissive about your opponent, you'll definitely be lying prostrate before them, groveling to save half a point."** If you do manage to escape with a draw somehow, this is only because they are indeed weaker than you and might not be able to grind you down.

Example 5

And here's a story from Lev Psakhis as I remember it. He had a +3 score after four rounds at a strong open – Dortmund, 1989. In the next round, he faced the old and sick Efim Geller. Geller offered a draw, Psakhis agreed – out of pity, even though there was everything to play for in the position and he really wanted to play on. And then he lost almost all his remaining games in that tournament, and his "triumphant march" also continued in his next tournaments as well. Caissa's law: **"Never agree to a draw out of pity."** (This story is different from Tal's case, as Tal's participation was completely symbolic, just to make the tournament more prestigious. Geller, on the other hand, played completely seriously and even won the tourney.)

Example 6

The fact that Caissa punishes **dramatic, fanciful and pretentious moves** is known to all chess players. It's more a rule than a law, but the goddess is often remembered in such cases – always after a loss. If they win, on the other hand, such moves are usually called "full of talent", "worthy of consideration", "a non-standard solution".

Nor does Caissa forgive you if you ignore common sense – instant karma usually follows. And she inevitably punishes a player who does not dedicate themselves to her fully, unconditionally, without reserve. Generally, if you show any kind of weakness, she will definitely notice. She's a woman, after all.

Belief in the unwritten laws of Caissa hangs over players' heads like the sword of Damocles. Even the most reasonable and healthy players remember "what's allowed and what's not allowed" at chess tournaments. That said, maybe it's not a bad thing? This in a way facilitates ethical self-regulation in the chess community...

Analytical Preparation

Suppose that you have worked so well on chess at home that you don't fear any opening: everything is comfortable for you, you're prepared everywhere. You love endgames, and you navigate the middlegame well. You're the king of attacks and strategic grinds! We won't even discuss that, it's all self-evident. By the way, Botvinnik considered analytical preparation as one of the four most important components of a chess player's strength, together with chess talent, personality and physical health.

What do chess players do at tournaments then when they say that they are preparing? Haven't they prepared at home already?

They are preparing for their next opponent. I'll tell you now what this preparation consists of.

Preparing for your opponent

> Before the game, it's important to study your opponent carefully, but don't go overboard with that, otherwise you risk accidentally making them too important

When a tournament player learns with whom they have been paired, they need to choose their character of play against the upcoming opponent. The character of play consists of the following factors: the type of position, opening and tactics against that particular player.

Every pro player has a computer with ChessBase installed, and so they can learn literally *everything* about their opponent in about half an hour. And their performances over time can be found on the FIDE official site – you simply enter the player's name on the "Ratings" page and open their personal information. If you are to play only a single game against them, rather than a match, the following info will be enough: how often they play in tournaments; how long ago they played last time; what's their growth trajectory; do they agree many draws. And, of course, it's important to determine the player's style, i.e. the types of position they like and dislike. The easiest way to learn that is to look through their opening repertoire.

Don't spend more than half an hour studying your opponent. Professionals usually do that in the evening, before sleep, after the arbiters publish the next day's pairings. Why is it better to do it before sleeping? Well, first, because this information is technical and you don't need a fresh mind here: you won't need to find any creative inspiration or to make good decisions. Even if you're tired, you can still type on your keyboard and search for the needed information.

Secondly, it can be useful to "sleep with that knowledge" and get a ready-made answer from your brain in the morning to the question of which opening to go for. Thirdly: it's simply silly to waste your precious preparation time on the game day on such things. Lately, I have often tried a different tack: I prepare at night, before going to sleep, and don't even touch chess on the game day.

But if you're so much of a psycho that you could actually lose sleep over your next opponent, then it's better not to look at the pairings at all. Go to sleep in blissful ignorance, with a calm spirit and innocent hopes that everything will be all right.

I have to do just that at important, tense competitions. You get so nervous towards the end that the only thing that you dream of is getting some deep sleep, at least a few hours per night. If your raw nerves also receive the information on your next day's opponent, you are virtually guaranteed a sleepless night. So, see for yourself what's best for you.

Opening choice

> The start of your endeavor is exceptionally important, it determines the direction of movement. Be mindful of your first steps: did you choose the right path?

Remember what Tal said of Fischer? He said, "Fischer seems to choose the continuations that are not too active, but he knows them through and through." In other words, he chooses the types of position where he is in his element.

Of course, if you're trying out a new opening or a novelty, then use them exclusively, taking a risk with your result. But if you need to gain a prize at the tournament, rather than simply improve your game, then go all out to win points. Usually this entails familiar positions where you know all the plans and where you have already won dozens of games. Also, when you choose an opening, look at the tournament position, both your own and your opponent's.

If you don't care what you play (you either don't know anything or, on the contrary, know everything), then take note of your psychophysical state. Perhaps you're in a deep depression – in this case, instead of 1.e4, it's better to play 1.d4, or even better 1.c4 – English positions are so sad. But if you are in a frenzy, like a stampeding wildebeest, then play any opening that can lead to a quick mate: risk, adrenaline, sacrifices, all that kind of stuff. In such a mood, you can play literally anything, even 1.a3.

I am baffled by chess players who have a limited repertoire and never change it. I once prepared to face a woman grandmaster. I looked into the database: she'd been playing 1.e4 her entire life! *Her entire life!!* Don't you want to learn what happens if you play 1.d4?! Or 1.c4, or 1.♘f3?! No, not interested. She learned 1.e4 in childhood from her coach and just plays it all the time.

I don't judge her — on the contrary, I'm a bit envious. She knows exactly what she is comfortable with, she has studied all these openings very deeply, she's happy. I think she's also very happy with her husband. A dream wife!

Nobody ever "plays against the pieces"

> You want some "pure art"? Choose painting, poetry or philosophy.
> If you have a competitor, you, sadly, cannot get rid of them. You
> are in the same boat.

"It does not matter whom I face today. I play against black pieces."
— Akiba Rubinstein

"I never play against an opponent. I play against their pieces."
— Svetozar Gligoric

The history of these quotes is as follows. In the era of chess romanticism, it was considered "unchivalrous" to defeat an opponent, or, more precisely, that is how the idea was framed. The most righteous and noble way of playing was to make the strongest moves and win the game. Your so-called adversary was sitting there as your companion and opponent, but not an enemy. This was called "pure art".

Emanuel Lasker was the first chess player to treat the opponent as a person that needs to be defeated. He was the first to study playing styles and psychological profiles of his opponents in his preparation. The public, of course, disapproved at first, but then everyone acknowledged that he was right. All players started doing that, and nobody was ashamed of doing so anymore.

Still later, when players started going a bit overboard with their preparation, they engaged in all those self-therapy mantras: "I play against pieces!", "I don't care whom I face," all that stuff. I think that Gligoric and Rubinstein were so sick of thinking of their opponents that they tried to soothe themselves somewhat with those mantras. (But this is only my guess!)

Everyone prepares for everyone else, you can be sure of that! Playing against pieces is a cherished dream for every chess player, but, alas, it's hardly achievable: you always take note of your opponent's personality, and their title, and their rating... It's much easier for people with mental illnesses and autistic spectrum disorders (or borderline conditions) not to pay attention to their opponents: they are only focused on chess. This is their great advantage. Maybe that's why there are so many of them in our sport.

The image of the next opponent is very important for the modern chess player. Now everyone prepares for a game as a fight against a particular opponent, not just a chance to "demonstrate their mastery". You need to outplay that person, trample them over, destroy, tear apart, humiliate, break, crush, them. That's a joke.

Or maybe it isn't. As we know, some players don't just study their future opponent – they start treating them as a sworn enemy. The shining example of that approach was Viktor Korchnoi's. He could only play at his best if he was in an angry mood. There are actually many players who play like that – Viktor simply admitted as much, while others don't.

But such an approach is not for everyone. For instance, David Bronstein loathed it: *"Making yourself hate your opponent, sacrificing the riches of your soul for a point in the table, is a poor man's chess."*

Yes, not all chess players are motivated by bloodlust. Those who are motivated by the desire to rise above their opponent are more numerous. These two desires – to destroy and to rise above another human being (and the whole crowd) – are the main motivational force for any sportsperson. "Creativity", "search for the truth", and "beauty" are simply side effects. They can help you play better, but they can't inspire you to win.

Another great motivating force is **professionalism**. Doing what you do the best way you can. This type of motivation is usually characteristic of experienced, mature players. Chess players exploit their professionalism until old age, grabbing prizes in big competitions even if they've already lost the ambition to be the first and the best and any desire to destroy or even create.

What else can inspire a chess player to win? Of course, there's also the concept that can be described with the fashionable phrase, "Becoming a better version of yourself." Or, to put it differently, self-exploration, pursuit of Force and Mindfulness through chess. It's something similar to alchemists: they were trying to invent the Philosopher's Stone, a life elixir or a panacea, but essentially they were trying to develop their inner Force. I fully believe that this motive can serve as the strongest flavoring in the smorgasbord of "motivations" for many successful players, or even all of them. They wouldn't have achieved much without it.

Nevertheless, even if you are mostly motivated by your professionalism or your inner alchemy, there's still the imposing figure of the opponent facing you. And you need to defeat them.

The first thing necessary for chess struggle is the knowledge of human nature, understanding the opponent's psychology. In the old times, they only fought against pieces, but we also fight against our opponent — his will, his nerves, his individual peculiarities and, last but not least, against his pride.
— Alexander Alekhine

Avoid too much preparation

> Intuitive and reckless people do better in important tasks when they are allowed to be spontaneous, when the ability to improvise comes to the fore. Over-preparation can "crush" them. If you are one of these people, don't prepare for important tasks and meetings too zealously. Only outline the main goal and the stages, and then plunge into the unknown, jump in with both feet.

In the last few years, I lost 90% of all my points in games I actually prepared for. I didn't even use the computer for more than 70% of my tournament achievements — I improvised as I went along... I often didn't even know the name of my opponent until I sat at the table. ??? I don't understand it myself!
— Igor Kovalenko

I agree with Igor's every word. I also play better when I don't prepare. This is characteristic of intuitive players who love exploration and risk. Such players are constrained by preparation. They feel much freer and lighter when they aren't burdened with the necessity of doing everything "properly".

Who is your opponent, anyway?

> Appearance is deceiving, everyone wears a mask, the opponent is unknown, the owls are not what they seem.

The overwhelming majority of our tournaments are not big European or world championships, but simple opens. Often, after discovering the "low" rating of your next opponent, you don't even bother learning who or what sort of person they are. How can you know what sort of person they are by looking at the name and rating, anyway? The only possible way to know is to talk with your fellow tournament participants.

Such "known unknowns" can sometimes lead to an encounter with an unusual opponent, which you lose because you weren't ready for such a shocking swerve. I'll give you my advice for every type of bizarre adventure.

Opponent: A player who's drunk out of their mind and can barely stand.

Description: He falls asleep as you think on your move, and when it's his move, he suddenly awakens and moves his piece, knocking over the others.

Problem: On every move, you hope that he won't wake up and just loses on time. But he has some kind of internal alarm clock and seems not to think on his moves at all. You hope that he won't notice your cunning plans, won't be able to calculate difficult lines, will get into time trouble, will fall asleep during time trouble... there are a lot of hopes. But the dude *always* wakes up on time and makes the move. And his move is intuitive and strong. And you get increasingly nervous, you're angry at him, at yourself, at the tournament, at the weather, at the organizers, at the whole of humanity and this imperfect world.

What should you do?
I had the misfortune of facing a drunk opponent once. My chess friends warned me: it's a difficult test. The key advice is to play your usual game. The guy sees everything, he plays quickly, spends the remainder of the time sleeping, awakening and adjusting the fallen pieces. Do not be swayed by his behavior.

UPD: As of late, tournament arbiters have acquired the power not to let a drunk player enter the tournament hall. My story is a blast from the past of sorts. But still, let it remain here as a historical anecdote.

Opponent: A gifted kid.

Description: A child so small they have to sit on books on their chair so that they can reach the pieces.

Problem: You think that the little urchin doesn't even know all the moves yet, but this is an optical illusion. This child is actually a monster, a bloodthirsty beast.

What should you do?
Lifehack from Anton Korobov. *"There's a method to meet it! Patience and a waiting game! You suffer for thirty moves in a worse position, then you equalize, and then you win."*

Opponent: A person with some kind of condition.

Description: Anyone who isn't totally fit and healthy. Including those who are coughing or sneezing, those who are bandaged up. Additionally, a pregnant opponent.

Problem: Some of you might not care, but I simply cannot play because I suddenly get overwhelmed by a feeling of pity. I seem to want to make their already difficult day/week/month/life at least somewhat easier. Compassion guides me, and my aggressive pre-game attitude gets flushed down the toilet.

What should you do?
I still don't know the recipe. I want to play against the proverbial pieces, but I can't. There are no tips, they will all be misleading. Simply try to play chess. This is truly an ordeal. And not only for soft-hearted people (of which there aren't many in professional chess). It's not that easy to play against sick people even for the toughest of us. In this case, different emotions are at play: "Now I'll beat him without thinking!" Or, "She can't comprehend anything in such a state." Or, "He's making me uncomfortable with that illness." It's hard to remain completely indifferent.

Countless games have been lost to players who were allegedly (or truly) sick with cold or flu (and now, the fear of COVID-19 has also entered the equation)! Or to players who were "upset" to the point of tears or "dying of despair" because of their lost position!

Oh, and don't make the mistake of treating visually-impaired players any differently: you might think that they can't see anything on the board, but they actually see the position even better than you, because they've been playing "blindfold" for their whole life, and you haven't.

There's no sense in giving you advice until you meet such an opponent at the board and experience that yourself. I can only encourage you: hang on in there, bro!

Opponent: A woman. Women's chess deserves a section or two devoted to it, and that's exactly what I'll do.

Women's chess

> Men and women are essentially different biological species

Chess requires a huge expenditure of energy. I am not surprised by the fact that male players are stronger. They can better withstand overstrain.
— *Anatoly Karpov*

Chess is a very difficult sport. You need to be in a combative mood and good sporting form, and men are generally better at this than women.
— *Garry Kasparov*

Women play chess more aggressively and go all out. They lack the deliberate calculating attitude of men.
— *Alexandra Kosteniuk*

The difference between the sexes is remarkable in chess, but not any more so, to my mind, than in any other field of cultural activity.

Women cannot play chess, but they cannot paint either, or write, or philosophize. In fact, women have never thought or made anything worth considering. It's got nothing to do with chess, let's not kid ourselves.

What's it got to do with then?

In the first place, there is of course the fact that women are much more stupid than men. That is why women are totally incapable of amusing themselves.
Useful work, especially in its everyday aspect, is the field where women are at home.
— *Jan Hein Donner*

A woman will never be able to play chess on equal footing with men, because she cannot sit at the board for five hours in silence.
— *Paul Keres*

Bobby Fischer on women: "Chess is better."

Playing against a woman is a special kind of chess. I agree with the ironic opinion that women and men are actually two different biological species. They have different brain structures and different metabolisms. Men are better organized, and a thought that has started must be finished. In women's heads, there's controlled (or uncontrolled) chaos, jumping from thought to thought. This is natural and explained by their brain structure. Chess is a man's game, a logical game, and if a woman wants to become an IM or GM (without the "W"), her main goal is to learn to think "like a man". Basically, to overhaul her whole nature. Female players who do manage that play at a high level. They have managed to reconstruct their thinking.

But they can't reconstruct their bodies. Thus, with some caveats, we can still say that they are feminine. "With caveats" — because despite their fair, well-groomed appearance, they are only interested in the sporting result, and they subordinate all their life to this goal. Yes, a win is the most important thing in chess, but this constant striving for victory is something distinctly unfeminine. As they grow older, most professional woman players start putting family first. Nature takes over after all.

Women's tournaments are a peculiar sight. Position evaluations jump at every move — yes, women are that illogical and brutal in their treatment of chess. It's not a fun task to be a woman player's coach, let alone a captain of a women's team. You need to have a forceful personality and strong nerves. A captain of a **men's** team can tell his guys after two or three hours of play, "We're going to score +2," but a captain of a **women's** team, even if they are highly experienced, cannot say anything even if the team consists of full grandmasters and international masters. This person knows that at absolutely any moment, on absolutely any board, anything can happen for unknown reasons. The result will be unpredictable until the very last move.

On the other hand, there's something good in this for women as well: they can also suddenly play a brilliant game against a male grandmaster. Perfect,

logical, matching the engine's first line. Or, maybe, she's just in a good mood today, and she will tear apart any king that has the misfortune to be attacked by her. And today, this particular king happened to be yours, and it was purely bad luck to face this particular woman on this particular day.

Male players have also told me stories along the following lines: you are playing against a female and then she suddenly resigns. She shakes your hand without explaining anything and goes away, and you sit there flabbergasted. Later, you ask her why she resigned, and it turns out that she simply "lost the desire to play."

Since women are much more resilient, cunning and sly creatures than men, it's hard to play chess with them for this reason. For instance, you have a big advantage, and she forces you to relax by playing possum. But as soon as you let your guard down, a trap emerges all of a sudden, you, of course, step right into it, and after that, nothing can save you.

Another reason that makes it harder for men to play women is the fear of losing. It's hard for me to understand, but all men I have discussed it with told me that yes, the result is exceptionally important for them. This is important for their *manhood*, which, of course, I only know about from second-hand accounts.

In addition to this "manhood", men have another weakness – the facts of life. Modern female players have solved this simple mystery and successfully use it in their nefarious goals. They openly and blatantly distract their male opponents from deep thoughts with their appearance. It turns out that the sight of an attractive, sexy woman subconsciously affects men's brains. On a physiological level, it's nothing personal. Hormones fluctuate, the brain gets distracted, concentration lowers, and suddenly you're in too deep. Some women use this huge advantage very successfully.

In the last few years, however, men have found a solution to this problem – they simply and clumsily, in their usual style, introduced an obligatory dress code that forbids woman players from looking sexy.

More on dress code towards the end of this book.

So, how should you play against a woman?

> When you have to deal with a woman, forget everything you knew beforehand. You're dealing with Mother Nature, the Earth, the Moon, the ancient gods, call it what you will. But it will be always stronger than Rationality. Simply relax and enjoy yourself. Set a goal, and it will fall into your hands by itself.
>
> A second method is for those who are very sure of themselves: come and take what you believe is your birthright. In such cases, this "temporal and ancient being" submits quickly, without a peep. But what should you do if you confuse the two methods and get punished as a result? Well, resort to an old anecdote:
>
> "Lieutenant, why are you so successful with women?"
>
> "I come up to them and immediately invite them to my room."
>
> "But you can get slapped for that."
>
> "Sure, but more often, they do come to my room."
>
> So above all, you need to believe in your own success, and then whatever happens happens.

I can give you advice that I usually give for any interactions with women, not only in chess.

Forget everything you've ever known about the fair sex: all your life experience, all the books you read, all the tales your friends told you. Any new woman should be a *tabula rasa* for you, because it's simply impossible to predict what awaits you. Act spontaneously, improvise, don't try to guess her thoughts – they jump around like fleas, you won't keep up. Relax and have fun. A woman is needed to create an atmosphere, not to search for the truth.

It's the same in chess. Did you prepare for the Ruy Lopez? She'll play the Caro-Kann, which she'd never tried in her life. Has she lost in every previous round? Surpri-i-i-ize! She might well destroy you without giving you a chance. Throw away your emotions completely, and may common sense guide your every move.

Chess players love telling stories about women's chess. For instance, the entire team spends a whole evening preparing a woman grandmaster who plays for the national team in an important competition (by the way, I heard this story from the original source). And the next day, she makes a different first move — 1.d4 instead of 1.e4. Well, just like that. She forgot, or changed her mind, or got mixed up — oh, please, leave her alone, she's just a girl!

In light of all the above, the main lifehack is this: **"Do not try to outplay a woman, she will do it for you herself."**

Play solidly, firmly, resolutely, without any fanciful or showy moves. Women's play is peculiar in that they eventually defeat themselves. You only need to wait for the right moment. Her emotions and pseudo-ingenuity will definitely prevail. "She'll get there by herself," as chess players say. And when this does happen, finish her off with strong moves, watching carefully for counterplay and traps.

If you don't know what you are doing, then your enemy doesn't know either!

If you're much stronger than her, or you are facing an old granny, or a little girl, or someone who hasn't played for a long time, try pressing from the very beginning. Use all your manly might to crush her before she realizes what has hit her.

If she's about your strength, on the other hand, be more modest in your play.

As we finish our pleasant discussion of women, I'll show you an example from my own career — and you'll learn a great idea in an opposite-colored bishops endgame in the process.

The game was played at the Tbilisi Women's Interzonal in 1999 (back then, the world championship qualifying path included Interzonal tournaments). My opponent in the last round had already secured a qualifying place for the world championship, but I had to win on demand to qualify.

Shortly before the second time control[1], I realized that winning was impossible: the opposite-colored bishop ending was completely drawn. The only thing I had in my favor was some mystical conviction that I would succeed in this tournament.

Rusudan Goletiani played extremely well and made no mistakes. Her coach, Zurab Azmaiparashvili, was watching her intensely from the hall. She was proving to be a fine student. Nobody could have predicted what would happen next.

Game 2
M. Manakova (2344) – R. Goletiani (2310)
Tbilisi Women's Interzonal, 1999

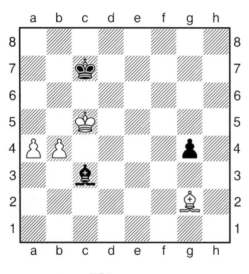

White to move

For the last ten moves, the black bishop had moved between the d2 and e1 squares, which was completely correct. I was ready to abandon all hope for the win, but then Rusudan, for a completely incomprehensible reason, put the bishop on c3! Would a man who simply moved his bishop along two drawing squares and

---

[1] Time controls have frequently changed over history. Back then, time control was as follows: 40 moves in 2 hours, then 20 moves in 1 hour, and then 30 minutes until the end of the game, with no increment. The second time control was hence once you had made 60 moves.

could secure second place with this back-and-forth movement just put it on c3 for no reason? Something tells me no.

You may ask, what's the difference between the bishop being placed on e1, d2 or c3? There actually is a difference! White now has a great chance. The position is not won yet, but there is now a dangerous trap. And Rusudan steps right into it.

60.b5! If the bishop were on d2 or e1, black could simply give a check along the a7-g1 diagonal. Now, however, black is forced to play **60...♗a5 61.♗e4**, and now the only continuation is **61...♗b6+ 62.♔b4 g3 63.♗g2** (black can also play g3 first but let's not worry about that). And so, the moment of truth arrives. The only moves that can save black are ♗e3 or ♗d4. But my opponent doesn't understand the difference (during the game, I didn't either − I only found the draw using a computer when writing this book). **63...♗f2??**

64.♔a5!! Many players I showed the game to missed this move. Rusudan did too, and when she finally saw it unleashed against her, she got terribly upset. Had black instead put her bishop on e3 or d4, she would be able to control the b8 square from the neighboring h2-b8 diagonal. In this case, her king then transfers to c5 through d6 and it's a draw. Now, however, white's position is completely won, and I finished her off: **64...♗e3 65.♔a6 ♗d4 66.a5 ♗e3 67.b6+ ♔b8 68.♔b5.** Curtains! **1−0.**

I shudder when I remember what happened with Azmai at that point. He flew onto the stage and had quite a few choice Georgian words for his pupil's play. The profession of a woman's chess coach is dangerous for your health.

> *Training a female player is driving the devil out of her*
> *− Anton Korobov*

On Your Marks

Allow 5-10 minutes to pump yourself up before the game

> Before an important battle, you should be fully concentrated on it. You are an arrow on a drawn bow.

The time spent on the starting block is crucial. The bow is drawn, and the arrow is ready to hit its target. The minutes before starting the clock are very important. My observations, however, show that every chess player uses this important moment differently.

Professionals: concentrate on the game, calm their spirit, mind and body. Some recall their goals and how to get there, remind themselves that they need to play rapidly and positively. Others don't try to recall anything at all, simply sitting in inner silence, accumulating energy.

Me: I run into the tournament hall 5–10 minutes late. Apologize profusely to my opponent and swear to myself for the hundred thousandth time that this is the last occasion I arrive late.

Some women players: banter with their opponents, complete with fake giggling and loud, unnatural laughter. If I somehow *don't* arrive late to my game, then watching this anti-theater causes me immeasurable psychological pain and throws me off balance.

Modern young coaches teach their pupils: give your opponent a small gift before the game, ask if they have ever visited our country or town, if they liked it there?... butter them up!

"Can you imagine?" a coach once told me. "I taught him all that, he comes to the game, gives his opponent a souvenir – and the opponent does the same. And then the latter also asks, *How is he doing? How does he like living in this great city?*, all that stuff... His coach also taught him that, LOL."

Alexander Grischuk: dashes late to the table, surrounded by a cloud of cigarette smoke. He might even sit at the wrong board and start playing the wrong opponent. (OK, this happened with Alexander only at a blitz tournament. OK...once.)

And now let's get serious. Because players treat it really seriously.

Most chess players get to the board 5–10 minutes before the game, settle down on their chairs, and fill in the scoresheets. Everyone is nervous before the game, no exceptions. And everyone tries to hide and control their anxiety, no exceptions. Everyone has their own way: talking to the opponent, talking to friends or arbiters, getting some coffee. Some just sit and glare at their opponent if they too decided to sit down rather than roam around.

In all these cases, concentration is enormous, adrenaline is rushing through your veins, but you cannot show that. I once jumped off a mountain with a paraglider at Krasnaya Polyana near Sochi. Well, the feeling on the "starting block" before an important chess game can be quite similar to that before jumping into the abyss from a mountain. The adrenaline load is so huge that I, as an overly emotional person, simply cannot cope with it. That's why I always show up late to games and important meetings. Hurrying helps me to "burn off" some of that adrenaline. That's a peculiar defensive mechanism of my body, as I wrote earlier.

With Svetozar Gligoric, match between the USSR and Yugoslavia, 2007. The USSR and Yugoslavia no longer existed but the match did! I helped to organize it

During the Game. Alertness

Cooper's Color Code

> When you leave home, try to be in the Yellow (alert) state,
> sometimes going into Orange (heightened awareness). This will
> help you to interact better with both yourself and the surrounding
> world.

You have probably heard that levels of danger are often labeled with colors: White, Yellow, Red, Blue, etc. Color codes are often used in areas where a rapid response is necessary: in determining risks from weather, the climate, heat, and, especially in recent times, terrorism...

In the middle of the last century, military and police officers realized that they needed a similar classification, with each color depicting the level of the person's psychological and physiological alertness. If they had such a system, they thought, it would be much simpler to teach people to recognize and prevent critical situations both in combat (for professionals) and in mundane life (for civilians). And it would be very useful for all martial arts as well!

Just such a system was created by Jeff Cooper (1920–2006, United States), a shooting instructor, small arms expert, and author of many books. To be fair, we should point out that he didn't come up with the color code himself, but he wrote about it extensively, developed it, advocated and promoted it as well as he could, and it eventually became known as Cooper's Color Code.

Cooper's colors
All living creatures have instinctive reactions to danger. Humans have them too: from full relaxation to a state of shock when it's already too late to react to the problem. Cooper gave all five states their own color code in order of increasing danger: White, Yellow, Orange, Red, and Black. A person's awareness can be changed by both external factors (for instance, a cop pulls you over: your pulse quickens, the whole body tenses, your legs feel like jelly, even if you are sure that you are completely innocent) and internal factors (when you sit in a dentist's chair you force yourself to mobilize and be ready for the "dangers" ahead).

Why does a chess player need to know this system?
You'll see why very soon. Let's first discuss all the states separately.

White, or "total unawareness", is the state of total relaxation. You lie on the couch at home and scroll your mobile device listlessly, or push the buttons on a TV remote; your brain is turned off, your thoughts are a chaotic salad, you notice nothing around and rest. Everything is peaceful and serene. It's as though you are sleeping with your eyes open, because there's no danger in sight. Everything is familiar, there's no need to concentrate on anything. There's next to no cortisol (stress hormone) in your blood, no adrenaline either. Lovestruck and drunk people also enter a similar state. At home, this state is very useful, like "sleep mode" for your computer, because the computer also needs to cool down and rest like we humans do.

Humans, however, have a bad trait. If any other carbon-based lifeform is taken by an unpleasant surprise, it usually either skedaddles or starts fighting – "flight or fight". Any lifeform, even amoebas. But not humans. We have got so lazy for the three hundred thousand years of our existence that when we face a danger and are hit with the fight-flight-freeze reaction, 75% of people instinctively try to play dead – "freeze", and the predator won't notice you. As if!

In our fun times, you can only truly relax at home. As soon as you go outside, you have to switch from White state to Yellow, i.e. mobilize, otherwise you might be surprised by an open manhole or a balcony falling on your head. Your body won't be able to react to something unexpected if it's not prepared.

Criminologists have noted that most misfortunes happen to people who remain in White state outside of their home. They text behind the wheel, cross the street with their faces buried in their phones... Zero awareness! Moreover, a person in White tends to be deeply immersed in their thoughts, paying little heed to what is going on around them. And so, a young man's legs carry him along the familiar path, although were he a bit alert and mobilized, he would certainly have chosen a different path, because it's 2 a.m. now, and there are some aggressive and loud drunkards on that route. But he doesn't hear them and continues on his way, straight into a morass of trouble and tragedy.

Yellow, or "relaxed awareness". Your consciousness is functioning: you see and understand what's going on, but don't bother too much. Your brain automatically watches for potential dangers. In this state, we usually drive our cars, cross roads, and walk cautiously near tall buildings in winter so as to avoid an icicle that might fall on our head (if we live in a snowy region).

A girl comes home late at night. Lots of assaults on people happen in the hallways of their apartment buildings, because they already allow themselves to relax into the White state in the hallway. Psychologists recommend retaining Yellow state right until you enter your own flat. If someone has followed the girl into the hallway, she should quickly raise her alert level to Orange if she hasn't done that already when walking alone in the night.

A person prays and meditates in the Yellow state. They relax their body, but their "inner observer" remains alert – that's how quality meditation is supposed to be. You should strive to make Yellow your default, natural state. It allows you to keep your grasp on reality at all times, to open your inner eye for other people's reactions, for random sounds, for surrounding details, for your own well-being, while it helps you to control your own thinking and stop the flow of unwanted thoughts. By the way, chess – or rather playing in chess competitions, where the price of every move is high – is very useful for developing concentration (Yellow and Orange states).

Humans can spend 10–15 hours in the Yellow state, then they need to rest a bit in the White state.

Orange is the state of full attention, almost combat readiness. The threat of an attack is very real, and the brain isn't just analyzing the potential danger – it is also preparing the body to react to a direct attack. Adrenaline and cortisol (hormones that mobilize the body) enter the blood in high concentration. The pulse elevates to 100 beats per minute. A tunnel vision effect may occur: the field of view narrows from 120 to 10 degrees, fully focusing your sight on the threat.

Orange state turns on in a driver who tries to overtake another car, in a security guard who hears a rustle, and in a chess player who experiences time trouble.

But there's a problem. A human can only remain in Orange for 40 minutes to two hours at most, depending on their training level – they simply can't bear more. The mind starts to slow down, first to Yellow and then to White, to get some rest and recovery. That's why patrol guards in the army are changed every two hours.

Red is the state of fight for survival, the reaction to an attack. The fight is on, and the mind instinctively chooses one state out of three: fight, flight or freeze.

The human brain has a special area that controls mood, motivation and fear. And so, when a person faces danger, this area sends the alarm signal through the hypothalamus and pituitary gland (in the head) to adrenal glands (in the belly), which respond by producing the vitally important hormones adrenaline and cortisol. This fearsome twosome bears the most responsibility for our survival. They cause stress for the body: suppress the activity of the parasympathetic nervous system (which controls eating and pooping) and drive the sympathetic nervous system into frenzy:

→ the heart beats harder, the pulse quickens to 160 beats per minute

→ gross motor skills are enhanced while fine motor skills get turned off; involuntary urination might occur

→ the skin turns pale, the pupils dilate

→ the pain threshold increases

→ frontal lobes stop working (the ability to think rationally decreases)

→ metabolism quickens: the liver actively breaks down glycogen to provide a large supply of glucose (neuron food) for the brain, giving the body energy necessary for survival

→ behavioral patterns kick in (there's no time for creativity and inventiveness when your life is in danger!). We cannot make reasonable, conscious decisions, so our reflexes guide us.

Black is the state of shock, which is close to death. The brain turns off, the sensory organs too, and the chances of survival are close to zero.

What's this all about?

Transitions between the colors should be consecutive. Any jumps (from White to Red, for instance) carry the risk of falling into Black, when the body does not have enough time to reorganize – it simply cannot work at such speeds. Reverse transitions should also be gradual: you can't return to the Yellow state directly from Red. This can be traced by heartbeat – it cannot slow down immediately, you need time.

To move smoothly along Cooper's Color Code, you have to be in the Yellow state at the very least: this will at least allow you to notice the danger. If you're wallowing in White vibes, however, you won't be able to react immediately. Neither your intelligence, nor bravery, nor ingenuity, nor academic degree, nor grandmaster title will help you. Thus, you need to develop your consciousness to at least survive in this mad mad mad world.

The classic example of this is the death of the famous poker player and gunfighter Bill Hickok. He terrorized the whole Wild West: he won his every gunfight and was unstoppable. One day, when he sat down to play poker, he, for the first (and last) time in his life, sat with his back to the door, because all the seats at the walls were occupied. He lowered his guard slightly, going from his usual Orange state to Yellow. A local drunkard entered the room and shot him in the head twice from behind. The combination of cards that Bill Hickok allegedly held in his hand (aces and eights of clubs and spades) got the name of "Dead Man's Hand" in poker.

But what about chess?

You cannot play in the White state, only in Yellow. In time trouble, rapid and blitz, you should play in the Orange state – try not to transition to Red, because it blocks rational thinking.

The problem of playing beyond move 40, when the time scramble ends, boils down to the fact that the player thinks that they can afford to go into the White state, to fully relax. They freeze for a bit, and then the second control suddenly approaches. Yes, your body needs rest from the intense bursts of Orange or even Red activity between the 30th and 40th moves, but you can't give it more than five minutes of rest (time control at big official competitions is 30 minutes until the end of the game with a 30-second increment). And to return the body into a working state quickly, you need fitness, a well-trained mind and the competitive ability to force yourself.

Do not slip into unconsciousness

Nature has allocated a special time for the "unconscious" state – sleep time. Do not "sleep" while you're awake. First of all, you are wasting your time, and, secondly, this is simply dangerous. (There's only one exception – when your energy batteries are exhausted. In this case, you need a short rest in a safe place.)

Here are the symptoms that show that you played a game (or a part of the game) in an unconscious, "White" state:

1. You cannot recall the game properly and mix up the moves.
2. You say, "I don't understand what I spent all my time on."

How can you catch yourself in such a state during the game? Of course, it's not easy: the brain is so relaxed that it's ready to do anything to prevent anyone from waking it up. It will deceive you in various ways: for instance, it will pretend to calculate lines. Or it will suggest to you that it would be "important to meditate" over the position, so that the solution "comes up by itself". Or it will attempt to convince you of the importance of calculating a concrete line and all its variations for 20 moves.

All you need to do in such a situation is to catch yourself lying. White state is forbidden in chess! (As I implied already, you *can* afford five minutes or so in this state after the time scramble, to help your body restore itself more quickly, but only when your opponent has the move.) **Wallowing long in line calculations should serve as an alarm signal to you.**

If you don't see the position clearly when you calculate, stop your analysis. It's a waste of your time and freshness. Moreover, your variations will be full of holes, because you are not mobilized. Pull yourself together, turn away from the board, eat a chocolate, then go back to the position, look at it clearly and tell yourself, "I will now identify three candidate moves!" Determine them and give yourself no more than 10 minutes to choose between them (5 minutes will probably be better, because you have already wasted enough time). After those 5–10 minutes, make a firm decision, without cutting corners.

Here's another useful thing. When your mind is numb after a necessary but long calculation of complicated variations, you could do the following. First, pause for a short time and distract yourself (as I described above), and then get back to the variations, but, instead of simply calculating, silently **verbalize** them. Yes, you can even actually whisper, moving your lips. Why do that? There's a fog in your head, your view is distorted, and verbalizing the moves allows you to perceive better and structure the lines.

Let's say it again. This is important: **full distraction from chess for 20–30 seconds after long calculation provides the brain with a quick energy recharge.**

The eighth world champion **Mikhail Tal** *once recounted a strange story. You probably know it, so I'll mention it only briefly: in a game with Evgeny Vasiukov, in a complex position with countless variations, he needed to calculate whether to sacrifice a knight for the attack. At that moment, Tal's unconscious apparently served him a fantastic way to distract himself. It reminded him of a line from a children's poem by Kornei Chukovsky (Telephone, 1926) about how hard it is to pull a hippo out of a swamp. Indeed, it didn't just remind him, but also challenged him to find the solution. He then spent forty minutes thinking about how to achieve it – with ropes?, or perhaps with a motor vehicle jack? Would they need a helicopter or was a truck sufficient? That's what Tal claimed anyway, explaining why he spent forty minutes over one move. After thinking for the full*

forty minutes, Tal claimed, he failed to come up with a satisfactory solution and decided "OK, let it drown." And at that moment, he decided to go for the sac even though the variations seemed inconclusive.

Work on mindfulness

Life as meditation is the ideal state for the Seeker

The ability to enter a mindful state is a very important skill, which can be developed. In fact, it develops on its own as you age and accumulate experience. Driving a car, practicing any sports (especially extreme ones), yoga, martial arts, fishing, cross-stitching, dance – all this helps a person to control themselves and their consciousness. It's as though you jump out of the pile of junk of your own thoughts and the chaos of random events around you into a "here-and-now" state (welcome to reality!)

Chess is also good for developing this skill, but the reverse is true as well: you'll be able to play chess much better if you play in a mindful state, not by fumbling your way around.

Some people are rather impatient: they don't want to wait for years of experience to grant them the desired mindfulness, and they work on it at an accelerated pace (or at least they think they do). These people are fans of the esoteric. They choose a path of mindfulness training with meditation (or even prayer). We'll discuss that some other time.

With Andor Lilienthal, also at the match between the USSR and Yugoslavia, 2007

Control the time, yourself and the game

> If you have a goal, you will always watch it with your inner sight

Control, control, you must learn control!
— Yoda

Now that we realize that we can more or less control ourselves, let's look at the things we must control during a chess game.

The result depends on three factors: the **game** itself (logic of the battle), the **time** you spend on it, and your internal **state**. This should be under constant, relentless control.

With my husband Miroslav Tosic at the chessboard. Late 1990s

Controlling Time

Magic shouldn't be sought in the absolute quality of your game these days, but in the speed of making very difficult decisions.
— Mikhail Golubev

At first I wanted to win without using black magic. When my position became untenable, I got into such severe time trouble that there was no time for black magic.
— Aleister Crowley on his 1897 game as the first board for Cambridge University in the annual varsity match. He lost as black, playing the Petroff.

There's a state called the "infinite time mode" (I first heard about it from my teacher, theater director Boris Yukhananov). It's ideal for any creative process. Even more importantly, a true creative process is impossible if it's limited by time. Any thought of "there's too little time" pulls the creator away from the creative process, and it's very hard to get back into it afterwards.

The person immerses themselves so deeply in their art that time, space and their inner state simply cease to exist for them. Only pure art remains.

That's why actors and directors rehearse all night, until the morning, and their "normal" spouses can't stand such a schedule and divorce them. That's why artists, as they create their paintings, stop eating, drinking, washing and sleeping, and their friends have to "revive" them afterwards, helping them eat and wash after creating another masterpiece.

That's how to create works of art. For an outsider, this looks suspiciously like insanity, but this successfully ends when the "baby", borne with so many difficulties, finally enters the world. Some say that chess is art, but it's not. There are some elements of art in it indeed, and elements of science too, but it remains a game, a fight. And this game is strictly limited by time. And, since the game is limited by time, creative masterpieces at the board will be a random occurrence, a "pleasant surprise". If we want a non-random chess masterpiece, it should be created in conditions when you are not bound by time — in home analysis.

In a chess game, Time is one of three most important factors, together with Moves and Energy. Loss of control over time most often leads to defeat.

Almost every chess player (exceptions are rare) is inflicted by "time-trouble disease" from time to time. And everyone fights it as well as they can. Some fight it successfully, while others don't and suffer from time trouble until old age.

I have studied this topic extensively because I've been suffering from time trouble for my whole life. I don't want to jinx myself by saying that I am totally cured from that disease, but the situation has certainly improved. I can tell you what helped me and share the tips of my coaches and friends.

Time trouble is the absolute evil

> You shouldn't get to the point where you risk having insufficient time. Because then it will happen.

Time trouble is a sign of lack of chess culture, and if you can't eradicate this altogether for some reason, at least try to reduce its frequency to some reasonable minimum.
– Lev Psakhis

I heard the following commandment from the same Lev Psakhis: "Time trouble is the absolute evil." This phrase has a strong aura of mysticism, and that's why I remembered it so well.

And, of course, **lack of culture**, yes.

Once upon a time, as any school kid knows, Wilhelm Steinitz came up with the criteria for evaluating chess positions: the position of the king, control of the center and space, pawn structure, piece activity, etc. Ever since that time, chess players haven't managed to come up with anything new – the first world champion's conclusions were so correct and complete. Coaches passed this knowledge onto their pupils, and it has been printed and reprinted in textbook after textbook.

However, another evaluation criterion has become important in the last few decades: time. No wonder – time is one of the greatest treasures in the life of any modern human. A clever chess coach will tell their pupil: the center, the king, the pieces, space... and time. And when the pupil enthusiastically tells them that they had a position "won twenty times over" (which they lost for some reason), an experienced coach will curb their enthusiasm with a single question, "How much time did you have left on the clock?"

The results of most games are decided in time trouble.

Your advert could be here, as they say. Or maybe anti-advert. I wanted to show some time-trouble blunders made by famous grandmasters here. But then I felt so bad for them! Let's omit the examples. Just take me on my word: even you wouldn't have blundered so badly, bwahahah!

Is it so hard to understand that time scrambles are pernicious? Why do people so insistently and voluntarily walk into this slaughter?

Because the reasons for "time-trouble disease" lie in the deep layers of the human psyche: their complexes, fears, illnesses, specific character traits... However, whereas normal, non-chess playing people eliminate their inner troubles with all possible seriousness – they consult with therapists, read books, do exercises – chess players prefer to turn a blind eye to their gluttony for time trouble.

Let's take chronic procrastinators, for instance. They get rid of this flaw with the help of psychologists and long, persistent self-improvement. But the "craving" for time trouble is often caused by the very same reasons as procrastination! You see? Common people get treatment, but chess players prefer for some reason to treat their problem as something that "will resolve itself". It won't! It never does. So, if you do suffer from "time-trouble disease", treat it with the utmost seriousness.

Do not confuse procrastination with simple laziness. A lazy person never regrets something they fail or neglect to do, that they wasted time, but a procrastinator feels incredibly guilty and always promises that this will be the very last time. But the same thing happens next time as well: they set a task, then waste an inordinate amount of time, which leads to more suffering and hand-wringing.

I'll leave a place here for a picture about procrastination, but I need to find a nice one. Well, they are all nice. OK, I'll put off this hard choice until later.

Below, I'll try to list all possible reasons for "time-trouble disease", both deep and not so deep:
→ Lack of self-confidence
→ Lack of over-the-board practice
→ Lack of self-discipline and willpower, the ability to get a grip on yourself only in extreme need
→ Lack of culture of calculating lines (or discipline)
→ Lack of chess knowledge
→ Dependence on the opinions of others: your parents, coaches, fans. In time trouble, the player gets an "excuse" for their moves
→ Addiction to adrenaline and time-trouble excitement, the desire to feel it again
→ Bad habit of thinking when you don't need to
→ Perfectionism, the constant search for "the ideal move"
→ The need to enter the White state during the game because of a pathological desire to enjoy life and do nothing
→ The desire to be an artist, not a player (which is tantamount to amateurism in modern chess), which makes one search for "the prettiest" continuation
→ *Time trouble is characteristic of "heavy thinkers", players with poorly developed intuition. (Mark Dvoretsky)*

Poor health, a lack of freshness, strong emotional pressure (for instance, because of the tournament situation) etc. − all these troubles are transitory. They can serve as the reason for time trouble in individual games, but they cannot cause "time-trouble disease".

As a rule, chronic time-trouble addiction is caused by several reasons at once, and the problem is more difficult than it seems. In addition to serious daily chess training (which expands your knowledge and makes you more self-assured) and regular tournament play, serious work on psychological issues is necessary. And, of course, constant control of your inner state and time during the game, even when it seems that development of this skill (constant control) is detrimental to your results.

But the most important thing is that the player should truly want to kick the habit. Otherwise, it's useless.

As proof of this assertion, I'll show you the maxim by psychologist Mikhail Labkovsky which he uses to make people quit smoking (he'd been a smoker himself for 35 years):

How can you stop doing something that makes you happy, that you like?! It's impossible. It's possible in the short term, but then you'll regress to your previous state. For starters, you should definitely understand that the thing you are doing is evil, and you are a complete addict who got hooked on that rubbish. Only after you realize that can you quit smoking.

There are a lot of grandmasters who spend their entire life in time trouble; they try to kick the habit, but to no avail, because they seem to enjoy time scrambles. They play at a high enough level, but can't progress further. There's even a chess commandment:

You cannot become a great chess player if you're a time-trouble addict.

There's only one exception: Alexander Grischuk. Many say that if he didn't get into time trouble so much, he would have become world champion. Or, at the very least, permanently stayed in the top five – he's just that talented.

Since there are many reasons for "time-trouble disease", and several of them are usually combined in one and the same person, every "patient" should be considered separately. But in this book, I'll try to give some universal advice that can help many. Consider them recommendations for serious individual work.

Let's begin!

Play rapidly

> When you are psyching yourself up to achieve a particular result, concentrate on the things that you want to achieve, not the things you want to leave behind. Tell yourself: "I'll be healthy" (instead of "I won't be ill"), "I'll be rich" (instead of "I'll get out of poverty"), "I'll be successful" (instead of "I'll stop being a loser"). Our brain is primitive and ancient like a dinosaur's jaw, it reacts only to the direct meaning of the word. Metaphors, hints, parallels, and other figures of speech are too difficult for it to comprehend.

The main advice is simple: play rapidly. Pay attention to the phrasing: not "avoid time trouble", but "play rapidly".

Let me remind you again about the precept of psychologists and various spiritual gurus: if you want to leave something behind or get cured of it, you shouldn't think about this problem or illness — you need to think about *what* you want to get *in exchange*. Let's remember our white monkey formula again:

You cannot stop thinking about a white monkey, but you can start thinking about a giraffe.

And the monkey will disappear on its own.

You want to quit smoking, drinking or overeating? Concentrate on a healthy lifestyle or a life goal. Forget about "quitting smoking, drinking and overeating"! Moreover, your entire lifestyle should be changed — since it is based on your bad habit. It's the same with time trouble. Don't think "My goal for today is to avoid a time scramble!" You'll get into time trouble for sure. Tell yourself instead, "I'm playing rapidly today, like in a rapid game."

How do you play in rapid tournaments (say, 15 or 30 minutes per player per game)? You get a grip on yourself for the whole game and don't let yourself leave the table or relax. You should play a classical game in the same state. If you're a chronic time-trouble addict and try to play a classical game like a rapid one, you'll suddenly realize that you're still almost out of time! Nevertheless, if you do save some time, then spend it on moves 35 to 40 — the most important ones.

Remember this state and play like that every time. Do not relax. Think of yourself as a chess engine. It's constantly working. It gets switched on before the first move and switched off after the last one. No daydreaming, no "meditations", no "There surely is a winning move!"

Give yourself permission to play rapidly

> Our fears and complexes don't allow us to make the steps we want to make. We simply don't give ourselves permission to follow our intuition easily and joyfully. How should we improve the situation?
> (1) Here's an experiment: forget about the result, make peace with the idea that you might lose, but make all decisions quickly and easily, following your inner voice.
> (2) Look at the result.
> (3) Feel the horror ☺

It's better to make a good move quickly than an unclear move very slowly.
— A grandmaster

At one of my tournaments, a woman grandmaster round-robin, I hadn't been playing particularly well and decided to go for a revolutionary breakthrough, a risky experiment (I had got fed up with having a low rating for years on end, so I had to come up with something radical). I decided to reply to my opponent's moves immediately, like in blitz. The result? I won all the games, even against the tourney leaders.

What happened when I replied to the moves so quickly?

First of all, I got my intuition working. My hand is much smarter than my head, but I tend to forget that. And if I do remember that, then I lack the courage to trust my hand. Secondly, my opponents got terribly confused, and this really disturbed them psychologically.

Thirdly, I would build up a huge advantage after move 25, but, unusually, I had more than an hour to convert it, not five minutes. At this point, I started using my head much more, because I know that my conversion skills are rather mediocre.

As a result, I had both enough time and energy to win games. I even finished them before the first time control ☺.

I simply gave myself permission to play rapidly.

Boris Postovsky:

At what moment do chess players make mistakes the most often? A chess player usually sees the move they need to make immediately. Thanks to that, blitz games are sometimes played at a very high level because nobody thinks on their move for half an hour in blitz, whereas in classical time control the player starts thinking: "Do I really need to make a move immediately? Nobody will understand if I make a move without thinking." And so, they start studying one move, then another, and both of them look quite good. But time passes. And as a result, they make some move that they didn't study much but looks playable. This is a very serious mistake, because, as a rule, the first move that comes into your head is the strongest move. And then, the player start thinking, "Why didn't I play that immediately, why did I waste half an hour?" Such mistakes are caused by indecisiveness — you should trust yourself more. And don't fear losing the game — a loss is not a tragedy.

Playing quickly is a great idea, but try not to lose control over the process, as once happened to my opponent.

Game 3
M. Manakova (2163) – J. Pein (2301)
Dimitrovgrad, 2023
Petroff Defense

He got to the game obviously determined to win. And to win quickly at that (time control was classical: 1.5 hours for the game with a 30-second increment). He spent about half a second on every move. And this continued until move 8.

1.e4 e5 2.♘f3 ♘f6 3.♘xe5 d6 4.♘f3 ♘xe4 5.d4 d5 6.♗d3 ♗e6 7.♕e2. Here, he either forgot something, mixed up the move order or simply blundered: **7...f5?**

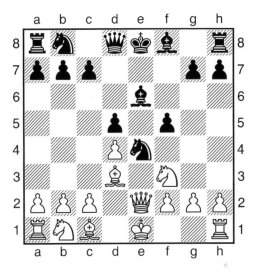

White to move

8.♘g5! My opponent raised his hand to reply immediately again, but suddenly stopped and started thinking. And then thought more...and more. And then he realized that he simply had no moves left, that he's in serious trouble. The best reply was 8...♘xg5 9.♗xg5 ♕xg5 10.♕xe6+ ♕e7 11.♗xf5 ♕xe6+ 12.♗xe6 c6, where he is doomed to suffer in a worse endgame a pawn down. Instead, he decided to "die beautifully" and sacrificed a piece for active play.

8...♕d7 9.♘xe6 ♕xe6 10.f3 ♕e7 11.fxe4 fxe4 12.♗b5+ c6 13.♗a4 ♕b4+ 14.♘c3 ♗e7 15.♕h5+ ♔d8 (not 15...g6 due to 16.♕xd5!) **16.♗g5 ♕xd4 17.♖d1 ♕e5 18.♗xe7+ ♕xe7**

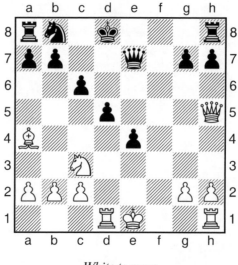

White to move

19.♘xd5!! cxd5 20.♖xd5+ (A queen check would do the trick as well.)
20...♔c7 21.0–0 g6 22.♖f7! (This move is probably the 60th engine line, or something. It's not the strongest, but the best choice! White gets a won endgame, which is a good way to make your opponent resign immediately.) **22...♕xf7 23.♕e5+ ♔c8 24.♕xh8+ ♔c7 25.♕d8** Check and mate. **1–0**

Some lifehacks for time control

- Recording the beginning of a process is great advice for any area of activity.
- The method of "sitting, waiting and meditating" for the solution to "come up on its own" works very well if you have all the time in the world. If your time is limited, this does not work. Nevertheless, you can use the essence of this method: calming your body down and plunging into the unconscious. At the same time, don't forget to set the alarm. This method doesn't work every time, but, unfortunately, I don't have any other option for you: meditation with a deadline is only half-baked meditation.

1) Recording time

This is a well-known training technique: after your every move, record the time you spent on it. This allows the coach to see later on which problems the pupil spent the most time. Do they have problems with the opening? Or maybe they are stunned when faced with an unexpected move? Some coaches are even sure that time-trouble addicts have no psychological problems, they simply lack knowledge of certain types of position. I disagree, so I think that recording time might help, but only partially.

Moreover, recording the beginning and the end of an activity is the main exercise recommended by time-management specialists for developing a "sense of time". Therefore, it will be easier for you to control time if you see concrete numbers on the scoresheet.

2) Recording the beginning of a long think

When you realize that you have reached a critical position and have to make a difficult choice, record the time when you start thinking. This should be a completely *conscious* action – you may even write it on your scoresheet, or another sheet of paper, or even on your hand! – such an unexpected action will surely be remembered by your body.

Never spend more than 20 minutes on a decision even in a hypercomplicated position.

Why 20 minutes? Well, there are certain rules based on experience and a huge number of repeat situations. For instance, you shouldn't spend more than 20 minutes on solving even the most difficult endgame study. And don't try to persist. Your brain has just turned off, and you won't get a result. Take a pause, return to the study the next day – and you'll see how quickly you solve it.

It's the same with thinking on your move over the board. Of course, it's cool to engage in a 40-minute deep analysis, but you'll lose the game in this case, because after 20–30 minutes of intense work you regress back to the White state, the freshness and clarity of thought go away, and your brain essentially turns off. You randomly shuffle the various lines, and as time passes, you gradually become nervous and then hysterical. You can avoid that only through herculean efforts of will, basically pulling yourself out of the swamp by your own hair. Why go there at all?

3) Wearing a watch

I have a big black watch with an inscription, *Whatever, I'm late anyway.* It describes me so well, I love it. No matter what kind of watch you have: it should pull you out of the "sleepy" state, when you have wandered into a swamp of variations and cannot escape on your own. The watch can be big and unwieldy, you can wear it on your wrist or put it on your table, but it constantly reminds you of the time. At some official competitions, wearing watches is forbidden as an anti-cheating measure, but this lifehack helps me a lot at those tournaments where watches are allowed. You can also use another object as your lifeline, not only a watch. Just look at it and snap yourself back to reality.

I asked Lev Psakhis: *"Why does the following happen? I sit for 40 minutes at some position, feeling that 'there should be something'. I penetrate the position deeply during that time, and voila, I do discover the necessary move! The 'only move' I was searching for!"*

And here's what he answered: *"All this is simply a fairytale spun by hopeless gamblers who come up with every possible excuse for their unconscious state, to which they have been long addicted and which they cannot escape. Even if you do find 'that move', does it really help? Ten moves later, you'll start panicking because of looming time trouble, and you won't be able to make rational decisions. And then it will become even worse: the time scramble will erase all your masterpieces and achievements.*

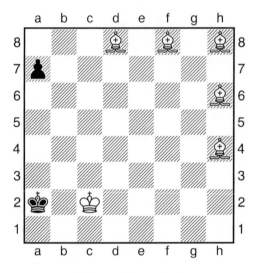

White to play and win

When this book was already finished, Vanya sent me this endgame study and, for some reason, said that it was difficult. Yes, it's actually not easy, but not so difficult that I should need more than ten minutes or so to solve it. Yet the solution evaded me in the first few minutes, and after twenty minutes, my brain refused to work. And then, the usual story happened. I continued to try to solve the study with a non-working brain because I stubbornly refused to admit defeat. Well, if the study is so hard, it's a challenge, right?

So, I sat there until midnight, then 1 a.m., then 2 a.m. I was determined to solve the position even if I died! I tried solving it sitting, then I tried lying down, then in my sleep... It only finally came to me at half past two in the wee hours. Yet had I delayed my attempts until the following morning, I would have solved the position in five minutes.

This is actually a slightly revised study by Alexei Troitsky (1915): 1.♗d6 c5 (if 1...♗b6 2.♗a1 a4 3.♗f6 a3 4.♗c3 ♗xa1 2.♗b4 (after 4...♗b1, the win is even faster) 5.♗b3+ b1 6.♗a1 a2 7.♗c3 ♗xa1 8.♗c2#.

By the way, after solving this study, you will have acquired a very important piece of knowledge. If you ever get five same-colored bishops, and the opponent only has a rook pawn, you will now know how to win this position. How incredibly cool is that!

Spend time wisely

We are accustomed to living by the Pareto, or 80:20 formula: we waste 80% of our time. Remember this as often as you can and try to act effectively at all times. (However, please don't consider proper resting a waste of time. It's necessary to recharge your batteries. But if you rest, you rest. Don't waste 80% of your rest time on other things.)

You can't possible know when you might need your time and energy the most, but such a moment will surely come in the future. Nevertheless, right now, you have to make reasonable moves at a relatively fast pace (1–2 minutes per move). If you spend three, or five, or ten minutes on each move, then later, when the game reaches a crisis stage and you'll need considerable time to think, say half an hour, you simply won't have it. And if you outplay your opponent and obtain a better position, then the looming time trouble, tiredness and lack of fresh perception will make mistakes simply unavoidable, and you won't achieve success in the game.
— Evgeny Bareev

Time trouble is experienced by those who think about the wrong things, not by those who think a lot.
— Gennady Malkin (a famous Russian aphorist)

Did you get it? You should spend time carefully and rationally. There will surely be positions in your game that require a lot of thought. These may include complicated, branching lines with sacrifices, or critical positions that determine the course of the whole game, including transitions into the endgame. For such positions, you'll need time and energy (!), which you have to conserve earlier.

Here are situations where you can save time and energy by **not** calculating at all.

1) Quick replies, because you are following theory (in the opening or endgame).
2) Quick recaptures after a capture.
3) Quick reply "because there's nothing more".
4) Quick reply because you already have a plan, and your opponent does not pose any concrete threats or simply follows through with their own plan.
5) Quick reply because literally millions of people have played that move before you, and you have made that move hundreds of times and there's nothing better: you have checked that at home.
6) Quick reply because you have already calculated this whole line several moves earlier and now you are just checking if you are blundering anything or if a better move has suddenly materialized.

In these situations, you shouldn't spend more than half a minute on the move (important: do not reply *immediately*, AAAAAAAH!!! You should always pause (breathe in, breathe out) and only then make a move. So many points are lost in chess because someone automatically recaptures a piece during a trade!).

Spend **1–3 minutes** on regular moves.

You can spend a bit more time, **5–10 minutes**, on positions that require some calculations, where the course of the battle changes somewhat, with lines leading to complicated positions or different pawn structures. You have to evaluate such positions and outline a plan, but don't engage in long concrete calculations.

If the course of the struggle changes drastically – the lines end with complicated, hard to evaluate positions, or with a transition into a difficult endgame, or with sacrificing material/accepting a sacrifice – then such positions are known as *critical*, and you can spend **15–20 minutes** on them. The ability to recognize critical positions depends on the chess player's skill.

Critical positions with calculations of complicated lines (and all the positions that occur in such lines) can take up to **half an hour** to evaluate. But only if you save enough time in the opening. Such positions occur only rarely.

Thinking for more than half an hour is useless and harmful. *This usually means that I don't know what to do (Magnus Carlsen).*

> *I slept through half a game. I don't know what I was thinking, but when I woke up, I had six minutes on my clock. My position was perhaps even slightly better, but with so little time after waking up, it was hard to convert. I didn't even try – I played as safely as I could.*
> *– Alexander Grischuk*

Save time in the opening

> Those who diligently prepare for a project have a huge advantage over lazy people. Joyful, careless laziness might work once, but in the long haul, a lazy person will be overtaken by hard-working ones.

In addition to purely chess advantages, opening knowledge is also useful for saving time. When you rattle off the first 15–20 moves in five minutes, you get 1.5 hours for the next 20 moves (with the 30-second increment, it's about 6–7 minutes per move). Many players do play like that. But masters of complications such as Alexander Morozevich or Richard Rapport force their opponents to think hard from the very first moves – at the same time, they also make *themselves* work hard as well. They love creating chaos on the board, where both opponents have to work from the very first moves. Don't expect them to give you an easy life. Of course, the kings of chaos prepare all this torture at home, it's easier for them. And their overall style is consistent with this approach: they are in their element.

To play quickly in the opening, you need **good memory**. By the way, many famous grandmasters have said that memory is one of the most important qualities for a chess player. Fischer, Averbakh and other greats even said that it was *the* most important. You can and should develop your memory, and there are plenty of techniques and exercises for that.

Train the "player" in you

> Life, like chess, is a fun game. Don't overburden it with your dullness, dogmatism and excessive philosophizing. And take action more.

The modern world is ruled by **results**, not process. Pragmatism has become fundamental to almost all areas of activity – including chess, of course. Success comes to those who treat chess as rationally as possible: including their position, tournament situation, and time consumption. Grandmasters don't look for the "best move" anymore. They make a move that is most comfortable for them and least comfortable for their opponent – this game tactic is more likely to lead to victory.

But wait, there's more. If you have a choice between two equally strong moves, one of which gives your opponent a choice and the other doesn't, grandmasters recommend to make the first move: let the opponent rack their brain over the choice, let them spend their time on it. The probability of error increases greatly in such a situation. But when the opponent has to find the only move, they will most probably find it.

In older times, they didn't play like that. Chess players tried to find continuations that were as beautiful and forcing as possible, striving for "pure art". But in our time, the competitive component of chess has completely overshadowed the art and science components. Playing time decreases, two games per day get played, there are official blitz and rapid ratings, and even some weird thing called "hybrid rankings"...

All in all, the romantic era of chess is dead, all chess players develop the player within themselves first and foremost, and only then work on their artistic and scientific skills. Such an approach allows them both to find the most rational solution and to expend time much more efficiently. At the expense of beauty, of course. We see such tendencies not only in chess, but in all other areas as well. We'll discuss this further in the chapter on move choice.

Brilliancies require time

> Create beauty when you have unlimited time available

So, professionals now come to games to earn points, and they don't look for brilliancies. Only amateurs still look for brilliancies.

By the way, now it's a good time to check if you're an amateur or a pro. There are four telltale signs that show that the player is an **amateur**:

1) Chess is *not* their day job, they don't focus fully on chess. Rather, they play and practice only occasionally. For them, "practicing" is how they get their kicks. For instance, playing online without subsequent analysis, or watching online commentary without analyzing the games themselves.

2) They are *not* obsessed with their score during tournaments. They simply play for fun, not caring about their opponent's style or their own tournament standing. They just play.

3) After the games, they do *not* draw any conclusions about what they need to work on. For instance, they don't study or improve their openings, improve calculation or evaluation skills or endgame knowledge... Again, they just play.

4) An opportunity to create a "brilliancy" at the board completely overwhelms their mind: common sense turns off, the remaining time is spent on devising some amazing lines (creating a "study"), and the move is chosen for its beauty, despite unclear consequences and the risk of squandering all their advantage.

If you see at least one of these four signs in yourself, congrats – you're a pure amateur!

And now let's expand on the last point. If you can't live without the aesthetic pleasure you get from chess, but it's hard for you to play because you can't withstand the tournament workload and time-trouble stress, you can always become a chess composer instead. There are no opponents, and you can take as much time as you want: you just sit there and create. For instance, study composer Nikolai Kralin takes a suburban train to work every day and composes studies in his mind on the way. And then he only checks them with a chess engine.

And Oleg Pervakov, the living legend of chess composition and perennial deputy editor of *64 – Chess Review*, composed studies during the famous "Roshal meetings".

Alexander Borisovich Roshal, the man who saved the most famous chess magazine in the world, revived and carried it on his back for years, loved to talk. His speeches were eloquent, clear and interesting – but very, very long. He would often call the editors into a planning meeting and speak to them for hours, sometimes 5–6 hours non-stop. Many of them couldn't stand it and had to come up with all sorts of coping mechanisms. When I asked Oleg how he managed to stay part of the editorial staff for decades, he answered, 'I composed endgame studies in my mind while Roshal spoke.' Such an unusual way to become mega successful in your field.

Conclusion. A professional treats brilliancies in the following way: they will not waste lots of time on a beautiful combination with unimaginable consequences. They will calculate for a bit, and then, when it becomes obvious that it's impossible to calculate fully, and the position is unclear, they'll just make an executive decision: either to go for it or not.

Chess perfectionism

> There is no such thing as "correct" or "ideal". Or, if these concepts do exist, the search for them takes so much time that ultimately there's no sense in pursuing them. You should just live.

The young generation doesn't need an explanation of what perfectionism is: in recent times, this term has "migrated" from psychology into blog posts and memes. In a nutshell, anyway: perfectionism is the conviction that results should be ideal in every way.

In general, perfectionism is a mental property, but if you don't control it, it might grow into a serious psychological disorder and cause lots of discomfort.

For instance, it's not enough for a perfectionist to simply write a letter to their friend: they need to meticulously check spelling, syntax and punctuation, and then rewrite it several times because "there's something wrong," or because "it's not ideal". Objects on the table should always be parallel or perpendicular to each other — at 90 degrees exactly, without any margin of error.

First Commandment of the Perfectionist Procrastinator: "Better do something well, but never, than half assedly, but today."

It's not enough for a perfectionist chess player to make a good move: he always needs to find the best one!

Yuri Averbakh on Vladimir Alatortsev:
Despite Alatortsev's numerous strong qualities, he had one big shortcoming. He was a perfectionist: he always wanted to squeeze the absolute maximum out of a position. This took him a lot of time, and he constantly got into time trouble. And time trouble destroyed all the masterpieces that he created so meticulously.

Poor Alatortsev desperately tried to eradicate that problem. He wrote articles on time trouble and even created the "Alatortsev Tables" that describe how much time one should spend on each move (like me in this book, lol).

My friend, IM Sergey Zhurov, who works as a coach, once complained to me in frustration:
My new student is a disaster! She thinks incredibly slowly on natural moves. Obviously, she constantly suffers from time trouble. I asked her, "What were you thinking about?" She answered, "I thought maybe there was a better move." And she tries to calculate decigrams of advantage on these scales of perfectionism... This is too much for my nerves! She'll never achieve anything!

So, how should you combat the problem of perfectionism?

Well, there is a way — get help.

What's wrong with that, anyway? When famous doctors or psychologists are asked how to combat a particular illness, they always reply with, "Consult your doctor!" Of course, the person

wouldn't even think about that on their own. I am the same. If you suffer from perfectionism and want to get rid of it, consult your doctor.

To be serious, there is a lifehack that worked for me. You should purposefully make things imperfect. Force yourself to settle for some workable solution without trying to make it ideal. After a time, you'll feel the changes, both in your feelings and in the results. It will become easier to complete tasks, to work, to live your life. You'll feel immense relief. I'm saying that so confidently because I have been there and done that.

If you are out of practice

> Maintain your fitness in every way possible. Meanwhile, think of apathetic periods as an ebb after a flow, this is normal. Watch the long-term direction of your life – it's a marathon, not a sprint.

Even if a chess player is not a time-trouble addict, if they haven't played for a while they may need a couple of rounds at the start to get back into form.

They will surely get into severe time trouble, and maybe their flag will even fall (OK – there are no flags on digital clocks but let's say, "they'll lose on time"). Lack of practice makes a person less sure of themselves – it may simply be too hard to move a piece from one square to another. During the third or so round, they finally see that it's not hard anymore – the pieces move easily. Even that skill has come back.

Why sacrifice the first rounds? It's better to avoid that. Therefore:

1)   Do try to play in tournaments regularly.

2)   If you haven't played for a while, start regular training about a week before the event. The training should preferably take place at the time the games are played at the tournament, or an hour later, so that your head gets used to working at this time of day. At these sessions, you solve endgame studies (preferably without looking at the board), study calculation positions, combinations, look through grandmaster games and try to guess the move.

3)   It might be rather useful to find a sparring partner for a few rapid games, 10–20 minutes per game. Play four or so games and quickly analyze them right afterwards.

4)   If you absolutely cannot prepare for the tournament to regain your old form, at least play online, but this can hardly be considered preparation – online and offline play is too different. This will serve as good training for your wrist, at the very least.

5)   If you can't prepare *at all*, then be very careful in the first two rounds and watch your playing tempo. Be as collected and disciplined as possible. Play rapidly. Do not grab tempting poisoned pawns. Avoid long complicated lines with unclear consequences, because you can both blunder and waste an inordinate amount of time on them. After you regain your normal form in the 3rd or 4th round, do whatever you like ☺.

If you spend more than 15 minutes on your move. Remember!

> – When you hurry, you look ugly.
> – As you lie dying, you will remember binge-watching TV serials 10–15 hours per day until you collapsed from exhaustion.
> – When you freeze on something for too long, uncontrollably and unconsciously, you lose energy.
> – When you freeze on something for too long, uncontrollably and unconsciously, know that you have simply frozen. Do not come up with a million excuses as to why this is "necessary". Maybe it is, but turn your consciousness back on and see what changes.

Another bunch of "Remembers", but now the topic is time trouble.

Remember! – That you are hideously ugly during time trouble. Both men and women are equally ugly. If lots of spectators gather around you at that point, it's not because you are playing beautifully. People simply love watching other people go insane. You're nervous, your hands are trembling, you shake all over, your movements are sharp and unsightly...

You cannot think with your mind in time trouble! When only seconds remain, a chess player can only think with their hand, and they only have time between raising their hand and moving a piece. The most they can do is to change the destination of the hand, that's all.
– Alexander Nikitin

Remember! – That in time trouble you would have given a lot for just one lousy minute, which would have allowed you to calculate a very complicated and important line. Here, you remember the time you unnecessarily wasted on pointless thoughts.
Remember! – That the more you think, the less fresh and clear your thinking becomes. You only make everything worse for yourself. Return to the position with a fresh mind, choose some candidate moves, and finally make a choice!
Remember! – That the move you're thinking over so much won't likely affect the result of the game by itself, but wasting time and energy probably will.

Whatever you choose, it will be a mistake

> For those who have problems with decision making: if you don't know what you want and don't know what you don't want, just make any decision. Any at all. It will still be a mistake, so why waste your time, energy and nerves?

I would like to share an incredible lifehack that helps me both in life and chess. I found it only recently and I articulated it myself. I can't remember exactly on what it was based: it may have been derived from quotes of great people, or from teachings of religious figures, or even from simple memes. This lifehack works for people whose parents would only accept success, victories and perfection from them. Perhaps you are one of those people.

One of my greatest weaknesses and the most painful of topics is making choices. Or, to be more precise, I always know exactly what I don't want, but I often don't know what I do want. Therefore, when I need to choose between several equivalent "wants", this turns into a supercomplicated problem. Sometimes it's so hard for me to make a decision that I delay it for a time, then delay it again and again, and this might drag on for years. For instance, should I throw away a toy that reminds me of my childhood or not? And so, this toy travels around the world with me, and probably only my children or grandchildren will finally throw it away after I die. The very next day after my funeral, no doubt.

It's hard for me to make chess decisions as well, and this is one of the main reasons for my time trouble.

After I came up with this lifehack, my life got a fresh coat of paint. And my chess playing too – it became so much easier to make moves! And time scrambles also became a rarity – they are more of an exception now. This is the lifehack:

Any decision you make will be a mistake

There's a well-known saying, "Any decision you make is correct." But it always did diddly squat to calm me down and motivate me. In fact, it doesn't work for me. Only the polar opposite did: don't fret, you might make mistakes. It doesn't matter what you choose. You're allowed to do anything.

Once I gave myself permission to make mistakes, I dropped the dead weight and took flight. Better late than never.

Time-trouble moves shall be erased from history

> You can't do anything good in a hysterical hurry. "When we are too focused on doing something in time, we can't even understand if we *should* do it in time. We lack sufficient awareness to evaluate the situation, check our priorities, and enjoy the process." (Sergey Kalinitschew)

As I already mentioned, I suffered from time trouble my whole life. I realized that there were several reasons for this "disease" of mine. I worked on the "treatment": my personality traits, complexes, psychological binds. Nothing helped. However, after one incident, I finally saw a small ray of hope that I would overcome this disease. Consider this the first stage of recovery. (I came out with the permission-to-make-mistakes thing later, and the first great leap in recovery happened thanks to this incident I'll tell you about.)

I showed my coach my annotations to a game. I was very thorough, I had worked hard on the analysis. When discussing moves after the 30th, I told him, "I made a mistake here because of time trouble. The next few moves are also imprecise."

He, like a true Buddhist teacher, smacked me hard over the head with a stick, or maybe it wasn't hard, or wasn't a stick, or he didn't smack me... But he definitely yelled! Or did he?... Anyway, he said the following in such a way that I remember it very well (or maybe I don't?): "OK, we won't look at your time-trouble play at all, show me your notes after the 40th move!"

This impressed me greatly. For him, a famous grandmaster and very experienced coach, time-trouble moves simply don't exist. For him, they lack any value or meaning. Thus, we don't waste time analyzing them. A superb coaching technique! (I have also started using it with my own pupils.) Of course, it's a bit of an exaggeration, but you won't understand that until you get smacked with a stick! You need pain. All my hours of analytical work on moves 30-39 are flushed down the toilet, we simply erase them from history. We deny their right to exist. Then I remembered this episode when I thought too long during the game: if I get into time trouble, I'll make weak and ugly moves not worth analyzing. Do I really need that?

If you have an advantage but little time on the clock, don't take risks

> In the end, he who has more patience wins

When the 40th move (and the danger of losing on time) approaches, a normal person's stress level increases. They move into Orange or even Red state. In this state, as I have already noted, it's much harder to control emotions and think rationally. The unfortunate player then wants to "go for it", "finally do it", it's "now or never", "nothing ventured, nothing gained"... in other words, they decide to change the course of the struggle. This is a common trap and even grandmasters step into it sometimes.

Since the decision to change the course of the game was made based on nerves, and not on sound judgement, the probability of error is 50%. Sometimes you get lucky, sometimes you don't. The player with better intuition has higher chances of making a good move. Is it right to do that?

The answer is obvious. If your position is **better**, there's absolutely no reason to play for all three results. Just hang in there until time control and then, with a calm and sober mind, make a decision on whether you really should change the course of the struggle.

If the position is **equal**, there's also no reason to take risks unless time trouble is mutual, and you desperately need a full point. In this case, this is a huge risk but there is also CHANCE.

If your position is **worse** – how much worse it is? If it's, like, very very bad, then it's a time-tested trick – get yourself into time trouble and then take random swings to make your opponent lose their cool and make mistakes.

If you have gotten into time trouble grab these tips

In life:
1) Do not make any important decisions in a panicked state. Cool down first.
2) In difficult situations, when your heart is racing, pay attention to your breathing. Normalize it, and your body will return to a balanced state. In addition, concentrating on your breathing will allow you to take a few steps back from what's happening and look at the big picture.
3) Also in difficult situations, do simple things. For instance, sit there silently. Or try moving smoothly and slowly, or noiselessly. These pauses are very useful; they will help you avoid worsening the situation and enable you to wait out the crisis. After them, it's usually much easier to make a decision, or it sometimes comes by itself.
4) In a highly emotional state, you cannot control your tongue. Simply stop speaking. Simply get up and leave.
5) When a person becomes too emotional, they do things that will ruin everything they worked so hard to create. It's better to wait, to sit in silence, to relax.
6) The world is a single being, everything is interconnected, every one of us is but a drop in this ocean. If something is "sick" in this world, then we'll eventually get sick, too. Therefore, love other people and help them out. Don't neglect yourself, either. Take good care of yourself: if one of your organs doesn't work too well, others will eventually break down, too. Take care of every component of your body.

1) Take risks only if your position is much worse. Otherwise, don't. Later, after the time scramble is over, you can calmly decide if you need to risk. Remember: if you're in the Red state, your emotions can drown out your judgement, even if you think that you are in control. This is the reason for the majority of chess losses. Postpone serious decisions until later.
2) Find a moment to make yourself aware of your breathing. If you spend at least 10–15 seconds to normalize it, your play will become more rational.
3) Try to make calm, solid moves.
4) Do not expose your king.
5) Do not make rash pawn moves, especially f2-f4/f7-f5. (I love such moves, although the position immediately turns from "better" to "worse" or even "much worse". Other players' hands always stretch for their g-pawn in time trouble.)
6) If you need to make a move, but don't know what move to make, try to find a piece that's not positioned particularly well. Or maybe its position is already good, but can still be improved. Start maneuvering with this piece. This is a well-known surrogate for a proper plan. Moreover, you will have made one more useful move on your way to time control.

When your opponent is in time trouble

> When there's mass or individual madness happening all around you, it's very hard not to join in. To continue acting at your own tempo, you need to have a sturdy nervous system and well-developed critical thinking.

Your opponent's time trouble can be as dangerous as your own. They have only 1.5 minutes to make, say, 25 moves! (Yes, there are people who love chess as an extreme sport.) How can you stay calm? It's impossible.

Your perception of reality is suddenly distorted. For instance, you start thinking that it's impossible to make so many moves in so little time, and they surely cannot be good. Thus you start hurrying too much or, alternatively, slow down too much. Your tempo becomes uneven and inappropriate, your moves are overly aggressive and shallow. It's as though you have joined your opponent in their madness. You have both gone insane.

What should you do?

You should play as though nothing is happening (one of those coaching tips that are impossible to actually follow). Professional chess players with a strong nervous system are able to do that. If you aren't one of them, let's get to concrete chess-related recommendations.

Playing in your opponent's time trouble

Your opponent's time trouble is like a couple of aces you get from a lucky draw in card games. Use your advantage wisely.

To understand how to get the most out of their time trouble, let's think about your opponent's condition. They're incredibly mobilized, concentrated, calculating replies to your main moves, they would love to find forced lines that help them make some moves in a row without thinking. They don't think strategically, they frantically calculate lines and search for tactics. Thus:

→ Avoid forced lines

→ Make non-obvious moves, but don't go overboard with flashy ideas

→ Try to pose problems with every move

→ Try to change the course of the battle, force your opponent to make important strategic decisions – this will make them panic at the very least

→ Pose your opponent difficult choices, especially those involving changing the pawn structure

→ Quiet moves with hidden intentions are great – they make your opponent anxious. The best course of action for your opponent in this case is to make some simple moves that improve their position, but it's hard to do that on an adrenaline rush.

Game 4
Z. Mamedjarova (2355) — M. Manakova (2268)
Women's European Championship, Vysoke Tatry, 2018

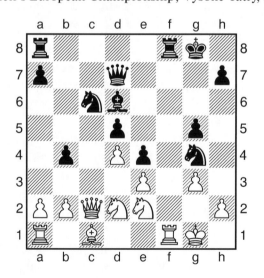

Black to move

I have a lot of excellent moves to choose from in this position. My opponent is in horrible time trouble, and her position is very difficult. I can go for a forcing line: 23...♘xe3 etc.

"But why do that?" I ask myself. "She has probably already calculated all the forced lines in a few seconds in her Red state. Better to get on her nerves, and you'll achieve a much better result!"

That is exactly what happened. I made a move that she likely hadn't even considered:

23... ♖ac8! A devastating move. Quiet, subtle. Another piece joins the play. Lots of new threats appear, and it's impossible to withstand such pressure in time trouble. When there are tons of threats on the board and only seconds on the clock, 90% of chess players capture something: **24.♖xf8+ ♖xf8** (now it's completely lost) **25.h3 ♘f2 26.♘f4 gxf4 27.♔xf2 fxg3+ 28.♔e2 ♖f2+ 29.♔e1 ♕xh3** End of, **0–1**

The magic 40ᵗʰ move

> The thin line between "Almost there" and "I can finally breathe easier, everything is over" is a twilight zone. The most horrible and inexplicable mistakes are made at that moment.

The hardest, the most fatal, the most decisive, the magical 40ᵗʰ move. Why does it have to be like that, dammit?! Why on Earth is the most important

decision in a game made on move 40? It would be one thing if you got about 15 minutes for this move, but no – less than a minute, sometimes literally a few seconds!

First of all, I should reassure you: this is a problem for absolutely every chess player. Secondly, the biggest blunders happen on moves 38–42: 38–40 because of great tension, and 41–42 because of "whew, we can finally relax." But why *the most* decisive moment has to happen on the 40th move, I don't know. Ask numerologists.

There's only one piece of advice. If you do have to make a momentous decision, and it's on the 40th move, simply laugh about it. Relax, release your subconscious, safe!

Game 5
F. Caruana (2792) – A. Giri (2772)
Wijk an Zee, 2022

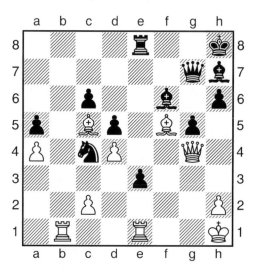

Make white's 40th move

The position is not simple. There's an only move that can maintain a balanced position: 40.♕h5!. It's not easy to find, but you can at least make "some move", right? Unfortunately, this was the 40th move, and this means that the move will be horrible. **40.♖b6??** The jaws of the whole world, watching the game online, dropped in unison. **40...♘xb6.** Even the inscrutable Caruana couldn't keep his poker face, such a blunder is a great rarity in elite chess. He resisted for about 10 moves for appearance's sake, and then resigned. **0–1.**

Game 6
R. Rapport (2776) – B. Deac (2671)
Bucharest, 2022

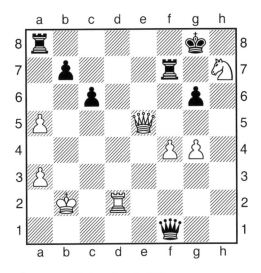

Make white's 40th move

Richard Rapport went down to a similar brain fart. Instead of the perfectly normal 40.♘f6+ (with an equal position), he played the horrendous **40.♘g5??**, overlooking a queen trade: **40...♕xf4.** This is hopelessly lost.

There are tons of similar examples, I only took these two because they are the freshest in my mind.

I also often got lost in this chess Bermuda Triangle, the 40th move that claims chess lives of both amateurs and professionals alike. In a game against Mariya Muzychuk, I failed to find the only, yet simple, move.

Game 7
M. Manakova (2273) – M. Muzychuk (2521)
Women's European Championship, Plovdiv 2014

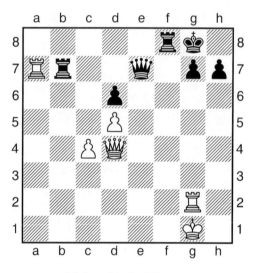

Make white's 40th move

Good, you found it. But I couldn't find it over the board. Mariya had previously made a mistake, too. She had grabbed my b3 pawn with her h3 rook to interpose on b7. And she did interpose.

The drawing sequence was pretty: 40.♕xg7+!! ♕xg7 41.♖xb7! I, however, played **40.♖xb7??** (I'm one of those chess players who try to capture a piece when they only have a few seconds left and don't know what to do) and resigned ten moves later. **0-1.**

The next two moves were made with the sole purpose of reaching time control. I was not actually in time trouble, but it's useful to do everything right even if it's not completely necessary – simply to develop the habit of following best practices.

– Boris Gelfand

After the 40ᵗʰ move, don't rush, chillax!

> There can be times when life forces you into the Red state (maximum mobilization). After you manage to complete your task (or a part of it) in this state, stop, catch your breath, calm your body down, take your time. In a calm, balanced state, you'll be able to make appropriate decisions and continue moving forward.

History is rife with mistakes made on moves 41 and 42. This is probably caused by adrenaline and other hormones that affect the brain in a way that is not conducive to making far-reaching, rational decisions.
— Alexey Dreev

After the time scramble, on the 41ˢᵗ move (!!!), check if 40 moves were indeed made. Check both your own scoresheet and your opponent's one. OK, the moves have been made. DO NOT MAKE THE 41ˢᵀ MOVE! Simply get up and move away from the board. Disregard the ticking clock, the decorum, the weird glances of your opponent and the audience. Go to the bathroom, eat a snack, drink coffee or whatever you like. I personally snack with coffee, chocolate and nuts.

Recently, FIDE came up with a new rule: you can only leave your table when your clock is ticking if the arbiter allows you. And the arbiter may not allow you to leave (this happened to my opponent at a recent tournament). In that case, make contingency plans: make your 40ᵗʰ move and immediately run like Hell from the hall before your opponent replies and the arbiter stops you. If you do get caught – well, you'll have to sit down and think. Need to go to the bathroom? The arbiter knows better what you need – sit down and think. What if you hid a mobile phone in a toilet booth?! Arbiters are vigilant guys who are always on the look-out.

Anyways, arguing with arbiters during the game is not a good use of your energy, it's better to maintain your concentration. If you are not allowed to leave the table, then stay seated, but distract yourself from the board entirely – don't look at it, don't think of it. Look away, eat a chocolate, forget about chess for a while, calm your mind and body.

Several wasted minutes won't decide the game at this point, but this small pause will allow you to leave the stressful Red state and gradually return to Yellow. With a calm head, you'll soberly evaluate the position on the board and plan the course for the remainder of the game without excessive nerves. Many continue playing automatically, but this is a grave error.

Moves 41 to 43: don't snooze, you'll freeze to death!!!

> When you complete a task successfully, there's a danger of
> hibernating, feeling too cozy. Drive out the sirens and their lulling
> song. You have rested a bit, now you need to go on.

There's a danger of hibernating at moves 41 to 43. You transition from the Orange state into Yellow – or even White: your heartbeat slows down, your breathing calms, and your body returns to its usual state. You look at the ruins of your game and try to comprehend the new, unexpected position. There's a danger of wasting an inordinate amount of time here. Some spend twenty minutes out of the thirty available in this state (back when we played with two time controls, you could snooze for 45–50 minutes... ah, the good old days!). Then something clicks in their brain, they wake up, get back to reality and realize with horror that time trouble has begun anew. But this is going to be the last one ☹.

Thus, you should first relax, get your body into a calm state, and then immediately order yourself to mobilize.

Of course, in games where you get 1.5 hours for the whole game, rather than for 40 moves, there are no opportunities to relax. No White states. Be ready to fight without rest.

With my coach Evgeny Sveshnikov, closing of the Moscow Open, 2012. Vladimir Barsky is also in the picture

Control of Your Inner State.
Concentration

Maintain concentration

> Concentration, willpower, patience and flexibility are the main ingredients of success. While belief in your luck is the key spice for this dish.

During a tournament, a huge chandelier fell on Artur Yusupov's table. It hurt him a bit, there was a lot of noise. I played at the adjacent board, but only learned about the incident in the evening.
— Alexander Beliavsky

For me, brought up on Botvinnik's scientific method, the ability to concentrate is the key to everything else. Seemingly a simple thing. But what about when you are in an extreme, crisis situation? Few people acknowledge that the ability to

focus one's thoughts during the decisive moments in a game is virtually the most important quality that a chess player can have.
— Garry Kasparov

There were a few times when I got so detached from reality that I was almost on the astral plane... Two or three times, I sat at the wrong board and tried to understand "when did I start playing the Najdorf?"
— Igor Kovalenko

At this moment, the waitress brought coffee. Alekhine thanked her, but continued to look at the board intently. Instead of sugar, he reflexively put a white pawn into the cup.
— Vladas Mikenas on his game against Alekhine in 1937

Chess is first and foremost a game for the autistic, those who can go into a trance and completely detach themselves from outside stimuli.
#fromtheinterwebz

My sister Yulia, who does not play chess, was invited to work as a photographer at an open tournament where I was playing. After the second or third round, I approached her in the press center, squeezed like a lemon, tired out of my mind... well, it's a normal state for a chess player after a difficult game. Her reaction: "Mashka, I'm shocked! You play in tournaments your whole life, talking about 'work', 'tension', 'tiredness'... This is the first time I have got to really look at you chess players. I'm impressed! Such huge concentration is required! How can you bear it? I wouldn't last five minutes under such tension!"

Only after seeing chess players' work from the inside do you really comprehend its essence. Ordinary people admire the obvious things: the ability to think logically and calculate long lines. This is actually the easy part. The hard part is the sporting component: being able to withstand incredible strain on your body caused by total concentration for long periods.

As you age, the ability to concentrate fully decreases. Kasparov confessed in an interview that he does not play "dynamic" chess anymore because this kind of play requires enormous concentration, and he can no longer do that. Away from an actual game, he can find the strongest move faster than the youngest and most talented players, but it's too hard for an older man to maintain the "electrified" state for hours. Thus, older players usually choose quiet play, where strategic understanding and extensive knowledge are more important than calculating lines.

By the way, I made an interesting discovery about myself. Previously, I thought that milk boiling over, forgetting that I had put the kettle on three hours ago, or other examples of poor memory, were caused by my general absentmindedness. But recently I discovered that the opposite is actually true – concentration is to blame! I get so concentrated on each new task that I completely forget about everything I did previously. I put milk on the hob, then pick up a mobile phone, and the milk boils over. I put a pot of soup on the hob, then sit down to work with a pupil, and the soup evaporates, only something mushy remains at the bottom of the pot. I go to write down something important in a notebook, but I start stroking my cat on the way...

The ability to concentrate fully on a task, entirely isolating yourself from all surroundings, is developed at home. And people on the autism spectrum don't even have to learn that, it comes naturally to them, without any effort.

This is a bit off topic, but I want to share a story. For eight years, I taught chess as a compulsory subject in a Moscow grammar school. And I had a pupil, a nine year-old autistic girl. Why her parents put her in an ordinary school is beyond me, as she was bullied by the whole class: they laughed at her, refused to be friends with her or even sit at the same desk with her. She took all that bullying stoically.

But when chess was introduced as a compulsory subject, it turned out that this girl was the most talented player of the lot. And she began to beat them all. Her classmates refused to play her at first, but I forced them under the pretext that this is a tournament, and they are obliged to play. Of course, when she started winning tournaments, she changed completely, and the classmates began to respect her, too. She got so enthusiastic about chess that she asked me for additional homework. I gave her positions for solving and worked with her after classes.

And that's how the story ended. At some point, the girl started to cry and complain to me that her mom wouldn't let her play chess and forced her to go to guitar lessons, which she hated. The more fascinated the girl became with chess, the more irritated her mom became. It came to the point that her mummy started to simply withdraw her from chess lessons to prevent her from playing. I don't know the subsequent fate of this family. Parents are, well, everything in a kid's life, and the teacher can only give advice, nothing more.

The root cause of blunders is loss of concentration

Hasidic wisdom:
You are where your thoughts are.

When does concentration decrease? Well, first of all – when you're tired. We have already discussed cases when you have wasted all your energy early in the game on calculating unnecessary lines and lost your freshness. Now, your head is tired and requires rest. Concentration weakens, and blunders become possible.

Secondly, when you are sure that your position is won and winning is simply "a matter of technique" [1]. Your body already begins to rest on its laurels, and even if your technique is the best in the world, relaxation leads to a loss of concentration, and you blunder.

Thirdly, when you are sure that your position is lost, but you don't have the heart to resign. Your concentration is zero, and you blunder.

Fourthly, when you haven't learned to concentrate on the game properly.

Professionals blunder much less often not only because they "see the board better", but also because they have learned to concentrate fully on the game. They don't get distracted by noises in the playing hall, or by their opponent's behavior, or by incidents concerning other players, or falling chandeliers, or even someone dying at a nearby board (that happens, too). The chess player plays on, fully immersed in an absorbing thought process. Conserve your energy, watch your state. Any blunder, even in calculations that you make in your mind, is a wake-up call that tells you that your concentration is not at its best. Perhaps you're not in the best chess or physical shape, or maybe you're too nervous.

And, by the way, if you blundered only in your calculations but not actually on the board, consider yourself very lucky. You haven't spoiled your position yet you uncovered an internal problem. It's your last chance to mobilize and pull yourself together.

However, if you have started to blunder at the board, then it's already crisis territory. You should immediately concentrate or offer your opponent a draw. They will sure as Hell refuse, but this refusal will force you to concentrate much more. This works, I have checked.

Someone asked Tal if he had sacrificed or blundered. "If I win the game, it was a sacrifice. If I lose, it was a blunder."

What should you do if you blunder?

> Give your all, regardless of what exactly you're doing. Most people spend most of their lives in a "permanent half-ass mode". But we are different, aren't we?
> "Nothing should be mediocre — from buildings to shoes. Mediocrity is as unnatural as lies." (Evgeny Evtushenko)

---

[1] Technique in chess is the ability to convert your advantage. It's usually based on strategic understanding, experience and knowledge of typical positions and methods.

If you blundered **in a particular game**, either on the board or in calculations, I repeat: you should do everything you can to pull yourself together. If you see that you are continuing to miscalculate, this means that you are not on form today. Of course, I'd like to advise you to finish that game as soon as possible, and to attempt to get a draw, but you wouldn't want that! I, for one, never want that. I play on, and confidently lose. The most reasonable conduct in such a situation is to offer a draw, but if the rules don't allow it (say, 30 moves haven't been made yet) or the opponent declines, make healthy, solid moves, avoiding complicated lines and positions.

I refer to such games as occurring on "bad days". Your head simply refuses to work, and that's all! Even though you were all right the day before and will be all right the day after. It's hard to survive a "bad day". The best strategy in this case is to try and avoid defeat at all cost.

If you blunder **in every round**, try to eliminate risks. Avoid playing long, complicated and tiresome games, keep your common sense and try to finish the tournament with a reasonable result, without dropping rating points. This is your goal. You can't expect much success with such bad form/health/nerves in this tournament. But a reasonable, practical approach sometimes works wonders: play without risk in every game, provoke your opponent to take risks themselves, and you might unexpectedly earn a lot of points.

I once asked the winner of a big women's tournament: "How did you manage to win? You've got a family, a business, how did you prepare for the tournament?" She told me: "Of course I didn't, I had literally no time – I just solved some puzzles, that's all. Since I had no practice for a while, I didn't know what form I was in... I simply devised a strategy for the event: do not attack at all cost. Your opponents will defeat themselves. I couldn't believe my eyes, but this is exactly what happened in every game, even against strong players. And so, I won first place without much effort."

If you blunder **in every tournament**, then you are a child or a beginner. That's all right, you are allowed to. As you develop your play, the blunders... no, they won't completely go away, but their nature will become subtler and more complicated. You won't leave pieces en prise anymore – now your blunders will consist, say, of overlooking a non-obvious move that leads to a strategically lost endgame.

Emotions

For years, people have been discussing the unique nature of Magnus Carlsen. And it's clear why: he has been showing his superiority for more than a decade in every chess variant (classical, rapid, blitz, online, offline...). And it's been noted that he completely lacks emotion during the game. There was even an experiment conducted on him, observing his heart rate during play. Here is how it went:

In 2018, an experimental match was held in Oslo between Carlsen and Nakamura, with both participants hooked up to sensors that observed the body's reactions. The results stunned everybody: Magnus' heart rate was exceptionally low and hardly changed at all, even in time trouble. There was a moment when the researchers gasped in unison: his heart rate dropped to zero! There was an uproar: calls, selfies, someone even ran to apply for the Nobel Prize... but then it turned out that the sensor had simply had a glitch and reset.

But no matter. At any rate, it was proved that Magnus was an absolutely unique man, something unreal. Some even asked if he was a reptiloid. (Probably one of those reptiloids who control our planet and who contacted Kirsan Ilyumzhinov.)

However, given the fact that Carlsen does some very human things after losing games (for instance, throws his pen on the table, draws a doodle instead of signing the scoresheet or similar stuff), this seemingly proves that he is not a reptiloid. Or... maybe he did that sort of stuff deliberately because we started to suspect the truth?

Carlsen's heart rate had finally reached 100 beats per minute — solely because he had to run to the bathroom after making his time-control move.
#fromtheinterwebz

Now, we're going to discuss ordinary warm-blooded humans, such as you and me. How and when emotions appear during the game and what to do with them.

When an emotional burst happens

> Emotional bursts happen to everyone — they are a healthy reaction to something unexpected. If you aren't in a dangerous situation where you should react immediately, then it's better to first calm down and then react. Learn to work with your emotions to avoid doing stupid things. Train yourself to first count to ten (or in other situations you can sleep on it) and only then react. Believe me, you won't become less charming or charismatic because of that, and you will protect yourself from serious mistakes.

When you're really anxious to do something, pause for a few seconds — this is enough to go from compulsiveness to Mindfulness.
— Sadhguru

Chess is not simply a battle of the minds — it's also a battle of nerves.
— Mikhail Botvinnik

I'll reveal a harsh truth to you: from the biological point of view you are simply an animal. And if you're healthy, then, as I said before, your body will react to unexpected things in a corresponding way: with a fight-flight-freeze reaction. It's an atavistic reaction, like when your pupils dilate or constrict or when you blink. An unexpected move can lead to an upheaval of the player's color state, usually from Yellow to Orange (on the other hand, if you were wallowing in the White waves, and your opponent suddenly sacrifices a bishop on h7, then you jump straight from White to Orange, or even straight to Red, and it will be much harder to calm down. Further proof that it's necessary to remain in the Yellow state for the *whole* game). Hormone production drastically increases, heartbeat and breathing quicken. And, as I have said loads of times already, rational thinking slows down. It's hard to evaluate the situation objectively — the process of searching for a balanced, sensible move is blocked.

All this means that you are not bad, you're just healthy. The only exception is Magnus Carlsen. But he, as we have already determined, is probably a crocodile in disguise (if aliens don't exist after all). By the way, he once let slip that crocodiles were his favorite animal.

You probably have a question: "How do I work with my emotions if I'm not Carlsen, not a reptile and not a reptiloid? What can I do?"

Well, let's first of all recall: when do we fall into complete disarray due to nerves? Let's look both at situations where we suddenly explode and quickly calm down, and, by contrast, at situations where emotions block your brain for a considerable time, shrouding your thinking in darkness:

→ When you face an unexpected move in the opening
→ After an unexpected move by your opponent, especially a sacrifice or a tactical blow
→ When you come up with something unexpected yourself, be that a cunning idea or a pretty line (this is more characteristic of weaker players, grandmasters don't get excited: they win in a cold, ruthless and practical way)
→ When you are sure that your opponent is cheating, using outside help or deliberately disturbing your thinking
→ When you are panicking because of looming time trouble
→ In time trouble
→ During an important game, when the situation in your match or tournament is very tense
→ When you are winning and know that your opponent can resign at any moment.

Women can also suffer from emotions for lots of other reasons, which are often not related to chess at all: there's a hole in my tights, I mixed up the move order, he looked at me weirdly, I forgot my lipstick at home, my nail broke, why did I make such a stupid move, how are the kids at home, there's something wrong with my hair, what will the coach say, why is she clicking her heels on the floor like a trotting horse... I could write a whole book just on this subject!

These are the main reasons for strong emotions, and you should pay special attention to such situations. But still, the most common reason for panic is your opponent's strong move that you overlooked. Let's discuss this in detail.

Spoiler: when your opponent makes an unanticipated move, you should recognize your own emotional burst, calm down and only then make a decision (this algorithm is useful in every life situation when your heart quickens in shock).

Catching excessive emotions in yourself is half the battle

> To be able to "count to ten" or "sleep through the night", you should learn to catch yourself when you enter highly emotional states. The ability to catch yourself is a very important quality, one of the greatest victories you can score over yourself. If you haven't reached such a pinnacle of your skills yet, simply remember a rule: if you need to make a difficult choice, don't react immediately.

Step one: learn to diagnose a highly emotional state in yourself. Let's call it "your heart quickens". If you forge on like crazy with this quickened heartbeat, if you cannot detect the changed emotional landscape inside you, it's very likely that you will make a wrong move. Let me remind you for the umpteenth time why. Because hormones have blocked your rational thoughts: you have lost your objectivity, your perception of the position is distorted. Therefore, you should say a safe word to yourself: STOP! + [safe word].

With that, half of your problem is solved.

Step two: calm down. Get your thoughts and nerves in order, normalize your breathing, and only then, with a sober head, should you evaluate the situation and make your decision.

Calm the heck down!!!

She is extra emotional. A woman of moods who cannot strike back if the tide of struggle has turned against her. Her mistakes come in series.
— *Mark Dvoretsky on his pupil Nana Alexandria*

Listen carefully: if you have made a mistake, there's a huge possibility that you will blunder again on the next move. Mistakes come in pairs! If you make a mistake, you should catch your breath, take a rest, and not hurry to make your next move. It's better to lose some time, but calm down and understand that the position has drastically changed; for instance, you stood better, but now you're slightly worse, therefore, you need to tune into a new frequency and prepare for persistent defense; you should never try to continue playing immediately. This is very important!
— *Boris Postovsky*

We have already mentioned breathing in the chapter on time trouble. Now let's discuss it in more detail.

Every chess player knows about normalizing breathing during play, but almost everyone tends to forget about it. Valentina Gunina, a brilliant blitz player, gave me a piece of advice a long time ago. She said that even in blitz, when you have very little time on the clock, you can still use a few seconds for a mini-meditation to catch your breath. And if you get too emotional, this is the first thing you need to do.

By the way, breathing is a good thing, with simple and clear "user instructions": it's enough to focus on it to get it back to the normal state, calming down the whole body in the process. Breathing control is the basis for most meditation, and it should be trained — preferably at home and regularly.

Don't make decisions in a state of panic

Please...

So, are we in agreement? Panic is bad. The chances of making a mistake in a panic are much, much higher. Maybe the position is not so bad yet, maybe it's even good, but you, dafty, are already panicking.

Step three: after you catch yourself reacting too emotionally to your opponent's unexpected move and calmed down, let's try to evaluate the position objectively: what has changed at the board, how unexpected was it, what are the advantages and disadvantages, and who is better now?

More advice from Dvoretsky: in that case, ask yourself, "Why is this move bad?" When you see the downsides of this move, it will become easier for you.

An analytical approach will help you look at the problem less emotionally, and suddenly, you'll be seeing the position in a more "three-dimensional" way.

If you can't calm down

> If you can't calm down but you have to make a decision, don't do anything radical or revolutionary. Try to have it both ways, to sit on the fence, to keep the bird in your hand. Such a decision will be easier to correct later, when you do calm down.

You understand everything logically: your emotions are in turmoil, but you can't calm down. What should you do? Choose a move that's as useful as possible. Something that "cannot be bad". Improve the position of a piece, for instance.

However... there are also situations such as in the following game Rapport – Caruana. What "piece improvement" can you possibly hope for if your opponent has just put his pawn under attack from five–and–a–half of your pieces?

Game 8
R. Rapport (2763) – F. Caruana (2820)
Paris 2021

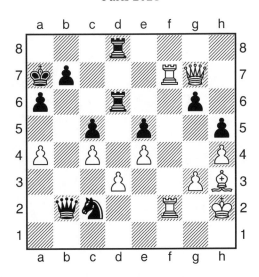

Make white's next move

36.d4!! Once you've seen it, it's easy to appreciate that this wonderful move is not just good, but the best! The black knight can't take the white pawn as his queen gets captured; the queen can't take it or the knight gets captured; neither pawn can take it because a white pawn will take its place, attacking the rook fatally; while the rook can't take it either because the white queen captures on e5 and the c5 pawn is loose. Black is in big trouble.

With Lev Psakhis, 2014

Energy

Consciousness and the brain are different things. If someone thinks that they control their thoughts or the behavior of their brain, they are deeply mistaken. You play chess both with your consciousness and your brain. And your brain can simply get overloaded and turn off at some moment. So, to avoid frying completely, it makes you play a move that leads to a quick finish. This is one of the reasons why we make mistakes. Chess players, like computers, can use various ventilation systems. Somebody may have a better cooling fan, but less processing power.
— Alexey Dreev

Even strong grandmasters sometimes make mistakes at certain moments that they can't explain later. As a rule, these mistakes are caused by tiredness. Of course, severe time trouble can also be a reason, but in general, these mistakes are made because the player loses control over themselves and their position.
— Boris Postovsky

Many said about Karpov that he was completely calm both during the first and during the sixth hour of play. After difficult games, he also liked to "finish off" his opponents in home analysis, securing a psychological advantage for the future.
— Grandmasters discussing Anatoly Karpov on Facebook

Energy has the awfully annoying trait of being expendable. As luck would have it, you have most energy when it's least needed, at the beginning of the game. And when you need it most desperately, it declines precipitously. You need most of your energy between moves 25 and 40, where the game is essentially decided. You also need it in the 5th and 6th hours of play, when you finish off your opponent or defend stubbornly. Remember the famous "Dvoretsky tragicomedies" where strong grandmasters blundered like the worst amateurs in the 6th hour.

Energy is a limited resource. Everyone has their own reserves, which are determined genetically. These reserves decline with age. But there's good news: you can influence the amount of energy — either increase or decrease it. Energy depends on sleep, food, physical form, sense of self, right interactions and other factors. During a tournament game, you spend so much energy that without good management, you will be simply drained. Your CPU simply burns out and turns off. (It's also important to distribute your energy during the whole tournament as well.)

The game of chess is similar to a long-distance run: if you take off as a sprinter at the beginning, you later simply fall and don't survive until the end. To have enough energy for the whole game, even the longest one, you should remember the rules of: 1) accumulating (storing); 2) expending; 3) restoring; and 4) preserving energy.

1. ACCUMULATING (STORING) ENERGY
– Good sleep before the game (deep and sound).
– Good health: lack of illnesses and malaises, being well-fed (but not overfed).
– Good mood.

2. EXPENDING ENERGY
What's more important: the quality of moves or saving time and energy? The answer is trying to make good moves with optimal expenditure of time and energy. Because if you make a strong move but spend lots of time and energy, you may lack the strength to actually win the game, while if you make a weak move without spending time and energy, this won't help either – you'll get a worse position. So, the priorities should be set as follows: 1) position; 2) energy; 3) time.

By the way, this is another piece of impossible-to-follow coaching advice. The understanding of how this works only comes with experience. But I'll still leave it here.

3. RESTORING ENERGY
It's possible to restore energy during the game if you know what serves as "food" for your mental work. It's **oxygen, water** and **glucose**. During the game, your whole body also loses **calories**, because your head was not the only organ that worked. You can replenish calories with energy-rich foods such as chocolate or bananas. Oxygen is replenished by normalizing breathing or special breathing exercises, water by regular drinking (of water, juice or tea), and glucose by eating chocolate or dried fruits. We'll discuss this further below.

4. PRESERVING ENERGY
The only situation where you can avoid deep thinking is when you are rated, say, 500 points above your opponent. In any other situation – don't even hope for that. The resistance is so strong now that even amateurs who play one tournament a year defend tenaciously – let alone the kids, who play so well and freely that you can't help thinking that chess has entered some new era where there's "No Country for Old Men".

And there will come a time when they create a problem on the board for you that will require both time and energy.

For such situations, you need to have a reserve of time and energy, a secret stash, if you will. Such stashes will come in handy both in the middlegame and in the endgame, where the fate of the game is decided, and you're running out of battery. Reserves are created first of all in the **opening**, and, secondly, thanks to **knowledge, positional understanding,** well-trained **calculation technique** and **thinking culture**. Let's look at these aspects more closely.

How to conserve energy

> Energy is life. Look at a smartphone with a low battery – there's nothing good to say about it, and you immediately panic: what if it doesn't survive until you get home? You can gain energy with sleep, healthy and tasty food, decent fitness, good sex, a feeling of inner peace, carrying out plans and achieving success. All these things cause beneficial hormonal processes that sustain life. Watch all these aspects and their balance closely, study yourself, fine-tune your own rhythms, create your own rules for your body. This is your energy, your life.

1) KNOWLEDGE.

The opening. You create the majority of your time and energy reserves in an opening that you know well. You remember the correct order of moves, the main ideas and structures for both yourself and your opponent – and so you spend hardly any time or energy, only checking the situation at the board fleetingly just in case. The opening is a shortcut that allows you to dash through a big stage of the long race without breaking a sweat. You go through the opening freely and quickly, and if your opponent is not ready for this particular line, it's a double achievement: you will deprive them of time and energy at the start of the game. These losses will definitely have an impact later.

The middlegame. If you know the standard ideas in a particular middlegame structure, you can search a bit for a more forceful and resolute plan, and if you don't find anything, you can always just go for the standard plan. That's why it's so important to study not only the piece structures in the opening, not only the move order, but also typical plans that are followed after you complete development.

If you know the main strategic ideas, you won't have to reinvent the wheel. For instance, what part of the board you should attack if the enemy king has castled long or got stuck in the center, what to do if your opponent launches a flank attack, etc.

If you know the typical tactics, you don't expend energy searching for them – they come up by themselves in your mind.

The endgame. You can't survive without knowledge here. Can you imagine not knowing the Lucena position, for instance? My pupils search for a solution for half an hour or more during lessons. Then we spend several more lessons memorizing the solution. It's impossible to find over the board. And what about the opposition rule? Or the knight+bishop mate? Or how to win with queen vs. rook? Or to which corner the king should run in a bishop versus rook ending? Or should you go for endgames such as rook vs. knight, rook and bishop vs. rook, rook and rook pawn vs. bishop, etc.? The endgame is the core of chess! The famous Soviet chess school teaches that you should start learning chess from the endgame. Or, as the Chinese say, *"the wise man begins at the end, the fool ends at the beginning."*

The opening has 20% annual inflation, the ending has 0%! Now think where to invest.
    – Igor Kovalenko

I didn't study endgames much because I knew that I would play endings a piece up.
    – Mikhail Tal

2) The second component of energy conservation is POSITIONAL UNDERSTANDING.

Grandmasters spend at least as much time on positional understanding in their home preparation as any other aspect. Positional understanding is a superweapon: it's not just an ability to evaluate the position correctly and create a plan, not just good technique to convert an advantage or the avoidance of strategic mistakes. Positional thinking allows the player not to think where it's not needed. A grandmaster, unlike chess engines, finds moves not by brute force, but because they satisfy the "demands of the position". And they don't calculate extensively: a couple of short lines to check if they aren't blundering anything, and then the move is made. And so a strong player only spends half a minute and minimal energy where a weaker player expends a lot of both.

If you have an opportunity to make a positional move, do it: it's faster and more reliable.
    – John Nunn

As I already said, when chess players get older, they try not to calculate lines at the board at all and avoid positions where they need to calculate. Not simply because their brains "are not the same anymore" and can't maintain concentration for long, but also because they are superior to their opponents in strategic decisions – positional understanding largely depends on experience.

3) Another way to conserve energy is well-developed CALCULATION TECHNIQUE.

I'm not sure that it can be developed "well" without working with a strong and experienced coach. That's unfortunate. If you do decide to spend money on an expensive coach, try both to use their knowledge and obtain important skills with their help, including calculation technique.

Now here's a question: what *is* "correct calculation technique"? This topic had been discussed for literally decades. Alexander Kotov was the first to explore it in depth, followed by Valery Beim, John Nunn, Mark Dvoretsky, Michal Krasenkow; this topic also appears in books by Valery Chekhov and Viktor Komlyakov, Mikhail Shereshevsky and other coaches and players. Still, even those coaches who haven't written a book on the subject always have something to say about calculation technique to their pupils.

Michal Krasenkow defined the essence of the calculation problem very well, in his article "Wandering in the Wilds". An amateur or average chess player

without good calculation technique jumps from one line to another, then back again for the umpteenth time, then forgets about the third line, thinks very long on the fourth, gets fascinated by the unexpected fifth one, then misses the win on the very first move or overlooks the opponent's simple reply on the second. There's chaos in their head, and their brain overheats in the middle of the game, starting to glitch and smoke.

I studied the arguments of various coaches on the right way to calculate lines, and, omitting the actual debates, came to the following conclusions.

How to calculate lines correctly

a) Candidate moves.

As you choose a move, always identify at least three candidate moves. To develop this skill, try finding three candidate moves at *every* move at first. You can even count on your fingers: one, two, three. And don't start calculating until you have identified all three. In more complicated positions, find five possible moves. After a time, this will become a habit, and your brain won't be satisfied with just one move, automatically searching for more interesting continuations.

b) Calculating candidate moves in the correct order.

While every coach agrees with the first point (that you should identify candidate moves immediately), the second point is hotly debated. I personally think that the order is not important at all. Start with the "CCA" moves (checks, captures, attacks), then go to those you like more, and then calculate the remaining ones.

Your calculations might start with a move that warms your heart the most, even though it looks totally crazy. Why? Because it will constantly vie for your attention: "Calculate me! Calculate me! I'm the best! All other moves suck, you should have started with me, don't waste your time! See, I told you so!"

In the process of calculating one candidate move, you might come up with another. *Put it off* for now – you should first finish with the move that you're currently calculating, this is very important. And then, of course, don't forget about the new one.

c) When you start calculating, calculate every candidate move just a few moves ahead to estimate what kind of position you will get. Maybe it's so crazy that you'll scrap that move immediately. In this way, you'll be able to decrease the number of candidate moves before delving more deeply into each of them.

d) Don't calculate deeply on every move. You should do that only in critical positions, at turning points.

e) Identifying candidate moves, calculating and everything else I just described is inefficient without understanding the essence of the position! This is usually done subconsciously, but sometimes it's useful to tell yourself outright: "OK, I need to save myself. It obviously cannot be done with normal moves, I have to come up with something unexpected." Or: "My position is absolutely strategically won, why should I engage in unnecessary tactics and give my opponent chances?"

By the way, this last point is very important. This is a common cause of losses. You overlook the main goal – to win, you forget that you have a huge advantage in both position and time, and you unnecessarily take a walk on the wild side, getting confused in the jungle of variations and losing everything. I often engaged in such seppuku myself – probably because I was not confident enough. I realized it all in my mind, but I couldn't stop myself.

You shouldn't start calculating immediately, without logical analysis of the situation. This leads to confusion and, as a result, to a waste of time and energy on unnecessary work.
– *Michal Krasenkow*

These are the main points for calculating lines correctly. If you follow them, you may be able to get the hang of it even without a coach. But the problem is that good calculation should become a *skill*, and this skill is acquired not only in play, but also at home – you should analyze games deeply, do specialized exercises... And it would be best to develop this super-important skill with an experienced coach.

4) The next important factor of time and energy conservation is your CULTURE OF CHESS THINKING.

Culture of chess thinking is understanding where you shouldn't spend your time and energy and where you should, when you need to calculate an entire variation tree and when it's enough to prune it to two or three moves. Culture of thinking develops with experience. But even if you're completely inexperienced, there's a great universal lifehack. It's called DAUT – Don't Analyze Unnecessary Tactics.

This great term was coined by John Nunn, and it's designed to combat one of the biggest scourges of a chess player: to calculate lines everywhere, in any position.

It's not even a bad habit per se, it's more like a relaxed state of consciousness. When a pro chess player looks at *any* position, their brain automatically engages and starts calculating lines *on its own*. Funnily enough, even when I look at a painting that depicts chess, the first thing I notice is not Virgin Mary and her child or the beautiful landscape, but the position on the board. And if the board is correct, 8x8, my brain starts calculating without my prompt, even if the a1 square, as is often the case in paintings and movies, is white.

Not to mention a TV series such as *The Queen's Gambit*, when you always look at the chessboard every time it appears... No, not at the main character, but at the chessboard, no matter what scene it appears in. And you start analyzing...

What should you do if you don't look at actual games with a holistic, mindful, "strategic" eye, but rather as a furiously working chess engine that sorts through innumerable lines? The same thing you should always do when you encounter a problem: use your willpower. You have to make a conscious effort to stop this madness. Because this pesky thing has another pernicious trait — it draws you in like a swamp, you sink into the depths of calculations and lose energy which is necessary to get out of the swamp. You simply *lose energy*!

So here are three related life hacks:

→   Do not calculate possible errors by your opponent.

It's a great, great temptation! "If he misses this blow, and I win his bishop, I can beat him a dozen times over! For instance... well... I can simply push the pawn... no, it's better to play for a mating attack..."

Hello, hello, Earth calling! Get back to reality! While you have been dreaming, your opponent has seen through your plans and won't miss your tactic! Don't overload your brain with useless fantasies that drain your freshness and clarity.

→   Act naturally during your game; unnaturalness drains energy.

A person produces maximum energy when they act naturally. What is acting naturally? It's the ability to move with the rhythm of your body, within the limits of your internal comfort. Any discomfort leads to imbalance and unfortunate consequences.

Some people like to sit at the board without standing up, others, on the contrary, roam around all the time, looking at other games. Some maintain a poker face for the entire game, others actively react with their mimics both to the opponent's move and their own thought processes. And this is great! All people are different, all move their own way.

If you have decided that expressing emotions is bad and you need to work on eradicating this putative "shortcoming" during a tournament, it's not the best decision, believe me. It's better to work on your traits and skills at home. At the tournament, this only leads to loss of energy, which you so need for victory!

$\rightarrow$ Remember that you can unexpectedly get a "second wind" in the 5th or 6th hour of play.

This is an incredible phenomenon, anyone who has experienced it can attest. It is well-known in many types of sport, and even exists in chess. Freshness of mind suddenly comes back to you, as though you have just started the game. You see everything, easily calculate complicated lines, and your brain starts working like a chess engine. I don't think that this phenomenon can be controlled at will, but it's likely linked to the chess player's fitness level.

Jump and pump, fitness bump!

Study yourself: when does your energy double?

> Energy boosts are usually driven by things that you like and that make you happy

It's only natural that a person's energy doubles when they are especially motivated. There may be different kinds of motivation, depending on your personality. Some get excited when they see a weakness in their opponent, others especially like wriggling out of losing positions – they literally beam with happiness, while others still see their energy double when they attack. Some players purposely get into time trouble because they only play at their best when they experience an adrenaline rush. Some play much better in team matches, while others do better when a big money prize is at stake.

A great energy surge allows you to play powerfully, to create, to make masterpieces, to move galaxies with your hands. If you know your special stimulus, you can steer your game in the desired direction. Your opening repertoire should reflect that, too. You should also play more in tournaments where luck comes naturally.

Resigning in a drawn position

> Sometimes, when a person's energy is depleted, they simply want to die. And subconsciously do everything to bring this about.

History is replete with tragicomic cases when strong players resigned in a drawn position – either in the middlegame when they fail to see a good defense, or in the endgame when they simply don't have enough strength to continue. In both cases, the reason is depleted energy. Without energy, you can't even lift your hand, let alone come up with the best move. And so, you resign.

Here's a well-known case.

Game 9
S. Khademalsharieh (2403) – N. Zhukova (2484)
Fide Women's Grand Prix, Tehran 2016

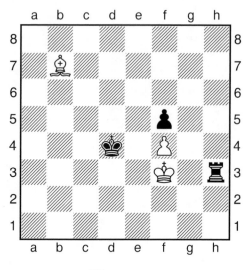

White to move

With her last move, **74...♖h6-h3+**, black erred. The winning move was 74...♖h6-b6, and then 75.♗a8 ♖a6 76.♗b7 ♖a7 77.♗c6 ♔c5 78.♗e8 ♖a3+ 79.♔f2 ♔d5. The white bishop cannot return to the long diagonal in time to control the important e4 square.

Incredibly, white... simply resigned in this position, **0–1**. Even though she had an easy draw. It's enough to control the e3 and e4 squares while having sufficient squares for the bishop on the long diagonal. For instance: 75.♔f2 ♖b3 76.♗g2 ♖b2+ 77.♔f3! ♖c2 78.♗h1! (white should always have a move in reserve) 78...♖c3+ 79.♔f2 and black cannot improve her position.

And one more case, this time from my own career, against a senior but awfully aggressive chess player:

Game 10
M. Manakova (2166) – M. Parvanov (1770)
Dimitrovgrad, 2023

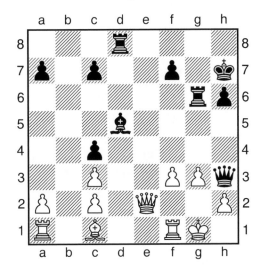

Black to move.
Show how white saves the game after 20...♖xg3+ 21.hxg3 ♕xg3+ 22.♕g2 ♕h4

My opponent was sure that he was winning (indeed, so was I, although in reality white draws in all lines and the computer shows 0.0 everywhere). So now he decides to play "spectacularly" and sacs a rook.

20...♖xg3+!? 21.hxg3 ♕xg3+ 22.♕g2 ♕h4. My opponent was radiating happiness and excitement. He was threatening ♖g8, and my position seemed hopeless. However, I pulled myself up by the bootstraps and found a way to draw.

23.♗g5! And now it was me who couldn't hide my joy. I was celebrating, even. His queen and rook are both en prise now. This move didn't just save the game, it put me the exchange up. He saw this, lost heart and... resigned. Which was totally pointless. Had he not descended into despondency, but continued with reasonable moves **23...♕xg5 24.♕xg5 hxg5** then we would have reached a position where white's pawn structure is so bad that it would be very hard for me to win, and the position would in fact be equal. However, the shock after ♗g5 was too strong for him... "my pretty sacrifice has failed, I made a huge blunder, got excited for no reason, yet happiness was so close, it's awful now, this game no longer has any point to it, I resign".

Learn to reset your mind and body during the game

> A new haircut, new home, new job, home decoration, emigration
> – this is all about the human's need to replenish and refresh their
> energy that has depleted, to support their life and to gain strength.
> A snake regularly sheds its skin to refresh. Be like a snake. A woman
> refreshes herself every month. Be like... OK, be like a snake.

The most difficult thing is to realize that you are tired. Your brain is so overloaded that it even refuses to let you know that it's overloaded. (This reminds me of a situation I have often experienced: I want to sleep so badly that I don't have the energy to drag myself off to bed.) But if you realize that you're tired, this means that you have a grip on reality!

The next step is to make yourself return to the path of easiness, fast play and common sense. In other words, to reset your mind and body. This will be a true feat.

It's very hard to do if your head is filled to the brim with moves and variations. If it's not your move, get up, take a walk, wash your face, drink some water. Have a break. Have a Kit-Kat. Mikhail Botvinnik (and he wasn't alone in that) recommended walking up to an open window and breathing some fresh air. Pay attention to your breathing, stretch your neck. Remember: you goal is not to regress back to the White state; on the contrary, you should be fresh and ready to maintain your Yellow state until the very end.

Celebrating Yuri Averbakh's 95th birthday with a song and not only, 2017

Freeing the Unconscious

The unconscious and intuition are both very important parts of chess, but I have no lifehacks for you here. I simply want to discuss this topic a bit.

The ideal state of a chess player at a tournament is complete immersion in chess. You are fully "there", in that virtual reality. For all nine (or even fifteen) days. You sometimes eat and sleep, but don't even notice that. You sit at the board in the same state, too. In this case, you don't need any

tips, any lifehacks, any "discussions on this topic". The dedication is total. We can say that a player enters a particular "trance" state, which serves as an important condition for creative work.

A Metropol Hotel waiter in Belgrade told me: *We had a chess tournament here, and I was struck most by Fischer. He always came to dinner with a pocket chess set. And he ate without looking away from the board. He studied even then...*

Creative trance

> Desire is the engine of life. If you truly desire something, if you love the process of moving towards that goal, you'll achieve it. And you won't even notice how it happened.

Well, I learned theater for six years under the guidance of the famous director and "guru" Boris Yukhananov (Grigory Zeltser was his deputy back then), and I was totally immersed in that world, with rare breaks for sleeping and eating. So I paused my chess career, obviously. For twenty four hours a day we, troupe members, made our own productions, acted in them and invited each other to act as well. Once a week, Yukhananov watched our "masterpieces", commented on them and created a big play out of them. Once the play was ready, we went public with it: it was added to the repertoire of the School of Dramatic Art theater, and we staged it at festivals and seminars, including abroad. I also had roles in productions of other directors – so my experience as an actor and director is rich enough to draw parallels with chess.

The most difficult part of acting for me was "turning my head off". It was constantly suggesting which feeling I should express in a given situation, which emotion I should use to say a particular phrase, or how to change my pose to do the scene "correctly".

I spent about three years learning to enter that "creative trance" where you don't think what to do next, but rather you are led by your nature, your unconscious. And your direction is determined by the *script* of the play, or rather the meanings that you discovered for yourself when you analyzed it.

At the same time, I realized that reaching such a state was the most important thing in any creative activity. This does not mean "losing your head", the head should always take an active part in the process. But you only need it to remember the words and the structure of the play, watch over the technical aspects of a performance and prevent you from going crazy. Because there is a danger of that.

The state of creative trance with an engaged consciousness is so wonderful that it can become an addiction for creative people. It becomes a "drug" for them, without which they cannot live.

Take stage acting. It's as though you enter the "acting corridor", and your nature drags you on. It's like you have died, and your soul is flying... It's hard to describe, but it's an incredible feeling! It's... kind of metaphysical.

Chess Trance

Chess is a special kind of creative work, and so, ideally, you should play games (and tournaments) in a special state of trance. All great chess players do so. Their moves are so perfect and beautiful that it's not possible to create them solely with a conscious mind! Moreover, if you give such a move to a chess engine to analyze, then it first evaluates it as "bad", but then, as it gets deeper and deeper into analysis, huffing and puffing, it eventually concludes that it's the first line. In other words, chess engines with their brute force algorithms can only find this move after a long think. (However, I must admit that neural networks of AlphaZero, Stockfish and others have lately learned to "think" like humans, almost nothing is impossible for them. In other words, chess faces a losing battle!)

Great masters find the strongest and most beautiful move rapidly, without brute-force. Why? Because when they enter the chess trance, they unleash their unconscious, which works wonders. It opens up the person's inner reserves and shows the shortest path to success. And I'm sure that you can reach the greatest heights in chess only if you learn to enter this state. Actually, anyone who has ever won a tournament, even a low-level, amateur one, can probably attest that they "could think of nothing else" during games, they even forgot to drink water. They only stretched their stiff necks instinctively. And they weren't "in the zone" only during games. Ask the player what they were doing before or after their games, and they won't remember! All questions, dilemmas, superstitions, thoughts, complaints, suspicions — everything just disappears.

Is this familiar to you? It probably is. You come to a tournament simply to give it all you've got. And, as a rule, you do win a prize.

Chess players get into various bizarre incidents because they live in that "parallel world" during tournaments. Some forget what hotel they were staying in (Lasker, for instance). Alekhine, as some say, once locked his wife in a hotel room and completely forgot about her. Grunfeld set an alarm clock to come to the game at five, and yes, he did get to the playing hall at five, but the streets were dark and empty. Only then did he realize that 5 a.m. and 5 p.m. were distinctly different things, even though the alarm clock doesn't care about such trifles. And sitting down at someone else's board and starting to think about their position — this has probably happened with almost every chess player! In this case, you sit and think, "Where has my extra pawn gone?"

How can you learn to always play chess in such a state? I don't know. This probably depends on a whole lot of factors: motivation, age, experience, level of opponents, psychological make-up of your personality... I'll leave this question open.

If I ever manage to develop a technique for entering such a state on demand, I'll surely file an application for a Nobel Prize.

True hunger is not a thing you can forget. It's a very intense experience. If you go hungry for 3–4 days, you won't even lift a finger unnecessarily afterwards. You'll be doing everything very carefully. You'll say only what is truly necessary. You won't make small talk, you'll be careful, because now your energy is limited, and you have to act in a certain way. You don't need any practice. You become quiet and calm simply because you are hungry. It's the same with the desire for something, it's like hunger: if your intention is strong enough, everything will fall into place, you won't have to specifically discipline yourself, you won't need to find a guru. The reason for a lack of such intention is too many snacks. People who constantly snack don't feel hunger.
— Sadhguru

Intuition

"Leaders" possess strong intuition, they hear it and trust it. Common people prefer to listen to those around them, to authorities and their so-called rational mind.

You should play on a balance of ease and concentration, on intuition, not willpower, do whatever you want!!!

I heard this advice a very long time ago from Alexander Morozevich. Let me remind you that the legendary Moro had an uncanny talent for seeing things in positions that other players were unable to see (I say "had" because he has almost retired from competitive chess). His moves were paradoxical, yet fully correct. And he shared his biggest secret with me: intuition rules.

Of course, you can and should trust your intuition, but when, how and to what extent? It's a very difficult question. And how can you tell intuition apart from common desires, carelessness and laziness? Where's the boundary that separates the ability to "see the future" and the narcissistic certainty that truth is what one considers right? The ability to recognize the voice of intuition — this is what I dream of, this is what I'd like to get as a birthday gift.

It's probably different for everyone, but this is how it goes for me: I do hear the intuition, but I fail miserably at heeding it. "I cannot do anything about this," I simply get carried away. So many times have I lamented and hated myself for not stopping in time and not telling myself, "Stop! Where am I going, what am I doing? Intuition tells me that I should just move the pieces back and forth and wait until control," or "Intuition tells me that this sharp move cannot be good," or "I've got a feeling that this unclear sacrifice will lead to great results." But no, I just forge on, and then I suffer from well-deserved grief and self-reproach.

Professional players have also discussed intuition. Some of them warn that relying on it is too risky, especially if you're out of form or facing a strong adversary. Others, on the other hand, regard intuition as the most important thing. Igor Zaitsev wrote in a book that future prediction is based most of all on professional knowledge. The more you know, the better your intuition is.

I'll give you some quotes, emphasizing the main idea, and will close the subject with this. After that, think for yourself.

The stronger your underline{opponent} is, the less you should rely on intuition and the more on calculation.
— Ilia Smirin

Mistakes are the result of tension.
— Magnus Carlsen

Your hand knows better than your head what to do. You only have to think seriously a few times in a given game.
— Aleksandar Indjic, in a private conversation

Sometimes I think with my hand. I probably should think more with my head, but it's not better organized.
— Zvulon Gofshtein

Psychological Problems

Lots of psychological problems and challenges come up during games. It makes sense to discuss them.

Think only about the game or don't think at all

> Any intrusive thoughts are destructive. They show that you're in an inadequate mental state.

When you think on your move, there should be no "extraneous" thoughts in your head. But such thoughts are always there, and, sadly, this is reality. Of course, the aforementioned "chess trance" is the best state for a chess player: you're so immersed in the game that there's no place for other thoughts or negative moods in your mind.

Usually, however, various thoughts wriggle in a chess player's brain, like worms. They become especially active if their opponent thinks for too long. A train of consciousness is not bad per se — this means that your brain is resting. But there can be some pernicious, destructive thoughts in this train as well.

Here are the three main types of *destructive thought*:

1) *Relaxing thoughts*:
– Okay, I win
– Why don't you just resign?
– Okay, I win this and then face Smith, or maybe Jones
– Ooh, they're all gonna cheer me when I leave the playing hall!
– I wanna sleep
– I'm starving
– I'm bored of this game.

There are also other thoughts that are not game-related but relax you: about your home and family, your loved ones, your appearance, your tournament position, your plans for the evening, and everything else that switches you from playing mode to "mundane" mode.

2) *Unsettling thoughts:*
– Okay, it's hopeless, there's no chance!
– He's too strong for me
– He knows the opening, and I don't
– Damn, he's fast
– What will my coach say?
– My head is killing me
– Why on Earth did I sign up for this tournament in the first place?
– The arbiters handpicked Smith to face me, the pairings are wrong.

Unsettling thoughts are worse than relaxing ones: they turn your mood more negative. And, as we already know, you shouldn't play in a bad mood! (Unless you are all fired up.)

3) *Intrusive thoughts*. These thoughts just refuse to leave your head, and you can't control them.

This reminds me of a well-known story from the Talmud. After the Jerusalem Temple was demolished by Roman emperor Titus, a mosquito somehow invaded his brain, grew in size and pecked at him from inside. It tortured him for years, no doctor could help. When the pecking became completely unbearable, the emperor ordered the doctors to open his skull and extract the mosquito. When the doctors cut the skull open, they found the mosquito, which had grown to the size of a baby pigeon. They extracted the mosquito, and Titus immediately died.

The most popular intrusive thoughts:
— Why have I made this move?
— I should have sacrificed that bishop, what a fool I am
— What if I had played ♘e4 instead of ♘g4?
— Why did I play this opening?
— He's cheating, that's for sure
— Someone is suggesting moves to him.

What should you do with such thoughts? Suppress them ruthlessly. Well, not exactly suppress... you can't stop thinking about the white monkey, right? You have to concentrate on the game. Not calculate variations, but think about plans, about whether all your pieces stand well, about how to improve your position and what trades you would like to make. It's very hard, but that's why you have willpower — to do what you think is right, not what your reflexes demand from you.

The game only ends after the clock is stopped

> *Finis coronat opus.* What's the "end" in your situation? Define it, name it and don't rejoice until you reach it. If you start celebrating beforehand, something will surely go wrong in a mystical way. Yes, right before the end. But there's actually nothing mysterious here: you simply relaxed. And how do you move forward without energy, even if only a single step remains?

You have to fight until the very end, even if your position is won.
— Garry Kasparov

The scourge of emotional people is celebrating victory when their opponent hadn't resigned yet. Some even start to think what they will say to journalists after such a "brilliant win." But it's only logical that, if your opponent doesn't resign, they are hoping to catch you in some trap, to make your life harder. And you're already super chill, seeing yourself accepting congratulations and giving autographs in your mind's eye... Your concentration has fallen considerably and is approaching zero.

That's why history is rife with cases when elementary traps in completely lost positions actually work — even in the games of very strong chess players.

Make an engraving on your forehead with the golden letters: "You can only relax after the clock is stopped." No won position is won until your opponent resigns. Be mobilized until the very end.

At this stage, it's not enough to feel that the game is won — you actually have to win it.
— *Boris Gelfand*

Here's an example from my own career. Actually, I have lots of examples — probably every second game ☺.

Game 11
M. Manakova (2268) — E. Hapala (2034)
Women's European Championship, Vysoke Tatry, 2018

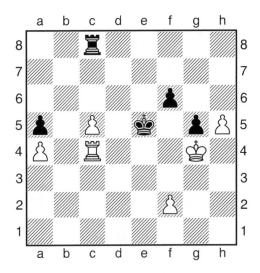

It's black to move and I have a completely won rook endgame. I love rook endgames and play them well. I want to play h5-h6 with the subsequent ♔h5. It's hard to understand how black is supposed to defend against that.

My opponent started thinking deeply. I was already tired of waiting, so I walked around the hall, with an internal dialogue going like: "OK, I get a point today and face a strong opponent tomorrow... stop, you don't have a point yet! But how can you not win the point?! You should be completely insane not to win in this position! She only has one reasonable move, 44...f5+, then I take on g5, she gives me a rook check on g8, and then I'll think. At the very least, I can retreat to h4, with an absolutely won game."

Of course, you should avoid thoughts of an easy win. But fantasizing feels so good! It's a European championship, after all. I had a good start to the tourney... My opponent now thinks on her move for 20 minutes, but I have already won both this game and the whole tournament in my thoughts.

So, she plays **44...f5+ 45.♔xg5 ♖g8+.**

Of course, 46.♔h4 wins easily. However, since I have "already won" the tournament, it doesn't really matter what moves I make. And so I totally lose my concentration and fall under the control of my emotions. And when emotions control me, I always start looking for something "beautiful". That is exactly what happened: "There's a beautiful and famous endgame study idea here! Can't it occur in my game? That would be so great!" Since common sense is turned off, my hand automatically plays **46.♔h6??**

You wanted beauty? Come and get it! Yes, this *is* a famous study idea. I knew it, and it seems that I desperately wanted to see it on my board.

Instead of the winning 46.♔h4, which I had planned far ahead (and which I also evaluated very positively when I looked at the position much nearer to the actual move), I play the suicidal 46.♔h6?? And so I got the study that I had desired so much: **46...♔f6! 47.♔h7 ♖g7+ 48.♔h8 ♖c7 49.♖d4 ♔g5 50.♖d5 ♔xh5 51.♔g8 ♔g5** etc. This was an upsetting, horribly upsetting draw! **0.5–0.5**

Get ready for a marathon game

> If your goal depends on external circumstances and other people, not only on your own efforts, be aware that you might not achieve it immediately. "I want it all and I want it now" is an infantile stance. A grown-up attitude needs patience, work and belief that you will succeed. But patience doesn't mean doing nothing. It means that you shouldn't get hysterical if not everything goes according to plan. Perhaps Fate has much more interesting plans for you. Wait and observe.
>
> To be fair, I should point out that people with the "I want it all and I want it now" attitude, who desire something badly, achieve their goals incredibly quickly and with luck at every step, to the envy of everyone. It almost seems that all doors open to them on their own. Why? Because they enter some kind of affective state and, like animals, obey their nature — they follow the path of least resistance, feel this "clear line" where everything favors them.

I fight for the win, and it doesn't matter how many moves it requires.
— Lev Psakhis

Of course, everyone is anxious to win the game as soon as possible, to avoid "toiling" for too long. When I come to my games with such an attitude, nothing good comes out of that: my moves are nervous, hurried, too ambitious. As a result, I get a poor position, suffer for six-plus hours and finish my game last.

There's a different approach, but I forget about it too often: being ready for a long game, until bare kings ("until tomorrow", as Nepomniachtchi said about his sixth world championship game against Carlsen). When you come to get a result, are ready to fight for it for as much as you need and have fun in the process, then... then your opponents usually blunder around the 15th move.

Be able to readjust psychologically

> Imagine that your life has just begun, from this very moment. As though everything else was erased and in fact never happened. Act and feel as though from a new starting point.

In chess, it's very important to know exactly when to strike and when to evade blows.
— Bobby Fischer

About turns await you in almost every game: for instance, you had a huge advantage, but then made a couple of wrong moves, and the advantage simply evaporated as though it never existed. Or you are now even lost. The ability to evaluate the change of circumstances objectively and set a new goal in the new conditions (for instance, saving the game instead of increasing your advantage) is a sign of mastery that comes with experience.

Experience — and also from work on your own games. If you analyze them deeply, you'll realize that many of your mistakes were made because you failed to readjust psychologically in time. You should clearly see the course of the battle and not have any illusions. If you see a drastic change at the board — breathe in, breathe out, calm down, evaluate the position with its advantages and disadvantages, and set new goals.

A poor player forges on in their inadequate state — attacking, lunging, instead of making calm, solid defensive moves. Or vice versa: they defended passively for the whole game, and now they simply can't see their own hurricane-force counter-attack or winning jab.

There's even a saying: the true mastery of a chess player is in their ability to quickly readjust psychologically.

Be flexible

> Yes, this is also relevant in life!

His exceptional talent lies in the fact that he feels who should be taken down in a pragmatic fight, and who in a creative one.
— Ljubomir Ljubojevic on Carlsen

His playing style reminds me of the Fritz 13 chess engine — he knows where to play mechanically, where to push hard, where to be aggressive.
— Garry Kasparov on Carlsen

The world's leading chess players are equally skilled in handling all chess weapons, and psychological factors often come to the fore. For instance, flexibility of thinking — switching quickly from solving positional problems to searching for tactical subtleties during the game, and vice versa.
— Evgeny Bareev

Switching quickly from a positional evaluation to calculation and vice versa is an important tool for destabilizing both your opponent's position and him as a person.
— Igor Kovalenko

It is not the strongest of the species that survives, nor the most intelligent. It is the one that is most adaptable to change.
—Attributed (perhaps incorrectly) to Charles Darwin

At the age of 40, I decided to learn a good opening for white, and I worked with a strong and experienced coach. He had me study the Rossolimo Sicilian, 1.e4 c5 2.♘f3 ♘c6 3.♗b5. He also recommended transposing into similar structures through 1.e4 c5 2.♘c3.

Of course, I wanted to try out this line in the first tournament after training. But this tournament was a strong mixed-sex round robin in Israel! It hurts to remember (I don't even want to check), but I lost almost all my games in this

opening, or maybe even all. Thankfully, I did manage to score some wins with black. My rating took a horrible dip, about 50 points.

And so I stood there at the closing ceremony, sad and dejected, and got talking with a famous Israeli grandmaster. I asked him, how could that be? What was my mistake?

And he answered, "I don't understand why you play the Rossolimo against strong male opponents?! The types of position that occur are ideal for men's thinking: it's almost impossible to stir up any chaos, and you have to play positionally and firmly. You should play such openings against women, because you're probably better than them in positional understanding." I remembered that advice for life. But how can you refuse the temptation to try out an opening you just studied?! So, this is the conclusion that I drew: even though I'm not a top grandmaster, my level is more than enough to be able to choose if I want to play solidly and positionally or boldly and a bit irrationally against my opponent. Every opponent should be approached differently, with different opening and playing style choices. I should treat this matter seriously as I prepare for every game.

Expand your toolkit (openings, technique, calculation, defense, understanding of material imbalances) instead of making it more polished and narrower. Flexibility trumps "correctness" today, because "correctness" is predictable.
— Igor Kovalenko

And if you do want to try out a new opening in your next tournament — don't be a wussy and be ready to lose 100 rating points. So if you lose only 50, consider it a major success!

Be persistent

Well, obviously...

Karpov said, "I came from the provinces, didn't know the openings and would immediately get a less than ideal position, but this helped me to become more tenacious in defense." Actually, all great chess players defend masterfully.
— Boris Postovsky

The most important things in defense are composure, presence of mind and persistence. Chess players who were famous for their defensive skills, such as Emanuel Lasker or Anatoly Karpov, had these qualities in abundance.
— Artur Yusupov

What's the difference between a world champion and other players? If he is slightly better, he'll squeeze you and grind you down, you won't escape easily. And if he is slightly worse, you'll have to suffer a lot to defeat him.
— Vassily Smyslov

Teach a sportsperson to fight for any place until the end, and they will learn to fight for first place.
— Larisa Latynina (Soviet gymnast)

No game was ever saved by resignation.
— Savielly Tartakower

When you think that there's no hope, simply remember the lobsters in the restaurant aquarium on the Titanic.
#fromtheinterwebz

There are two options in difficult positions: you either resign or continue to resist with all your strength and fury. If you have lost heart, but continue playing, you're doomed. Chess players have finely tuned instincts: they can immediately see if their opponent has already given up, in which case they finish them off mercilessly.

Persistence is a very important trait for a chess player. It's possible that circumstances of one's childhood and teenage years play as much a role as genetics in this. I had pupils from rich European countries, from prosperous families. They were incredibly lacking in tenacity! And nothing helped: no admonition, no persuasion, no examples. They simply weren't used to fighting for survival.

I compare them with their opponents. Here's a poor boy from a poor family, from a provincial town in a poor country. And he is playing in his national championship. Grabbing a qualifying place for a world or European championship is the only chance he'll ever get to succeed in life. And he faces other kids who also grew up in difficult economic and housing conditions, with an unstable family life. They are not kids though — they're piranhas, bulldogs, wolf cubs. They fight for every half-point until their last breath, searching for random chances even in hopelessly lost positions.

And my... uh... snowflakes face those wolf cubs. My pupil has a drawn position, but he resigns — solely because he doesn't want to salvage a passive position! What?! Resigned?!?! LOLWUT?!! You!! How could you?!! It's hard to describe my emotions at that point. A coaching job is nerve-wracking, indeed.

Stubborn chess players often get invited to teams. For instance, I heard great praise for Ruslan Ponomariov from his teammates. I heard it a long time ago, but remember it well. Even if he's completely lost, his teammates don't abandon hope. Or if they do abandon hope and go out to dinner (because there's "absolutely no chance" left in the position), he still manages to snatch a draw or even win. Nimble, flexible, tenacious, patient, resourceful — that's how he was characterized.

Obviously, if you are not persistent, you give your opponent a big advantage. I'll say even more: non-persistent people simply don't achieve much in chess.

And those grandmasters who do achieve a lot differ from each other in intensity and style of their persistence. One player "digs for treasure" in lost positions – tries to find a study-like situation and wriggle out in a pretty way. Another willingly goes for time trouble and manipulates his opponent psychologically, provoking a mistake. The third tries to wear his opponent down. The fourth starts playing super-aggressively. While the fifth plays easily and relaxed, following his intuition. Fifty shades of grit.

With Vishy Anand, at the 2016 candidates tournament

Control of the Game

So, we have discussed the topic of controlling yourself during the game (concentration, energy, physical and psychological shape) as well as the clock. Now let's talk about controlling the game itself.

A look from the "outside"

> Create pauses in your life: stop, pull away from everybody and think in silence. Ask yourself, "Where am I? Where am I going? Do I feel good? Is my current life what I dreamed it would be? What's right, what's wrong? Should I change something, and if I should, in what direction?" Don't lie to yourself, play games or cheat when answering these questions. Nobody hears you, nobody will criticize or shame you. Such pauses in life are the best navigator. They should be at least one day long (several days are even better).

You should see the big picture, like an artist.
— Alexander Alekhine

If you get confused by the web of lines and immediately reply to your opponent's moves with your own, without understanding the logic of the game as a whole, you will lose. You condemn yourself to "looking from the inside", and this always brings trouble.

In any process, a look from the outside, mindful and comprehensive, is necessary. This look develops during your whole life, even if you don't notice it. That's why older people are considered wiser. That's the main reason. They have an ability to see the big picture as a whole, not as fragments.

How to look at the "big picture" of a chess game? There are signposts that show the right direction. And these signposts are called — you wouldn't believe it — *positional evaluation*.

Yes, it's that simple. It turns out you cannot become a successful player without it.

Professional players always have the positional evaluation process turned on in the background; it naturally turns on when the game begins and turns off after they sign the scoresheets. After basically every move, strong players scan briefly for changes in the position, because any move inevitably changes the course of the game in some way. But sometimes they stop at the "crossroads" for a longer time to think deeply.

When do these "crossroads" appear? When the direction of the game changes significantly: the pawn structure has changed, mass trades took place, one player outwitted the other and gained material. In this case, the grandmaster will stop and evaluate the new position. He won't look at concrete lines, the important thing here is to look at the big picture, finding the good and bad points of the position, outlining the plans – both your own and your opponent's. When you control what's happening, you won't be fumbling around like a blind kitten. For instance, you were better, but then you saw that your advantage disappeared after mass trades. Clearly, the logic of the game got disrupted after some move (don't think about which move this was now, it's better to determine that in home analysis), and now you have to play in new circumstances.

If you aren't a strong grandmaster yet, you'll have to force yourself to evaluate the position, engaging your willpower to gradually make this skill automatic. If you learn to control the game's logic, you won't simply reply "move by move", you'll push the game in the right direction, you won't look for the "best" continuation, but for the one that brings you closer to the goal – the win. Your style will become increasingly effortless and confident, and your mind will be open to risk and joyful play.

There are three stages in a chess game: the opening where you're counting on getting an advantage, the middlegame where you think that you have an advantage, and the endgame where you see that you're lost.
– Savielly Tartakower

Nobody can teach you correct positional evaluation – you have to learn it yourself

> Every thinking person makes "navigational pauses" when they reach a critical age and every 31st December. The ability to make such pauses on other days allows them to proceed more mindfully.

A 2200-rated player often evaluates the position roughly. They rely on conjectures. Sometimes this works – they make a correct choice in a critical position and defeat a much stronger opponent. 2500-rated players, as a rule, know positions of every type, and their evaluations are much more precise. The

thinking of a 2700-rated player is more ordered... By "order", I mean that
their thoughts are under better control.
  — Alexander Mikhalevsky

Positional evaluation is a fundamental skill for a chess player, almost the most important one. But it cannot be taught. You have to learn it yourself. I'll explain why.

Kids are told: you should evaluate the position using such factors as material balance, king safety, pawn structure, control over the center and open files, space advantage, piece activity, etc. But I know from experience that pupils fail to do that. They say things like, "I'm better because I have more space, I have the center, and the king is safe." But then I ask, "What about the only open file, the b-file? Who controls it? Look!"

They are baffled: what about the center, the space, the king?

And then I realized what the problem was: the priority of the factors! This is the secret of any position. In other words, not the ingredients, but their proportion. Like in every recipe. What's the most important element in Coca-Cola, for instance? The proportions, of course, not the composition. If the Coca-Cola Company published the actual proportions, everyone and their little dog would have copied the drink. That's why we only see the list of ingredients and nothing more on the label. No "secret knowledge" on the proportions.

The "secret knowledge" of chess is understanding which evaluation factors are the most important in a concrete position. And this knowledge can be acquired only by serious individual work.

This reminds me of the Kabbalah. It contains: 1. common knowledge accessible
to everyone; 2. secret knowledge accessible only to the few best pupils; and 3. the
knowledge of the "Chariot of Elijah the Prophet", which is knowledge that "cannot
be shared".

As they grow and develop, chess players study more and more new positions, or "chess images", as Dvoretsky refers to them. (By the way, I heard from a strong grandmaster that these "images" hold the key to success in chess. The more "images" a chess player knows and remembers, the better they can navigate the ocean of positions of different types.)

A professional player doesn't simply study their own games — they look through classical games and top players' games as well. And they don't simply look at them — they analyze them carefully, read the annotations... And so, as they look at the position at the board, they just *know* its evaluation, based on their acquired experience and intuition.

Let me explain using an example from my own career. It's not necessary to play through the opening, you may start with the diagram.

Game 12
N. Nguyen (2625) – M. Manakova (2320)
Indonesia Open, Jakarta 2013
Grunfeld Defense

1.d4 ♘f6 2.c4 g6 3.♘c3 d5 4.♕b3 dxc4 5.♕xc4 ♗g7 6.e4 0–0 7.♗e2 a6 8.♗f4 ♘e8 9.♘f3 b5 10.♕d3 ♗g4 11.♖d1 ♘c6 12.e5 ♘b4 13.♕d2 ♘d5 14.h3 ♗xf3 15.♗xf3 c6 16.♘xd5 cxd5 17.h4 ♘c7 18.h5 ♘e6 19.♗h6 g5 20.♗xg7 ♔xg7 21.h6+ ♔h8 22.♗g4 f5 23.exf6 ♖xf6 24.♔f1 ♕d6 25.♖e1 ♖g8

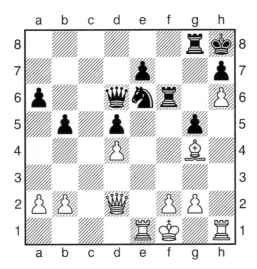

White to move. Evaluate the position: who is better and why?

I remember making my last move, 25...♖a8-g8, and being incredibly satisfied with myself. I was thinking, "Black is probably better. My king is safe, the rook is strong on the f-file, I can also seize the c-file later, I have a strong knight and active pieces. The white king has failed to castle, and the h6 pawn can become a weakness..." That's what I was thinking during the game. That was my effort at evaluating the position: you go, girl!

And here's what happened:

26.♕e3 ♖gg6 27.g3 ♕b6 28.♔g2 ♘xd4?? (28...♕xd4 was a decent move that led to a worse, but totally defensible position) **29.♖c1 ♖xh6 30.♖xh6 ♖xh6 31.♖c8+**. Black resigned, **1–0**.

Ngoc Nguyen was a nice guy, he offered to analyze the game together, which rather flattered me. I remember our post-mortem analysis in every detail. The main question for me was, where did I make a mistake? Everything had gone so well, I had a good position, and then I was even better! What was the wrong move I made in the end? He, on the other hand, mostly said that white had an advantage from the beginning, and perhaps he could have even played better on some moves. And after 25...♖g8 ... "The rest is not interesting." And yes, black should have captured with the queen, this would have allowed me to defend. Wait a second! I'm sorry? After ♖g8, it's "not interesting"?! And here I was, thinking that I was finally better!

After the analysis, I went back to my room thinking, "Some 2600 player he is! His evaluation is just so wrong!" But I still had my doubts...

At home, the computer confirmed Nguyen's greatness and my total lack of chess understanding!

Can you explain why this position is **better for white**, not **worse**? Probably you can: because of the pawn structure! Since the black rooks are tied to defending pawns, they can neither seize the c-file nor launch an attack along the f-file (the very same factors that I thought made my position "better").

So it turns out − attention, please!!! − that the pawn structure factor outweighed all the other evaluation factors! How was I supposed to know that? Only from experience. After playing that game and analyzing it extensively, I will become familiar with this type of position and its evaluation. Nguyen, on the other hand, had no doubts at all! He went through that stage much earlier, that's why he was and is a 2600+ player.

Something similar happens to me, too, when I get to face a much weaker opponent. I get a better position out of the opening because I know this particular line. In the early middlegame, my opponent makes a terrible strategic mistake and suffers for the whole game. Eventually they blunder, and only then do they start to suffer visibly − they're simply inconsolable because of that blunder! Almost in tears, then crying and ash sprinkled on their heads. You, however, look at your opponent and don't understand what the fuss is about: they blundered in an absolutely lost position, and only after spending all their energy on a difficult defense for almost the whole game!

And so they wail after the game, how could they have blundered like that! You tell them, well, your position was poor to put it mildly. Moreover, for the whole game. But they strongly disagree and argue. Well, let's look, then.

A completely useless analysis ensues, where everything is clear to you, but they are still sure that they were better for the entire game. You usually fail to convince that opponent, because they don't want to learn (there are exceptions, but they are rare). Of course, the time spent on this "analysis" is time wasted.

So, let's get back to our discussion of positional evaluation mastery.

Here is another example of how all laws get violated in the name of another, more important law:

Game 13
M. Carlsen (2834) – W. So (2792)
Wijk aan Zee, 2018

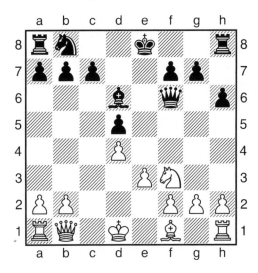

White to move

Here's a position. White cannot castle and his pieces are not well-developed. He is slightly worse. What move would a normal person make? Develop the bishop, for instance. Or improve the queen's position. What else? Think about where the king should be hidden and hide it there.

That's how any chess player would think.

But not Magnus. He played... drum roll...

11.e4!!??!??!?!??!!!??!??!!?

Huh? What on Earth is this? He exposes his king, opens up the whole position, loses a tempo, and weakens the center. Hah!

The computer is shocked by this move at first, but then, after a deep think, comes to the conclusion that yes, this *is* the strongest move, and it proclaims equality! Wesley So was probably also dumbfounded at first, but then realized that this was the strongest move. However, he failed to find precise replies and lost. (If you want to look at this game as a whole then try to consider which evaluation factors were behind this monstrous, almost reptiloid move.)

By the way, take note. We live in a seminal time when all the reference points have been broken, and chess is also undergoing tectonic shifts. Kids who only recently learned the rules of the game amazingly manage to select the computer's first line even in the most complicated positions. They don't even think of positional

evaluation, prevailing factors, long-term plans... They simply make an intuitive move, and it turns out to be the first line of the engine. I show some pupils of mine positions from games by, say, Capablanca, and ask them to guess the move. They do the assignment. I tell them, "Capablanca made a different move, but you, as usual, found the strongest move, the inhuman one, the first line of the computer. Now, however, try to guess the *actual* game move."

Yes, chess changes, but chess teachers are slow to catch on. Therefore, we teachers continue teaching the old ways. Even though we have also started to play games that horribly violate all the laws of "correct" play.

Now I'm going to show you my game from a recent tournament, noting, just for fun, which laws are violated on a move by move basis. Well, if you really are a stickler for the letter of the law. The computer, on the other hand, praises the game, the whole play was consistent with its first lines. That's how chess is played now ☺.

Don't try this at home.

Game 14
A. Jovanovic (1929) – M. Manakova (2146)
Serbian Women's Championship, Senta, 2023
Sicilian Defense

1.e4 c5 2.♘f3 ♘c6 3.♗b5 d6 4.0–0 ♗d7. Black persistently ignores the development of her kingside.

5.♖e1 a6 6.♗f1. Two moves by the same piece in the opening.

6...♗g4. And again, two moves by the same piece in the opening. If white can, why can't I?

7.c3 e6 8.d4 ♗xf3. A more valuable bishop is given up for a knight. A pinned knight, for that.

9.gxf3. Deliberate doubling of pawns. White went for this "disrupted" structure when she played 8.d4.

9...♕h4. Early development of the queen.

10.d5 ♘e5. Leaving the queenside completely undefended.

11.♕a4+. White liked the early development of black's queen and decided to repeat her feat.

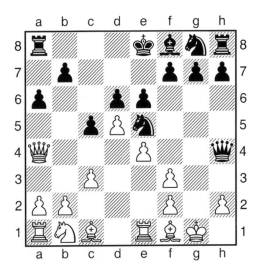

11...♔e7! Oh, the horror! The horror! Giving up castling, the black king moves towards the center of the board, blocking the path of its own bishop (the poor priest doesn't make a single move in the entire game, remaining a living witness to this monstrous encounter).

12.♗e2 ♘f6 13.♕a5. Instead of developing *all* her forces, white continues to play with the same pieces.

13...g5 14.♕c7+ ♘fd7 15.dxe6 fxe6 16.♖d1 ♔f6!?. This is the engine's second line. The first line is the even more insane 16...♔f7, leaving the knight on d7 both pinned and effectively unprotected.

17.♘d2?. For the first time in this game, white decides to play a "correct" move — first develop a knight and only then the bishop. And this was a serious mistake: 17.♗e3 was stronger (even though white's position remained difficult). She needed to continue this masochistic suffering and make moves that would prompt all the classics of chess to collectively spin in their graves.

17...♖g8 18.♘f1 g4 19.fxg4??. White had a defensive resource, but my opponent failed to find it. Probably because she'd already given up in her heart: 19.f4 ♘f3+ 20.♔h1 ♕xf2 21.♗e3! ♕xe2 22.♕xd7, and white can still thrash around a bit.

19...♘xg4 20.♗xg4 ♕xg4+ 21.♘g3 ♕xd1+ 22.♔g2 ♕a4 23.e5+. The last swindle attempt.

23...♘xe5 24.♕xh7 ♖g6. A trap. For some reason, I had no doubt that my opponent would overlook this idea in time trouble. How would 99% of people play here with their hand? Correct.

25.♗e3?? ♕e4+ 26.♔f1 ♕d3+ 0–1

The seventh sense

> The sense of harmony is an important sense, as important as the other six. Good news: it can be developed.

I immediately see the essence of the position and I know what to do in it. Others evaluate, but I just know.
— Jose Raul Capablanca

Positional sense is a special "spider-sense" of chess humans. We can call it the "seventh" sense (after the known six: vision, hearing, taste, smell, touch and balance). Ordinary people have an "aesthetic sense" instead. Which organ controls this sense and where it's located, I don't know yet. Perhaps it's everywhere, in every cell of the body. But it's completely obvious that some players already possess this sense naturally (such as Capablanca, Karpov or Anand), while others have to work a lot to develop it.

The chess human with a strong seventh sense thinks, "well, the position's kinda cramped," or "the king is too exposed," or "the pawn structure is too fragmentary, I can't be better." Or rather, he doesn't *think* that, he simply knows it.

If you haven't reached such heights in mastery yet, here are some guiding principles that will help you with evaluation:
1. The position contains all the necessary information. Evaluate the position objectively, without emotions, without "rooting" for one side, as you always do.
2. Evaluate the position according to the classical principles, but don't be too dogmatic, don't forget about your own "positional feeling".
3. Your main guideline is the pawn structure. It largely defines the evaluation and subsequent strategy.
4. Never forget about the king.
5. Piece activity: think of the chessmen as though they each have a soul, they want to move freely, to work, to enjoy life, to dance. Especially the rooks and the bishops: they are mobile, freedom-loving introverts, they

need space.

Respect the character of your pieces and their strong qualities. And always remember Tarrasch's principle: *"One piece is bad, the whole position is bad."* All pieces are equally important. But some of them are more important, like in life.

And Paul Morphy used to say, *"Help your pieces, and they will help you."* Get them into battle, and they'll get you a win.

6. Don't forget about passed pawns as you evaluate the position. Just a reminder.

PS: As he worked on the book, my translator informed me that Emanuel Lasker also spoke of the seventh sense of chess humans, calling it "the ability to anticipate how my opponent will reply to my opening move."

Well, I never claimed to be the originator of the idea (they are all there in the air, we only need to hold out our hands to catch them). I took this information as a compliment: look, *Lasker and* I came up with almost the same idea. Well done, us. OK, well done me.

And Lasker too, to be fair.

Choosing a Move

All that matters on the chessboard is good moves.
— Bobby Fischer

The main problem with chess is that you have to think.
— Alexander Grischuk

And the second problem is the problem of choosing a move.

And this is horrible: you have to think for yourself on every move! I sometimes can't even decide what to do with an old pair of trousers — throw them away or leave them be, and I freeze for half a day, but here, you have to think on *every* move! Here's the steering wheel, you take it, and wherever you turn, that's where you end up.

Yes, you were taught to sacrifice when possible, to pin a piece if there's a piece to pin, to give discovered checks, even to attack. But what should you do if you played the opening well, and your opponent did too — unfortunately? They didn't create any weak squares, they even castled, they didn't cede the center to you, they developed the pieces well, and generally did a lot of terrible things that completely thwart your plans.

The position is equal, nobody is blundering anything, nobody has tried to complicate things. What should you do, heh?

When you are playing in such a difficult duel, you constantly have to choose between several almost equal continuations. One move is a bit stronger, the other is a bit weaker — how can you feel that?
— Evgeny Bareev, annotating a game against Karpov

There are also other questions:

How and when to make a plan? When should you take a risk? How should you play in complicated positions, and how should you play in simple ones? What should you do in situations where "neither opponent can do anything"?

There are answers to these questions, and they are hidden in chess books. Unfortunately, you'll have to read those books to find answers. They contain great tips, deep analysis and lots of examples. I can't give you a magic potion containing the best lifehacks that will somehow help you avoid serious work for many years.

But I'll try ☺.

Chess practicality: rather than searching for the "best" move, choose a move that leads to victory

> The key to success in every endeavor is action. Start to act, and you'll be surprised by new opportunities that arise. It's as though the whole world starts helping you. Kabbalists confirm: you can reach the goal (the Keter stage) through a complicated path, through all the stages, thinking and planning, or you can take action (the Malchut stage), and you'll suddenly get a straight shortcut to your goal.

In certain positions, some move might lead to a position that's comfortable for me and awful for my opponent. In this case, this move might be the "best".
— *Ilia Smirin*

If the line is objectively good but doesn't fit my style, I won't go for it.
— *Yona Kosashvili*

A second-rate move is often the most precise one.
— *Savielly Tartakower*

When I played Carlsen, I would get the impression of facing a clever adversary. In complicated situations he makes clever moves rather than the best ones, it's hard to explain this.
— *Alexander Morozevich*

Lately, I came up with a new amusement for myself: I tell a casual chess fan that professionals don't look for the strongest move – they look for a move that's comfortable for them and uncomfortable for their opponent. The reaction is invaluable!

Even though the thought is so simple and familiar to a chess player!

You came here to win – why should you search for an ideal continuation? A human being sits in front of you, a mammal, a carbon-based lifeform that is prone to anxiety and mistakes, and your goal is to checkmate their king. Strong moves are not the only way to reach that goal – you can sometimes make second-rate moves that cause your opponent much discomfort. You constantly have to pose problems that make them nervous, or panicky, or desperate, or spend a lot of time thinking... basically, you have to force them to make a mistake.

This is the practicality of modern chess, this is, as I already said, the main difference with the chess of previous generations. The strongest move, the engine first-line move, is not always the best one. Perhaps it doesn't fit your style, or maybe your opponent anticipated that reply in their home preparation and prepared for it specifically – and you feel it. The search for the "strongest move" is a very difficult task. It will rip all the energy from your guts, it will eat up all your time, and in the end, it won't even settle anything. The game is decided further ahead, in the late middlegame or endgame – or in time trouble, when your resources are already depleted.

So, here's a rule for you:

Attempts to find the strongest move hinder you on your way to victory

I couldn't find a move that would completely satisfy me, but in an over-the-board game, this is a very difficult, almost impossible task. Time is limited, and you'll need time reserves after the inevitable opening up of the game to solve the purely tactical problems. And so, you sometimes have to play a logical-looking move quickly, understanding that it might not be the strongest one.
— Boris Gelfand

Rational and effective – that's the chess we play now. But you can continue searching for the strongest moves all you want. Look what happened to Jozsef Szily in his game against David Bronstein.

Game 15
J. Szily – D. Bronstein
Budapest – Moscow match, 1949

Black to move

The great David Bronstein is to move, and he desperately wants to sacrifice his bishop for the h3 pawn, but, of course, only if white castles. Intuition told him that his opponent would definitely castle and blunder this sacrifice. Of course, black can make all sorts of useful moves now, and it would definitely be "stronger" than the one Bronstein played. But he went for **23...♗e6!?**

Here's how he explained his choice: *"If we suppose that the rules allow you to make two moves in a row, then I had a good move prepared in case white castled, but I was to move, and I had to conceal the prepared tactical blow... And so I calmly led the bishop away from the obvious goal, the h3 pawn."*

24.0–0 ♗xh3! 25.♘g3 ♕g6 26.gxh3 ♗xg3 27.♔h1 ♕h5 28.fxg3 ♕xh3+ 29.♔g1 ♕xg3+ 30.♔h1 ♖f3 31.♖xf3 ♕xf3+ 32.♔g1 ♘xc5 33.dxc5 ♕g3+ 34.♔h1 ♖f8 35.♕e1 ♕f3+ 36.♔g1 ♖f6 37.♗f2 ♖g6+ 38.♔f1 ♕h3+ 39.♔e2 ♕d3#.

Forget about brilliancies!!!

> Don't intentionally try to create "beauty". Beauty is when your soul sings, when you're inspired. If you work in this state, you'll create masterpieces. But if you try to "force" it intentionally, you'll fail.

My coach Vladimir Bagirov used to say, "You have to play chess correctly!"
— *Alexei Shirov*

4.h3 is, of course, very creative, but... this violates a basic chess principle, "Don't play rubbish".
— *Alexander Khalifman*

You ask what you should choose, a pretty sacrifice or a simple decision? We've already discussed that in the chapter on controlling time: the desire to find the most beautiful move eats up an inordinate amount of time and energy.

But you do want to play spectacularly!

When football players come on the field, they don't think about scoring a beautiful goal. They simply want to score goals and win. Sometimes they score incredibly beautiful goals, but they happen *randomly*, and this hence requires *luck*. And in this case, the whole world enjoys the "beauty of football".

In the chess of long ago, romantic players such as Greco, Philidor, Morphy, Anderssen, Marshall, Kieseritzky and other "evergreens" played the opening in such a way so as to achieve the quickest and most brilliant mate possible. Their opponents didn't yet know how to resist. Steinitz, Nimzowitsch and Fine wrote their golden rules only later — or they weren't taken seriously at the time. And their opponents were true romantics as well, they kind of played along with the great masters when they went for a brilliant attack or sacrifice, and then, instead of resigning, they preferred to get checkmated and become "co-creators" of a masterpiece.

In our pragmatic and cynical times, such an approach doesn't work. Only rarely do you get lucky with an opponent who generously allows themselves to be checkmated to make you happy. Actually, this did happen to me at a tournament in the recent past.

Game 16
M. Manakova (2252) – M. Pap (2431)
Serbia Open, Belgrade 2021

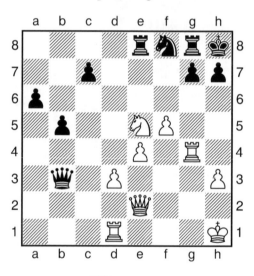

White to move

After **35.♕c2!!**, it suddenly turns out that the a2-g8 diagonal is too short for the queen, who has to defend the f7 square. Misa Pap, a decent, strong Serbian grandmaster, realized that there was no defense and decided to make me happy: he took my queen and allowed me to give a checkmate on the board. **35...♕xc2 36.♘f7#!** Smothered mate! Smashing! ☺☺☺. By the way, this was a classical game. I just got lucky.

The level of play in modern chess in general, and of defense and opening knowledge in particular, is so high that a crushing opening attack is a great rarity. More often, you have to make do with a small opening advantage and gradually increase it. Therefore, a professional will answer your question along these lines: if you have a choice between a "pretty" and "non-pretty" continuation, choose the one that leads to a more certain win.

I am essentially a creative player. And you can't even imagine how many points I have lost because of my desire for "beauty". About 40% of my lost or drawn games should have been won, but I let them slip through my fingers because of my "love for the art". Where are those games now? Who will remember them? Future generations will look at and admire only my won games. And if they don't look at those I didn't win, then, when someone writes my obituary, and they need a few games of mine for it, they'll look into the database and choose those I won. They won't even look at my losses – even though it was in those ones that I created masterpieces! And then... lost while attempting to convert my advantage because I ran out of time and energy.

Even famous and experienced grandmasters sometimes allow themselves to relax and switch to "pure creativity" mode:

Game 17
Kramnik (2807) – Deep Fritz
Manama 2002

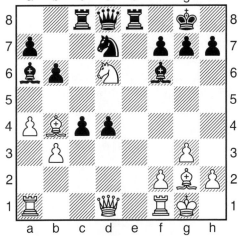

White to move

After 19.♗d5!, white has a big advantage. But Kramnik wanted to create a "pretty" win, and he played **19.♘xf7!?** This move is spectacular, but doesn't give white anything better than equality. And white ultimately even lost.

"I was in a creative mood. I just wanted to have fun with the game. At least I played like a human," Kramnik would later say in his defense.

When you have too many options, make the most useful move

> When the choice is too wide, and you are confused because of that, turn your brain on — your intuition is currently sleeping. Make a choice that at least doesn't spoil anything. Or try the following. Imagine the future: how it will look if you choose option number one, how it will look if you choose option number two, etc. Create an "image" of the future. This is an effective method.

Try pushing the responsibility of making a decision onto your opponent.
— Genrikh Chepukaitis

What should you do if you have a great choice of good moves and you look at them in awe, like a kid in a candy store? You first try to analyze more deeply — you can't find a win in this line even though it seemed at first that you should. And that line gives you too little... The clock is ticking (electronic clocks tick silently), you need to make a decision, but your head is spinning from all these possibilities and variations. You lose time and energy, there's chaos in your head, and it's growing with every minute — together with panic. What should you do in such cases?

If you can't see a direct win, and all moves look roughly equal, then you have to make a decision and simply make *the most useful move*, the one that "cannot be bad". Some improvement of the position: the placement of a piece or king, or the pawn configuration, or it may be useful to make a prophylactic move, create a luft, for instance... You don't win immediately with this move, but you don't spoil your position, either. You sort of pass the right of move to your opponent and gain some room for your overworked brain and body, tired from thinking for ages, to rest.

In such cases, when I analyze or play with my pupils or coaches, I tell myself, **"Play positionally, dear."** During tournament games, this phrase comes to my mind and, at the very least, calms me down. And it might even bring me back to reality. I didn't come up with this phrase myself — I inherited it from my coaches back when I was a kid.

If all moves are equally good and useful, make *any* move. Just make yourself do that.

I repeat: *any*!

Before thinking deeply, find a "reserve continuation"

> If you're on a deadline, it's useful to have a solution that is "at least workable". After you come up with this, you can engage in looking for a "good" or "best" solution. (Half-assed work? Indeed, it is. But you're on a deadline, in time trouble! So, don't let it come to this.)

It's important (and this is a skill of professionals!) to find a "move that doesn't spoil anything" at the very beginning in complicated positions requiring calculation, and hold it in reserve. Because usually, after 20, 30 or 40 minutes of fruitless thinking over a position, you want to either make a move that you didn't consider at all (and it's often awful – a blunder or a gross strategic mistake) or choose the wildest and most desperate continuation (which is incorrect in 90% of cases; if it were correct, you would have played it immediately).

Start working on this skill as soon as possible – to have a useful move in case it's time to make a decision. This continuation will be your anchor to reality, your lifeline. When, after lots of thinking, your brain gets bogged down by the variations and turns numb, you'll remember this "normal" move and make it. Because it came to your head back when you were in a relatively sane state.

To risk or not to risk

> Risk!

If you don't take a risk and sacrifice a bishop, you'll regret this decision for at least the whole game, which, without a doubt, will affect your play. So if you can't make up your mind whether to sacrifice a piece or not, the only correct answer is YES.
— *Lev Psakhis*

Sometimes it can be good to burn bridges, both in chess and in life. In such cases, you know what you are doing, you play rapidly and don't hesitate in your choices.
— *Boris Gelfand*

To risk or not to risk? This depends on various factors. For instance, you should always take risks in lost positions (what else do you have?). It's not simply a chance, it's also additional motivation.

Here's a small table I made for you.

When It Makes Sense to Risk

Factor		Yay or Nay
Tournament situation	You are one of the leaders	Nay
	You are close to the leaders	Yay
	You're middling or a tail-ender	Yay
The opponent	is much weaker than you	Nay
	is a bit weaker than you	Yay
	is equal to you	Yay
	is a bit stronger than you	Yay
	is much stronger than you	Nay
Your fitness or chess form	Good	Yay
	Bad	Nay
Lucky streak	Yes	Yay
	No	Nay
Time trouble	Your opponent's	Nay
	Your own	Nay
Position	Won	Nay
	Better	Yay/Nay
	Worse or lost	Yay
	Equal or a bit better	Yay/Nay
Your personality	Adrenaline junkie/choleric/romantic/psychopath	Yay
	Pragmatic/phlegmatic/senile/paranoid	Nay

OK, OK, I was joking with this table. Or was I?

The main advice: **take risks when you want to and don't take risks when you don't want to.** But do this mindfully. That's all.

The players for whom risk taking is like breathing have lots of fans: Shirov, Rapport, Jobava, Nepomniachtchi, Grischuk, or Tal, Kasparov and Morozevich in earlier times... I don't want to make an extensive list, so I'll stop at that. My childhood friend Alexander Gelman (he's a YouTube streamer, his Russian-language channel is called "Joyful Chess") takes risks and makes sacrifices every time. He plays beautiful and joyful chess, and so he's a favorite of tens of thousands of subscribers.

A separate topic is bluffing. Some chess players are simply hardwired to bluff. They are gamblers, both in life and on chess. Such players are often hooked on casino or poker. And they are hooked on chess, too. It's hard to play against them (because they are unpredictable and love to create mayhem), but it's possible, especially if you know for a fact that their crushing blows and brilliant sacrifices are simply bluff.

And another thing about risk. Risking is not just about being ready to play a move with unclear consequences, but also about the choice of opening or variation, or about refusing a draw offer in a worse position.

To summarize: take risks, be bold, forget all those tips, simply enjoy life. But your risk should be conscious, with you taking full responsibility for the consequences — not of the kind "What the Hell's gotten into me?"

Don't fear ghosts

People love creating ghosts and illusions in their head. The latter are born from our fears and complexes. Psychologists call such fears "dragons". These dragons have no bearing on reality, but they can make your life much more difficult. They scare you, they slow you down, they whisper in your ear telling you to fall back — they're basically pains in the ass, not dragons. There are techniques for banishing them from your body. But first you have to learn to recognize them.

One of the most common reasons for losing games cited by many players is that they "imagined things". This essentially means that they weren't concentrating enough when calculating lines, they lacked energy for a clear and precise calculation.

Here's an example from one of Mark Dvoretsky's books.

Game 18
A. Khakpoor – S. Dolmatov
World Junior Championship, Graz 1978

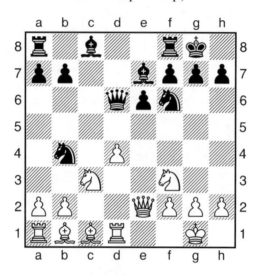

Black to move

In this position, Sergey Dolmatov intended to play 12...b6, but got scared of 13.♘e4. He immediately saw a reply to that as well: 13...♗a6!

His brain was apparently tired already, and so, his emotions prompted by the possibility of 13.♘e4 totally drowned out common sense, together with the already-found reply ♗a6. Therefore, he decided against the great move 12... b6 and chose another continuation. In his annotations, he wrote, "I got scared by a ghost." These visions, fruits of imaginations, are called "ghosts" by chess players. The stronger the player, the fewer ghosts they see. I often hear from my students, "I didn't castle because he'll attack me there!" "With what?" I ask them. "With his finger gun?" (One of the late Evgeny Sveshnikov's favorite sayings.) "Show me how his attack will develop, with which pieces?!" The student cannot show anything, because his conviction is based on emotions (fear in this case) which create illusions.

Another example:

Game 19
C. Goering – A. Anderssen
Leipzig, 1877

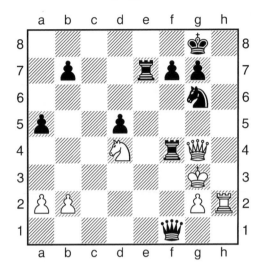

The great Adolf Anderssen agreed that he was lost when his opponent demonstrated to him in the tournament how he was going to mate him here: **35.♕c8+ ♘f8 36.♕xf8+ ♔xf8 37.♖h8#**

So what optical illusion did both players suffer? Where's the hole in this line?

Solution: After the queen check black first blocks with the rook: 35...♖e8!!, and only after that with the knight. This allows the king to escape to e7.

So, the cause of illusions is emotions that drown out common sense. My advice: be meticulous like a scientist. Have you seen them working on test tubes and beakers or on microbes under the microscope? They have *zero* emotions about what they're mixing and what they're looking at. They simply observe, find patterns, draw conclusions, classify. They feel no fear, no anger, no joy, no sadness, no love for their object of observation. They live in reality, they don't escape uncomfortable facts, they look at the situation in all its aspects, both positive and negative. Chess is, among other things, a science. Be like a scientist.

And sleep well, of course.

No passivity!!!

> No passivity!!!

In our time, nobody settles for passive, defensive structures where you constantly have to suffer. The new generation of modern players has studied the history of chess and has come to the conclusion: passive defense never brings you success. Search for counterplay at any cost! It doesn't matter if you lose in 3 or 10 moves: but fishing in troubled waters may yet bring you a positive result.
— Lev Psakhis

Professional chess players are awful sadists. They love it when their opponents defend passively. In this case, they slowly cook you on a fire (there are lots of examples on this subject, especially by those who play in suffocating, spider-like style: Rubinstein, Alekhine, Karpov... by the way, my late husband GM Miroslav Tosic also played in a similar style).

With their constant pressure, they break both your position and your spirit. How long can you suffer and find only moves? When will you start making at least small mistakes? Very soon, don't doubt it. It's psychologically hard to withstand slow, relentless pressure; tenacious people do it better. But this requires character, willpower and experience. I have won games like that in my career, and I'm proud of them. No less than beautiful crushing attacks.

And another thing. When you constantly expect threats and search for ways to thwart them, you expend double the usual amount of energy. It runs out quickly, and then you simply blunder. Or sometimes you commit hara-kiri not because you have run out of energy, but because your body subconsciously wants to end this suffering and sends you a command: make a suicidal move. You are caught between a rock and a hard place. Avoid passivity.

Defensive play, expectation and repelling threats, increases your qi (energy — M. M.) expenditure. Thus, in amateur chess, where both skills and qi reserves are not great, aggression wins more often.
#fromtheinterwebz

Pose your opponent problems with your every move

> Power should be felt in everything you do

My friend, an amateur player, once asked me to play a couple of online games with his Candidate Master friend. They play regularly, and his friend almost always beats him. "Don't fret, Masha, I'll tell him immediately after the games that it was you who played, not me. I simply want to look at his reaction."

While I played, my friend was in complete shock. He sat there beside me, watching me play and exclaimed, "I don't understand it! Why is my friend playing so badly?! Why isn't he attacking?! What happened to him?! He doesn't play with me like that." And I explained that the reason wasn't him, it was me. I simply predicted my opponent's intentions and didn't let him carry them out. And I forced my *own* game scenario upon him with constant threats.

Problems, problems and problems — that's what your opponent's head should be working on from the very first moves. You should attack and set traps. And remember: the main goal of your traps is not actually "catching" your opponent — this is very unlikely, unless they are a beginner. Our intention is to make them expend lots of energy on solving the problems you pose them. At a certain moment, your opponent will simply get tired and start making mistakes even where it seems impossible to make one.

It would be good to enrich your repertoire with some opening traps (against opponents at CM and FM level) as well as subtle novelties (for opponents above CM). You have to study them or come up with them yourself with home analysis. Chess is inexhaustible, there are still a lot of novelties hidden in the openings: don't be lazy, you have to and go discover them. And then pan them for gold. This is what grandmasters mostly do in their home preparation.

Every move must have a point

> Invest your lifetime (which is not that abundant, as you will realize nearer to the end) only in meaningful things. Avoid:
> — Time eaters (people and processes)
> — Pseudosacrifices (if you do a good thing, but with a heavy heart, better not to do it at all)
> — The paths you take "to prove something to somebody" (you'll quit sooner or later anyway)
> — Jobs you hate, people you hate, places you hate, things you hate

I have a great exercise for beginners. I play a game with my pupils: they have a full set of pieces, and I only have the king and pawns. If I move my king into check five (three, seven, one...) times, and the student doesn't notice that, they lose. And another condition. At any moment I can ask: what's the point of your move? And they have to answer.

And I noticed: the lower the player's level, the more often they make moves just for the sake of making moves, for the heck of it. Club-level players also do that, but much less often. And grandmasters never make pointless moves, they know everything you need to know about the importance of Time. Time, in this case, doesn't mean the clock – I'm talking about the **purpose** of every move made, its mission. Any tempo lost is time lost.

The legendary Svetozar Gligoric spoke about that when I interviewed him. To my question what's the most important thing in chess, he said, *"For me, the most important factor in chess is time."*

Make natural moves, avoid flashy ones

> Don't show off

If my opponent went for an unnatural structure, I would search for a refutation. I believe in justice in chess.
– Yona Kosashvili

In every art, there's a distinct difference between "originality" and "flashiness".

Originality, unconventionality, and paradoxicality are all great! New ideas and discoveries lead to the development of civilization, thoughts, and spirit. Flashiness, on the other hand, is far removed from beauty. Flashiness is unnatural. It's characteristic of graphomaniacs (graphomaniacs are either beginner "creators" or hopelessly untalented people). Since they are graphomaniacs, they lack the ability to evaluate their "creations" objectively. They declare themselves Superior, Genius, The Best, Unsurpassable (one "poet" literally used all these epithets when describing Himself – with a capital H) and consider their creations true masterpieces. And, since they are so great, they need to be different from mere mortals in some way, to break the old templates, and so they start doing "original" things, using some quirk or other.

Great masters of art also go through a graphomaniac stage, and it's only normal. When a person embarks upon some area of art, science or any other activity, they go through the following stages:

1. I am a genius!
2. Well, I'm not as great as I thought.
3. I can't do anything good.
4. I totally suck.
5. Yes, I do suck, but I want to continue working!

At this point, they might create something truly valuable.

It's the same in chess. Beginners adore their own moves (and they only lose accidentally, because the opponent is a jackass!) and love "originality". However, nature abhors unnaturalness and loves harmony. Grandmasters try to create harmony in chess with common sense, logic and the laws of play.

Of course, there are some players whose sole purpose seems to be breaking the mold. They constantly play antipositional moves, go for "unhealthy" positions, and their games quickly drown in chaos and suspense regardless of what opening they choose.

I am one such player. Outside of chess, too. People like me have been showing off since the very beginning of their life's journey until the end. And I have some advice for them. Set yourself a special goal: try to find the right things instead of avoiding them. In this case, such players can successfully move towards mastery in their own special way. To comprehend the harmony of chess, I am sure that you need to develop an aesthetic sense, a sense of beauty. There's harmony and completeness in the paintings of great artists, in the music of great composers, in ballet, in theater, in movies, poetry, prose, and meditatively watching the natural environment. Studying various form of art − especially with deep immersion − develops good taste and a sense of beauty, which will definitely impact your chess performance as well. And it will teach you to detect graphomania and run like Hell from it.

Play tough

> Fear of success, fear of failure... Success only comes to those who believe in it wholeheartedly.

Imagine that a viper slithered up to your baby (or younger brother/sister) with obvious intentions. You have to kill that viper in one blow. If you don't put enough will, energy and intention to kill into your blow, the viper will get enough time to bite the baby. You clearly won't be thinking of details such as, "Maybe I should wrap it in a sheet and release it in the woods? ☹ ", any more than you would be thinking "What if killing animals is bad?", "What would Mahavira[1] say about that?", "What if I fail?" You have to be tough and even cruel − with clear intentions, without an ounce of pity or reflections on the meaning of life.

---

[1] Mahavira (599−527 BC) was a wise man, a preacher and the founder of Jainism − a religion that preaches doing no harm to any living being.

In chess, you should ideally play tough in every game. But while it's hard to be tough in the opening or the middlegame (for instance, there are various positions where you should engage in mysterious and boring maneuvers, lulling your opponent, or chaotic positions where paradoxical looking moves turn out to be the strongest), toughness is especially necessary when you are converting your advantage.

Before you start converting your advantage, you should switch yourself (as you switch a TV channel) to conversion mode. This moment should be conscious, you shouldn't blindly rush headlong. You have to say a "safe word" to yourself and switch to another playing mode.

What's most important for advantage conversion?

1. Anticipating your opponent's intentions and preventing them (prophylaxis).

2. No brilliancies or showy moves (unless they are 100% correct).

3. Avoid weakening your own position (unless it's necessary for defense or it's a part of your attack).

4. Play confidently, both inwardly and outwardly.

I always enjoyed the fact that you can unerringly determine the mood of a chess player by moves they make: confidence or lack thereof, doubts, suffering, happiness, desperation, misery, sadness, optimism, inspiration, ecstasy, apathy, laziness, indifference... In the overwhelming majority of positions, the choice of possible moves is huge, yet a chess player chooses only one – and this one move is a dead giveaway. And so, if you are converting your advantage, you should only play confident moves, otherwise you'll lose the psychological initiative.

One of my main weaknesses is that I often get utterly confused when I need to calmly convert a won position. For instance, an extra pawn or two in the late middlegame or endgame. Of course, the most important thing here is positional understanding, the result of meticulous home study of strategy and endgames, deep analysis of classical games. In theory, I have enough knowledge to convert an extra pawn even in a game against a full grandmaster. But I still get confused even against weaker players. I probably suffer from "fear of not winning". I start thinking on every move, even the most obvious ones, for 10–15 minutes, the moves I make are uncertain or, on the contrary, too active, and so I get into time trouble and, in the best case, manage to scrape a draw.

Now, when I get a won position in an early endgame, I try to collect my thoughts and remember that I failed in 80% of such games, and so I have to play rapidly and confidently. It doesn't matter if I lose. It's better to lose in a new way than to lose again in the old way. I would have at least tried to change something.

Tough play is the main difference between men's and women's chess. Men most often manage to convert won positions, women most often do not. I don't know of any stats, but I think that men convert about 70% of their won positions, and women about 30%.

How can we claim women play a tough game when the evaluation changes on virtually every move?! The position is completely won, the opponent has no chance, the coach steps out of the room to smoke a cigarette, and when he comes back, his pupil is already desperately trying to save the game. He stands beside her in a semicatatonic state, demonstratively studies her scoresheet trying to figure out what exactly has happened and to show her how "bad" she is and how angry he is at her play. She's already disgusted with herself, but now she also feels guilty. Just leave her alone, let her catch her chances. Her opponent is also a woman, she'll definitely make an epic blunder in a couple of moves as well, and it'll be her coach's turn to faint...

Calculate 2-3 moves ahead, not more

> Don't try too hard, you're not giving birth here

Ordinary people are amazed at chess players' ability to calculate many moves ahead. Their favorite question is "How many moves ahead do you see?" This very question was once asked of Richard Reti, and he answered, "Zero!"

Reti was joking, of course. He decreased the actual number by two.

His ironic answer describes the essence of the chess master's deep approach. Are you so monstrously strong that you can calculate extremely long lines on any move? 15–20 moves ahead, with every branch? Good, buy yourself a medal. Your brain will get so tired while still in the opening that you won't be able to play much further. You're not a computer to calculate absolutely everything. Human beings possess intellect so they can prune everything that's unnecessary, only concentrating on what's essential, be guided by common sense and general considerations, and set strategies and plans. Calculating concrete moves is only used to check if they missed anything.

Am I repeating what I wrote on the subject of energy conservation? Well, practice makes perfect. You were welcome not to read that bit if you didn't want to.

OK, sorry, too late.

Do not abandon the line

> Don't be lazy! Don't half-ass it! If you have accomplished the feat of getting up from the couch and getting to your job, then do your job!

And now, here's an opposite lifehack for complete cognitive dissonance.

You have to calculate lines for the whole game. Of course, chess players joke when they say that they don't calculate anything. Everyone calculates everything, this is the chess player's *job*. If a chess player doesn't do his job, he's half-assing — and this will quickly turn into a zero in the table. Instant karma.

But true mastery is knowing where and how to calculate. The ability to recognize those positions where it's only necessary to calculate those cherished "two or three moves ahead" is characteristic of International Masters and above — i.e., not for you or me. I think that they calculate about every third move deeply, and the other two out of three very quickly. As Samuel Reshevsky once said, *"Good players possess a tactical instinct, the feeling for what's possible or probable and what's not worth calculating."*

Well, many losses are caused by the fact that people are simply too lazy to calculate the line until the very end, they leave it halfway. They convince themselves that "everything is clear afterwards". They half-assed the necessary work, they actually felt they were doing so, but just didn't bother finishing! And only back at home after the game did they come to realize that yes, they didn't calculate enough. They realize that — and then make the very same mistake in the next game!

Of course, you shouldn't calculate every possible variation until bare kings, but stopping calculating where the evaluation is unclear is half-assing it.

Catch yourself when you are lazy, finish the job, don't abandon the line halfway, pour more energy into it. Only stop calculating when the position "can be evaluated". Both stopping and evaluating should be done consciously. This is the most important thing.

You should always be ready to make a crucial decision

> Always waiting at the sea for good weather is what losers do. "A ship in port is safe, but that's not what ships are built for." (Grace Hopper)

You must possess a sporting spirit, go for forced lines and take risks.
— Bobby Fischer

Some time ago, I decided to train with a super-duper-famous coach. I gave him my games to look through. He studied them and shocked me with his conclusion: "You fear making committal decisions, you fear going forward."

What?!?!?!?!
I do what?!?!?!
Yeah, it's true... ☹.

Then he adds, "Look at your moves in positions with a big advantage – you're afraid to take responsibility for changing the pawn structure, the whole course of the struggle. But you can't win a game without it. And so, your advantage slowly evaporates." (I immediately recalled the classical chess law: *if you don't attack, you won't maintain the initiative.*)

But going forward does not necessarily mean unleashing a crushing attack on your opponent. Going forward, translated from psychological parlance, means leaving the comfort zone.

Yes, this is me, but who likes to suffer? Here you have a good, even better position. You achieved balance in your soul, you're comfortable and happy... why do you even need to move anywhere at all?

But you cannot win a game (without your opponent blundering horribly) if you aren't ready to leave the comfort zone, if you aren't ready to take risks and make committal decisions. It's the same in life – you cannot evolve and grow spiritually if you don't make leaps from the zone of comfort and happiness into the area of the new, unknown and confusing. Unfortunately.

> **All progress takes place outside the comfort zone.**
> **– Michael John Bobak**

This weakness is characteristic of many players, irrespective of their playing strength. For example, the super-GM Andrei Sokolov also suffered from it. Mark Dvoretsky coached Artur Yusupov to the candidates final in 1986 against him, and identified that Sokolov liked to ride the waves in his comfort zone in better and even won positions. Indeed, he failed to convert a position two pawns up into a win in game five. After that, Yusupov couldn't stop himself and exclaimed "If two pawns aren't enough for him, how does he intend to win at least one game?! Is he waiting for me to blunder?"
Actually, the final stage of the match was amusing – Sokolov did indeed wait for Yusupov to blunder, and he eventually won the match 7.5 – 6.5.

> **When you are converting your advantage, there always comes a moment when you have to switch from gradual improvement of the position to concrete actions. You should not miss this moment, you must concentrate, calculate precisely and find the strongest move – sometimes the only correct move.**
> **– Mark Dvoretsky**

Some positions require concrete calculation – general considerations don't work.
– Lev Psakhis

Leaving the comfort zone means you need to concentrate and calculate lines. But you should be careful: we are often swayed by our emotions (for instance, we "fall in love" with the idea of sacrificing a piece, or we are too upset by our hopeless position), and this may lead to mistakes in calculation. Try to play according to the famous formula: with a hot heart, but a cool head.

The position in your head and the position on the board are two very different things

Every new action opens a path to a new reality. This is fascinating at the very least

Never forget to check your calculations after every move you make – perhaps the position will open up from a new perspective!
– Lev Psakhis

Don't rush through your calculated line: regardless of how well you saw the position in your head, it will still look different on the board, in 4D (3D with the important addition of time!). Therefore, it's always useful to look at the actual position. Maybe some new opportunities will appear.

I often dream of chess positions during tournaments. And so, I solve them, find ingenious solutions, tackle the chess problems I set myself before going to sleep. In the morning, I wake up – hurray! – and I just need to check that my solutions were correct. I try to set up the position and then realize that, in my dream, the board was broken up abstract-Cubist style – fractured, overturned, extended, as though on a Picasso painting or in the movie Inception with DiCaprio. There are no normal chess pieces, let alone a definite position!

I remember seeing Karpov in action in my childhood – how he played and did a thing I'll describe to you. I remembered that very well. He has an array of continuations in some position. Then he chooses to trade pawns. For instance, supposing it was 15.exd5. The opponent also has to reply 15...exd5, because he has nothing else. Many chess players who don't want to reveal their intentions to the opponent make this trade in their head: I capture the pawn, he captures the pawn, and then... And then they calculate long lines.

Karpov acted differently. He immediately took the pawn, his opponent also took the pawn, and only then did he start to think! Of course, he made it a bit harder for himself because he revealed his hand (he might not have gone for this trade at all, leaving his opponent in the dark). But, on the other hand, he made it a bit more comfortable for himself: he created the actual position on the board and then started calculating.

Don't hurry

> A sign of mastery

So many won endgames weren't actually won only because the stronger side wanted to win as soon as possible and neglected simple improving moves before going for decisive action. By following the principle "Don't hurry", you can fight for victory in positions with a small, but lasting advantage. Only in this way can you force a weakening of your opponent's camp, mask your game plan, and blunt your opponent's vigilance.

– Mikhail Shereshevsky

"Do not hurry" is a principle known to every chess player. There's no need to discuss it in detail — almost every chess handbook mentions it in some way. However, since my book is a collection of useful reminders, I'll leave it here, too.

You shouldn't hurry in the following cases:
- When you are squeezing your opponent
- When you are barbequing them on a slow flame
- When you don't know what to do.

More concretely:
→   When you are converting your advantage
→   In the endgame
→   When you have a clear and solid positional advantage
→   When you are maneuvering in an equal position.

Move repetition is a very effective technique, one type of the "do not hurry" rule. Of course, the last thing you need is a draw, but this doesn't stop you from misleading your opponent: "Draw? Well, maybe that's a draw, why not?" In such cases, they may relax and become less vigilant. This is precisely the moment to shake them up with a sudden sacrifice or some tough moves that show your confidence in a quick win. This is a powerful and effective technique. Chess history is rife with cases of its successful usage.

Sometimes this technique is used with a different psychological intention: to show your opponent that you are so confident about your position that you definitely have a draw in your pocket.

> *The purpose of these back-and-forth maneuvers is to show my opponent that I have everything under control, that I can obtain a draw if I so want. This puts certain psychological pressure on black, forces him to avoid move repetition, which does not benefit him. Moreover, I didn't have a clear plan at this point, and move repetition is a well-known way to save time.*
> *— Dov Zifroni*

However, you should be careful with these "non-hurrying maneuvers" to avoid screwing up and accidentally getting an *actual* threefold repetition. That once happened to me way back at the girls' world championship in 1992.

Game 20
M. Manakova – S. Buervenich
U18 Girls World Championship, Duisburg 1992

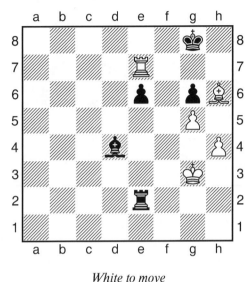

White to move

One of the last rounds, we are playing on a top board. The price of each point is huge, my position is absolutely won. I saw the way to win, everything was OK...

52.h5 ♖e3+

...but then I decided to maneuver for a bit:

53.♔g2 ♖e2+ 54.♔h3 ♖e3+ 55.♔g2 ♖e2+ 56.♔f3 ♖e3+ 57.♔g2 ♖e2+

And then my opponent claimed a three-fold repetition. I angrily disagreed. We investigated the position for quite a while, reconstructed the game at an adjacent board, and it turned out that yes, there was a three-fold repetition.

After that, the second, main part of the drama unfolded: I started to cry. I cried loudly, uncontrollably, with moans and sighs. All participants from all the other tournaments gathered round to watch the scene (and there were a lot of tournaments going on simultaneously: girls of all ages, boys as well... an entire indoor stadium of players). As he watched the scene, Alexander Sergeevich Nikitin remarked, "With such a nervous system, you'll never become a great player!" And he was correct. I never rose above the WGM title, even though my talent and other qualities might have taken me much further.

And then, I was consoled for a long time by the tournament arbiter Geurt Gijssen; we've reminisced about this episode many times since then, with a hearty laugh. To clarify, the chief reason for our laughter is different: during that game, I also managed to rescue a tiny spider crawling on the arbiter's table. I put it on a sheet of paper and let it out the window. Geurt, one of the most famous chess arbiters in the world, helped me in this good deed.

There are no plans

> "He followed his dream since childhood and, of course, achieved it," they write in books. In actuality, every path to success is so thorny, so meandering, full of doubts, wishes to quit, actual acts of quitting, returns, sufferings, trials and tribulations... only true dreamers reach the end.

Everyone simply plays move by move, and then, after the game, they say that they followed a plan.
— Joel Lautier

When I wrote books and annotated games, I said that I had a plan. But the plan only appeared after the fact. There are no plans, you have to think about what your opponent wants.
— Alexey Dreev

Everyone has a plan, until they get punched in the mouth.
— Mike Tyson

Wait, what?! You've been reading your whole life about the brilliant plans of legendary chess players, you were sure that you would be able to make plans, too. But here's what actually happens: you sit at the board, try to come up with a plan, plan everything, and then it's all ruined at the very next move. Your opponent somehow doesn't play that way, doesn't play like Capablanca's opponents, he doesn't meet your expectations. Your ingenious plan has gone to the dogs, you simply forget it because the game has turned in a completely different direction... Where did you go wrong?

Lol, you were deceived. Well... not exactly. Let me explain what happened. As you studied the classical games, with their clear strategic constructions, you got to understand what a plan is and learned to create plans on your own. It's an important skill, well done. But the thing is, a "long-term" plan is a utopia. It's unreal. It does not exist.

Here's what Dvoretsky said about plans: a plan is simply a direction, a general line of action, small strategic operations. If they are successful, then, as we play through the game afterwards, they merge into a consistent plan in our eyes.

In very rare situations, occurring once per several thousand games, your opponent's position is so cramped and hopeless that you can literally do anything with them. In such a case, your long-term plan may work. There were more games like that in the old times, because the resistance level was quite low. In our times, though, players defend dynamically, boldly, with counterplay, cunning traps and non-standard ideas. Nobody gives a rat's ass about your plan.

So, here's my advice. Figure out the general direction of play. For instance, a queenside attack, or seizing weak squares in the center, or a d6-d5 break in the Hedgehog Defense. Make a general plan for the next 10–15 moves. And to realize this plan, think in mini-plans, such as "don't let my opponent attack my king," or "untangle the knot of pieces on the queenside," or "get the knight stuck on a3 closer to the center," or "open the a-file after doubling rooks on it," etc. Tasks, ideas, piece structures, regrouping, prophylaxis – that is what's most important in modern chess, not a plan.

And use these guiding questions during the whole game:
— What does my opponent want?
— How should I position my pieces?
— What pieces should I trade for my benefit?

Trust yourself

> If you don't trust yourself, then whom can you trust at all?

For me, trusting yourself involves trusting your intuition. But all people are different. Perhaps you think that intuition is simply an esoteric invention, or aren't ready to discuss such serious, 18+ topics yet. In this case, I've got a great piece of advice for you.

In a chess game, if you follow the laws of the opening and common sense, you shouldn't have serious problems with your position. It may not be better, but it's certainly not worse. Let this serve as your guiding light. The same notion is true for the middlegame. If you have made competent, solid moves, you can be calm and confident. If you're still anxious, it's possible that you have been swayed by fear or overestimated your opponent.

If I play logically, my position cannot be worse.
— Yona Kosashvili

Here's another great litmus test for your moves. If you see concessions from your opponent, then you're doing all right.

Trust yourself – you can't succeed in chess without it. You are who you are now, with all your virtues and vices, and you chose this particular move in this particular position. This is your own Path, and everyone else can go screw themselves (including me).

With Ljubomir Ljubojevic, Elista Olympiad, 1998

Never play for a draw!

> If you desperately need a peace treaty, then actually getting it is akin to a victory. It comes as hard as a victory, and you have to make a huge effort to deserve that peace.

What should you do if you desperately need a draw, but you opponent doesn't want one? (By the way, preemptive draw offers are usually made either before the game, or right before making the first move.)

The main commandment is known by every and any chess player: YOU. SHOULD. NEVER. PLAY. FOR. A. DRAW.

When you play for a draw, your brain goes foggy with this single goal. You become disfunctional, you lose the ability to play easily, a realistic perception of the game and the ability to evaluate the position objectively. Your moves, therefore, will be as in disfunctional as you are.

So here's what you should do. Just go and play the game as usual. Develop your pieces, attack, defend as you always do. There will come a moment, a critical position, where you'll have a choice: to go for a drawing line or not. Then, go for it! And if critical positions don't occur, just sit there and maneuver, let your opponent bite off more than they can chew if they want to.

> *You only have the right to recall the result you need in certain rare moments – for instance, if your opponent offers a draw, or if there's an opportunity to force a dead drawn position – in other words, only once or twice during the game.*
> *– Mark Dvoretsky*

Draw offer as a psychological trick

> When your situation completely sucks, there's a tried and tested way to fight for survival: feign confidence. Convince everybody (including yourself) that you're happy, that everything's fine, gucci, and that you don't care about the outcome. This actually works.

During battle, there are situations where you absolutely cannot remain who you used to be, for instance, a proud lion or a soaring eagle. Those who can transform into a cunning fox, a scurrying cockroach or a dead sheep, survive and win.

I will forever remember the following story about political prisoners in Solzhenitsyn's GULAG Archipelago. Some cunning folks (mostly smart and well-educated, "intelligentsia") turned into bums in the prison camps. They didn't talk to anybody, wore ten items of clothing at once, did not wash themselves or their clothes and smelled so awful that even the wardens were too squeamish to approach them, let alone hit them. And if they did hit them, the multi-layered clothes cushioned the blows. They deliberately cultivated a scruffy image (even though these "bums" had been dandy urbanites just recently). This trick helped them survive and then get released after 20–25 years. Many memoirs contain the stories of prisoners in German concentration camps, who feigned being totally defenseless, but then, drawing on all their strength, ran away at the first opportunity. The guards weren't as vigilant around those who were docile.

Chess players have their own arsenal of tricks that allow them to achieve the desired result in a roundabout way, but without violating the tournament regulations. Some of these tricks are considered unsportsmanlike, but many still use them, so you have to know about it. One trick is offering a draw as a method of psychological pressure.

When is this trick used?

→ When you have a **very poor position**, and you need **motivation** to resist further. You get that motivation when your opponent declines the offer. And if they accept, then you get your (un)deserved half-point.

→ When you are **worse**, and your opponent clearly **doesn't know** what to do next. Your offer unsettles them further.

→ When your position is **bad**, and your opponent is in **time trouble**. Professionals reply to draw offers correctly: either with the strict "No!", or softly — with a negative gesture or "I'll think about it", and then continue playing as usual. Inexperienced players, however, lose wa-a-ay too much time on such offers... and most often agree. Because they don't have any time to play on. Here's also advice if you are the one who's been offered a draw in this situation. You simply play as you did, and whether to agree or not... you probably shouldn't, your opponent probably isn't trying to "sell" you this draw for the fun of it. Still, take the time left on the clock into account — it's also an important factor in a position's evaluation.

→ A variation on the previous point: when you are **completely lost**, and your opponent has **less than 5 minutes**, but they're not in severe time trouble yet. As in the previous case, an inexperienced player will spend at least two of those five minutes struggling with themselves — you simply **buy time** for yourself. You offer a draw not actually to get a draw (you are 100% sure your opponent will decline it), but to win some time.

→ When your head simply refuses to work that day. Well, "dark days" happen. If your opponent refuses, this will **give you strength**, and your head might even actually get to work. If they accept, it's bad, of course, but good at the same time. You may have wanted to play, but couldn't. In this way, you at least save a half-point.

If offering a draw before the 30th move is forbidden, but your head isn't working, then calculate less and play with your hand more. Take fewer risks, make fewer bizarre moves, play as naturally and sensibly as possible. Vassily Ivanchuk says that on such "dark days" he usually plays the English or Reti. And that's excellent advice: you hide the king in the f2-g3-h2 cave, cover it with the bishop, and then you stay where you are and wait until your body finally switches back on. However, Vassily didn't explain what to do if your head refuses to work but you have black, and especially when your opponent opens with 1.e4.

→ It would be wrong to forget another popular reason for offering a draw. The position is completely equal (or maybe you were better), but then you suddenly make a mistake and **see a winning move for your opponent**. They, on the other hand, haven't seen it yet, so they sit and think. It's high time to use your last chance.

I played in several games that illustrate this point, but I prefer to show a famous example here.

Game 21
P. Svidler (2713) – V. Anand (2781)
Dos Hermans, 1999

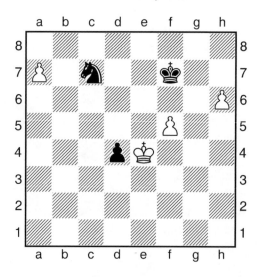

White to move.
Would you agree to a draw in this position if Anand himself had offered it?
If not, how would you continue?

A few moves before this position, Anand did have a draw, keeping his king on the squares g7, g8 and h7. However, he then moved the king along f7 and f6, allowing white's h-pawn to reach h6. At this point his king should have been directly in front of the pawn, but it was only to the pawn's side. Vishy is famous for his poker face. I'm sure that he didn't flinch a muscle on his face when he noticed that he had ruined his position and had no way to draw, as white has a forced win.

So it was just the right time to try his luck and offer a draw. After all, it doesn't cost anything. It's also possible that he didn't actually see white's forced win at this point, but whatever the situation, having just played **69...♔f6-f7** he now offered a draw. I'm sure he did this calmly, with disdain on his face even, giving the appearance that a draw here was obvious and the only logical outcome! That's what players usually do. Some amateur players even extend their hand in this case: "Well, a draw?"

And then Peter Svidler, a great and experienced player, got convinced by Anand's assuredness and agreed. Yet he risked nothing by playing on! Well, he just needed to play a couple more moves to make the position clearer, and then the winning trick would have fallen into his palm by itself. It's impossible to miss:

70.♔xd4 ♘b5+ 71.♔c5 ♘xa7 72.♔b6 ♘c8+ 73.♔c7 ♘e7 (73...♘a7 74.♔d7 ♘b5 75.h7! ♔g7 76.f6+!)

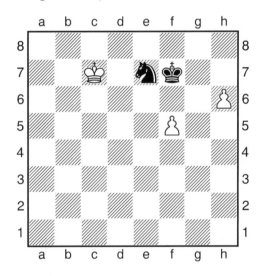

And here it is, the trick:

74.h7 ♔g7 75.f6+!! and white wins. So there you have it, a draw offered in time.

I should say that I personally almost never use draw offers as psychological tricks. Because... well, screw that draw! "The gods love me, they will make sure that I get lucky and win." This is my innate hope for a lucky break, unfounded by any facts or stats. I simply have an infantile personality.

And, to be honest, if the Soviet coaches from my childhood had seen these "drawing tips", they would have spanked me and forced me to drink tea without cookies. Offering your opponent a draw to unsettle them?! Such a disgrace.

Actually, I'm sure that everyone did that earlier, too, but it was considered utterly unethical to discuss it openly. Thou shalt not mess with thy opponent, even indirectly! That's how we were taught. It was considered that the coach, like a second father figure, had to instill common decency together with knowledge and skills in his pupil. He could tell you that it's reasonable to offer a draw in a worse position just in case, but to explain why... To unsettle your opponent?! No, in the old times, people were decent and well-mannered, so they didn't tell the truth.

But now? Do your worst! Whatever you want!

Famous players only offer draws in lost positions

> Don't expect "gifts" from those better than you. They are almost always motivated solely by their own benefit. If you understand this, you'll be able to make a more rational decision whether you should accept this "gift" or not.

If your opponent offers you a draw, try to work out why he thinks he's worse off.
— Nigel Short

Do not grab the hand of your famous opponent the second they offer you a draw. With such an approach, you won't get very far and will soon be relegated to playing old geezers in the park. You should understand one thing: when a stronger opponent sits down opposite you, they think that they already have a draw in the back pocket. They are sure that no sane player would refuse to gain 5–7 rating points given for that draw. Thus, they play until they reach a position beyond which it would be embarrassing to offer a draw. And then, at this threshold, they "save" the game by offering a draw. Their position is usually so bad at this point that even you (heh heh) might be able to win.

Here's an example from my own career that shows exactly how long stronger opponents can delay a draw offer.

Game 22
E. Moradiabadi (2571) – M. Manakova (2306)
Negroponte Open, 2010
Slav Defense

1.♘f3 d5 2.c4 c6 3.d4 ♘f6 4.♘c3 dxc4 5.a4 ♗f5 6.e3 e6 7.♗xc4 ♗b4 8.0-0 ♘bd7 9.♕e2 0-0 10.e4 ♗g6 11.♗d3

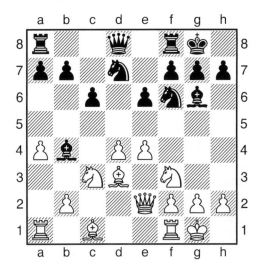

11...♗e7?!

11...♗h5 would be a typical and natural Grunfeld move. So I still can't recall for the life of me why I needed the bishop on e7. I would have followed up ♗h5 with c5, and white could not reply with d5 as the bishop on b4 would have served its purpose fantastically by capturing the knight.

12.h3 ♗h5. But now it's a bit late. White can get in g4, either immediately or after ♗f4, and then the grandmaster gets an easy game.

13.e5?! So I got lucky.

13...♘d5 14.♘xd5?! cxd5 15.♗d2 ♘b8! 16.♕e3 ♘c6. And now black is definitely not worse – I've equalized!

17.♘h2 ♗g6 18.f4 ♕b6 19.♗c3 ♗xd3 20.♕xd3 a6. 20...a5 was better. And if black doesn't play it, then white should.

21.♘g4

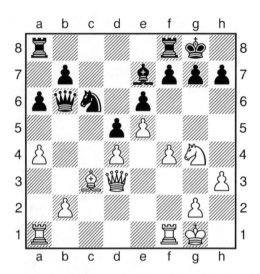

21...f5! A fine move, slowing down white's kingside attack.

22.♘e3. Obviously, in the event of 22.exf6 I recapture with the bishop, and certainly not with the pawn. In fact, white should have gone for this position, it was equal: the weakness of the e6 pawn is compensated by the weakness of the one on d4.

22...♔h8 23.g4. Ooh, that scares me! (not).

23...g6 24.♔h2 ♖ac8 25.♖g1 fxg4 26.♖xg4?. Oddly enough, it was this, totally human move, which my opponent unleashed instantly, that turned out to be the losing error. He urgently needed to evacuate his other rook from a1. But only my computer was able to find this move, at home. Everything seemed so natural in the game, except that we couldn't pinpoint where it went downhill for white. Well, it was here. Had white moved his queen's rook away, then black should not capture on h3, as the h-file would open; moreover, my queenside attack would not be dangerous when I am not threatening a queen check on b2 shortly after the bishop is exchanged.

26...♗b4! With this move I begin counterplay on the queenside (counterplay – what a delicious-sounding word!) and at the same time free up e7 for the main protector of my gates – my knight.

27.♖ag1 ♘e7 28.♖1g2 ♗xc3 29.bxc3 ♕b3 30.♘d1 ♕xa4 31.h4 Only now did my strong grandmaster opponent offer a draw. Note by the way that he made a rather menacing move when he did so. So that I wouldn't inadvertently decline his offer.

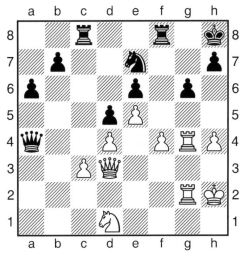

Black to move

The position's evaluation is very much in my favor. But the problem is not the evaluation per se (some grandmasters continue playing even when they are −5), but the fact that the white king is very weak. And I, a woman, played this whole game very well and can probably attack him to death. Moradiabadi decides not to tempt fate by playing on and risking defeat.

Or maybe he already realized that he was lost but offered a draw because it was a chance to save half a point? And also to obtain some motivation and unsettle me in the process? (I told you about this trick a bit earlier.) Whatever. What mattered was the fact that he delayed the draw offer until the point where anyone would have refused. Even you (heh heh).

31...♕b5 32.♕h3 ♖f5 33.♖g5 ♕f1 34.♘f2 ♖xf4 35.♕xe6 ♖xc3 36.♖h5
Or 36.♘h3 ♖xh4

36...♖xf2 37.♖xh7+ ♚xh7 38.♕xe7+ ♖f7. White resigned.

I could never understand why amateur chess players so gladly agree to a draw with a strong opponent! It's clear that the said opponent either has a lost position, or feels unwell, or maybe can't think of anything because he's suffering from a bad hangover... but they never offer draws without a reason.

So, why *do* lower-rated players gladly agree to draws without thinking?! Doing so is totally incorrect! Don't do that, ever! It's obvious that such players are exceptionally unambitious and don't think long-term, even though their thoughts are rather rational: indeed, "5–7 Elo points don't grow on trees."

If you do think that your advantage is not enough to defeat such a monster — well, then agree to a draw. But still, if you want to grow and become the strongest player in the world, it's wrong to agree to draws in better positions. Or even in "slightly more comfortable" ones. Only the bold and aggressive succeed, those who defeat opponents stronger than themselves. And then those strong ones fall down to give way to the new leaders.

"Our places were simply switched. That's the law of Sansara, the cycle of humans..."

Never agree to draws at all!

Neurotic people who suffer from problems such as "I can't choose" or "It's too awkward to refuse" will be best served by the following rule: keep going until the end, without ceding any middle ground. It's easier to say "no" that way. And you have much better chances of winning with that attitude.

My super-duper-famous coach gave me a piece of advice: if you have any trouble with the question "Should I accept the stronger player's draw offer?" follow this rule – never agree to a draw with anybody at all! Always play until the bare kings. In this case, the problem will just solve itself.

With Boris Spassky, Evgeny Eletsky and Valentina Kuznetsova, Moscow, 2008

This really works, I checked. Such an attitude brings wonderful results. I'm not sure that it works for everybody, but it definitely works for neurotics such as me, always anxious about "what to do", "it's too awkward to refuse", "poor guy/gal", "I don't know what to do", "there's nobody to ask for advice", all that fun stuff.

Simultaneous display against artists in the Tretyakov Gallery, Moscow, 2012

Your Opponent

Your celebration starts when your opponent is defeated. You're happy when your opponent is unhappy. It doesn't occur only in chess, it's in every sport — one's happiness is built upon another's unhappiness. But it's especially pronounced in chess.
— Alexey Dreev

Some chess players stop greeting their opponents after losing, others after winning. The former are much nicer.
— Ashot Nadanian

I always envied my friends who perform classical music. They strive for mastery, improve, achieve success and recognition, and at the same time they have no opponents, no enemies. Everything the musician has on stage is their instrument, the public and the music. Mikhail Baryshnikov could say, "I do not try  to dance better than anyone else. I only try to dance better than myself." A chess player cannot say that.

In chess, unfortunately, you have an opponent. And your goal is to defeat them. Only through defeating other people can you achieve mastery, perfection, success and recognition.

When I joined a chess club at the age of eight or nine, my character was already hardened by constant rivalry with my older sister: in endless fights and emotional explosions at the first opportunity. I don't know from where I got such a defiant and nasty personality (my sister is two and a half years older than me), but I didn't give in to her in anything. Well, I tried.

I still have audio recordings of when I was a year old and she was four, I hadn't even learned to talk yet (except for reciting poems, singing, dancing and speaking English). But as soon as my parents started praising my sister for a poem she recited, I started squealing like a pig, demanding that they listen to me, too: I'll recite that same poem better, I'm greater, I'm more talented! I'm listening to these recordings now and just can't believe what I hear. I was a toddler, probably still in my diapers, but so horribly ambitious!.. To cut a long story short, I showed up "prepared" for my chess lessons.

Psychologists have discovered that most people who stay in professional sports had family difficulties. Either they wanted to "escape" their home and so ran off to endless training sessions and tournaments, or they wanted to "take out" their tears and humiliation on others, or they wanted to "prove" something to someone. At least this happened in earlier times – maybe something has changed in the modern world. But it's very clear that only "warriors" stay in professional chess.

The presence of a real opponent is the most important condition for growth in chess. This has also been confirmed by recent events. During the COVID-19 lockdowns, all chess players flocked to the Internet, including such stars as Carlsen, Nakamura, Firouzja... The spectators were ecstatic at first, then the joy subsided considerably, and after a while, social networks were filled with posts about the incredibly weak play of the world's greatest grandmasters. And fans drew the following conclusion: physical presence of the opponent is an incredibly motivating factor for strong play!

In this chapter, I'll tell you about some peculiarities of playing and give you tips about your opponent.

Prophylaxis

> Anticipating your enemy's next step is an incredible super-power (all maniac mysteries are built upon this premise). In chess, a poorly developed sense of danger only leads to defeat, but in life, it can deliver tragedy. My observations show that people with a marked sense of danger live longer.

Prophylactic thinking is not synonymous with passivity, it has to do with simultaneous reckoning of both your and your opponent's resources, with clear calculation of short lines. It's very hard to oppose such a manner of play – you should be as adept as your opponent at solving each other's intentions.

– Mark Dvoretsky

We are used to thinking only for ourselves. Both in life and in chess. First us, then them. We shouldn't do that. It should be the other way around: first them, then us. To make a right decision, you have to think about the opponent. Your thinking should be based on what they want, not what we want. Those who have only started to play chess often tell me: well, I have this plan here. What plan?! Stopping your opponent — that's your plan. But they always have some plan, both in life and chess.

If you want to make God laugh, tell him your plans.
— Alexey Dreev

Neither attack nor defense, in our opinion, is the purpose of positional play; the essence of the latter is energetic and timely prophylaxis.
— Aron Nimzowitsch

Deprive your opponent of moves!
— Anatoly Karpov

Since prophylactic thinking is not an item of "knowledge", but a skill, and a very important one at that, it should be developed from the very beginning of your chess career. You have to learn to ask yourself constantly what your opponent wants, how would they play if they were to move, always look at the position through their eyes. Of course, your purpose is preventing all these plans that you see. Coaches teach their students this skill in analysis and training games. There are also lots of tactical puzzles on the same topic. And, of course, analysis of your own games is critically important.

When you analyze your own games, you come to a conclusion that the reason for most losses is negligence towards your opponent's intentions. They, like you, were taught to make their every move meaningful, they also create secret plans and cunning traps, and you should anticipate and solve them.

By the way, top grandmasters also mostly lose because they underestimate their opponent's intentions. It's commonplace. That's why they advise (everyone and themselves): "You should spend 70% of your time not on your own move, but on the moves that your opponent can make."

The most upsetting defeats happen in games when you are completely winning, but your opponent doesn't resign for some reason; you relax, and your prophylactic thinking gets dulled. (I've already shown one of my illustrative games.) Remember: your opponent is like a wounded lion now, at their most dangerous! But human nature, emotions, take over, and we start celebrating inside before even finishing the game.

The famous **"sense of danger"** is born out of prophylactic thinking. All grandmasters have it. They feel what kinds of positions they shouldn't go for even if this is not proved by concrete lines. Some players have an innate sense of danger, which is part of their personality. Petrosian and Karpov are the most prominent examples, symbols and role models.

> *His play is very impressive. First of all, in his approach to decision-making, his prophylactic attitude. With each move, with each movement he calculates his opponent's intentions and fights them.*
> — *Artur Yusupov on Karpov*

I can say about myself that my inner voice often whispers me the right things: be careful, don't go there, don't drink that Kool-Aid, but desires and emotions overpower it, the joy of approaching victory is intoxicating, the mind gets clouded... And then a thing familiar to all chess players happens: "The Devil made me do it!", "It was as though someone else moved my hand!", "I didn't want to do that, I swear!" As a chess player's skill develops, their alarm sensor also improves, increasing the intensity of the danger sign.

Therefore, you should always remember two things when you're playing, especially if you have a won position:

Composure and *patience*.

And here's a cool tip from Igor Zaitsev:

In better positions you should be as supermobilized as in moments of mortal danger.

Friends relayed that advice to me when I lamented the fact that I gifted points left, right and center at a tournament. Ever since that moment, I've often recalled it when I have a big advantage. Or, rather, it comes up on its own in my brain, coming to my aid in difficult times. Thank you, Igor, I'll say it publicly.

Be respectful towards your opponent

> Respect your rivals!

Before discussing who respects their opponents and who doesn't, I'll tell you briefly about the structure of the Chess World. Imagine it as a huge layered cake...

Top tier: the highest caste, the elite. Top players, the unreachable ones, the Chosen Few. They only play against each other, so they drop out of this caste quite rarely: either because of old age or some folly. For instance, you may play badly in several opens, your rating drops 50–100 points, and that's it, you're out of the club, no longer at the party. It will be incredibly hard to get back among the gods of the Chess Olympus.

Closed elite round-robins with participation of those 15–20 deities are held regularly. There are hefty appearance fees, five-star hotels, and, what's even more important, all participants are your "buddies" who won't go too far in their attempts to win, and so you play without much risk. That's how games are usually played there: they go through the opening and then check if their opponent remembers this certain line. He-remembers, I-remembers, all-remembers, everyone-remembers, why don't we make peace? "OK, the war is over, thank you all, you are free to go."

That's why there are so many draws in these round-robins. Journalists and fans have seriously discussed the "death by draws" of chess, and FIDE officials are trying to come up with new rules that make chess less predictable. And they're all deadly serious. Hello-o-o, what are you talking about? Have you forgotten that risk-free play is only possible at the highest layers of the atmosphere, at the tip of the iceberg, and the rest of us chess players, the mere mortals, still exist, too?!

Middle tier: 2600-rated players. The dream of every one of them is to become one of the Chosen Few. If that were to happen, they will no longer be constantly required to play in continental championships and opens; the organizers of those tournaments do provide conditions,[1] as well as opportunities to compete for decent prizes, but still, they are completely incomparable with guaranteed starting fees in the elite round robins.

Also, they are a lottery. For instance, you play in a strong open and get paired with some child prodigy from India. He is rated about 2400, 200–300 points lower than you, but does not settle for a draw. You're super-cool and super-fearsome, but here, you have to work a lot. I mean it. You'll have to sweat your guts out. This is exhausting, intensive work without any guarantee of a positive outcome.

You also shouldn't forget that all higher caste members have several sparring partners/coaches and a few ultra-powerful computers. This all costs a lot of money, but your appearance fees and prize money are only enough to provide for your spouse and child, and a bit for yourself. OK, you can also afford one coach.

Dammit, the life of a professional chess player is harsh and depressing!

Low tier: everyone who calls themselves a "chess player". A huge concoction of human bodies and monsters, like the ones on Bosch's paintings. Most of them hadn't earned any money from anything but chess until recently, and even those earnings were tiny and irregular. I don't understand how they survived at all.

---

[1]   Conditions are to incentivize the player to take part and usually include travel and lodgings and/or appearance fees.

When the whole world went on lockdown and chess tournaments stopped, they had to "retrain" as coaches and streamers. They horribly crashed the chess coaching market, and while the average hourly rate was $40–100 before the pandemic, it dropped to $5–50 after this nomad invasion of hungry chess players.

In this third tier, you can find everything: scandals, fights, gossips, cheating and baseless accusations of cheating, even court cases. Crazy "chess moms" primed to rush into a fight and defend their precious child from anyone they consider suspicious. Incompetent arbiters, downtrodden by their dismal life who by chance gain a sliver of power for the duration of the tournament. Mobile phones with running chess engines hidden in toilets. Everything, everywhere, all at once. And – I would especially highlight this fact – this layer of the atmosphere is inhabited by chess players who purposefully disturb their opponents.

And don't even start all this nonsense about "What's with the hasty generalizations?", "Why are you dishonoring our chess clan?!", "This is all so rare!"

I'm not talking about whether this is a rare or frequent phenomenon. I only mean that, in the **two highest** tiers, chess players respect their opponents (at least superficially). Take elite players, for instance. They either make that choice themselves, or the tournament organizers force them with their harsh contracts and fines, but they at least try to uphold a "bohemian" image.

Only recently, this "aristocrat" was a mere schlimazel[1] but now he's elite: dress code, sponsors, signed contracts, press conferences, interviewers, photographers, fans, girls...

The Chosen Few get up and smile when they shake each other's hands before the game, and they talk a bit after the game ends. As I noted, many of them are friends with each other, so that's also why it's not hard for them.

They are rather haughty towards the fans and journalists, but, of course, they love the attention from the media and common public.

The second-tier players are much nicer: they are not stars yet, but already solid experts. They aren't as haughty as the elite yet, but are already very well-behaved. They are most pleasant in conversations. They aren't too fed up with attention from fans and the media, so they gladly give interviews, autographs and smiles for selfies. They eagerly engage in post-mortem analysis with the losing opponent and are very respectful towards them.

Yes, they do glare at each other. "Hypnotizing" your opponent has become acceptable at the top. And at the bottom, too. Indeed, what can you do with a

---

[1]   "An extremely unlucky and weird-acting guy" in Hebrew and Yiddish

person who only looks at you, never doing or saying anything else? "I'm doing no harm — I'm not playing games, I'm mending the Primus[1]." You'll never prove that they are lying. Or that they look at you with an unblinking, withering stare when you are to move (some only glance at you furtively, but do so constantly). It's illegal to rebuke your opponent directly, you can only do that through the arbiter. I do directly address my opponents actually — up to now, this has worked.

In the old times, players also glared at each other. For instance, Karpov glared at Korchnoi. Korchnoi even resorted to playing in mirror shades because of that, so that Karpov "could only see his own reflection." However, the glare from Viktor's lenses started to unnerve Karpov, and a conflict arose...

Recently, at a women's round-robin tournament, I noticed one player constantly glaring at her opponents. This clearly unsettled them, they tried to block her stare with their hands, and they suffered in anguish.

On the day when I had to face her, I had a choice: to make a fuss or to wear sunglasses. At the start of the game, she audaciously stared at me. I asked her "Why are you staring?" with my own look. This didn't work, she continued to glare. Then I put my sunglasses on. She stopped glaring. She did try at first, but it seems that normal sunglasses hide your eyes as well as mirror shades, so she quickly stopped. And, by the way, sunglasses didn't hinder my play a bit. As a result, I destroyed that girl with black in 20 moves. Several tournaments were played simultaneously, and all participants, of course, noticed that I played in sunglasses.

Rumors spread immediately, and her coach, a well-known, respected player, apparently had a harsh conversation with her when he found out. The very next day, she didn't "hypnotize" her opponent. So, I made my small contribution to her education. And ever since, I always bring sunglasses to my games against younger women. Just in case.

I was personally taught the commandment "Do not disturb your opponent" by my coach Sergey Gertrudovich Grabuzov. He is known for his high moral principles, and he instilled them in me as well. But there are (and always were) some coaches who teach their pupils dirty tricks or, at the very least, turn a blind eye to them. For instance, you can stand directly behind your opponent's back to unnerve them, put chocolates and flasks on your part of the table and rustle the wrapper, kick your opponent under the table, or even cough and sneeze without covering your face.

---

[1] A quote from Mikhail Bulgakov's *Master and Margarita* — intended literally, this has become a metaphor in Russian for "Leave me alone, I'm doing nothing wrong"

In general, everyone who uses such dirty tricks at the board is an asshole. Take care of your karma, and may the Force be with you. Chess is just a game, and life is long, who knows what might happen.

Ah, yes, I forgot about the fourth tier.

Fourth tier: chess fans. They are everything to us. The whole pyramid of the chess world is held together by them. If they didn't exist, who would need us at all?..

Underestimating a low-rated opponent

> Respect your *every* rival

In our times, everyone can play. They have studied openings, calculate lines very well, are bold, have practiced hard in online chess, may avoid gross blunders in some games, and even surprise you from time to time.

Often, when a chess player has a much higher rating than their opponent, they treat the said opponent as a lower form of life. This does work: it puts incredible psychological pressure on the opponent. *Nolens volens*, they feel like a deer in headlights. I wrote about this matter when discussing domination.

On the other hand, it's too easy to go overboard with this. If you *actually* treat your opponent with disdain rather than *faking* it, you risk losing your concentration. And this, as we have learned from previous chapters, can be severely punished. Therefore, you can act as condescendingly as you want, feigning your surprise at the fact that your opponent hasn't resigned after ten moves, but inside you should be fully mobilized, as though you are playing against a very strong, or at least equal opponent. And don't forget to turn on your "prophylactic radar".

By the way, keep in mind that weak opponents don't like to go for complicated lines, they trust you, and you can exploit that.

Overestimating your opponent

> "As a rule, you pull your finger out when it becomes more important to earn someone's approval than to do good and enjoy yourself." (Sergey Kalinitschew)
>
> I have seen that in myself: both my voice and behavior change when I talk with people from whom I need something. When we don't overestimate a person or a situation, we are relaxed, and our beautiful self expresses itself best when we are in a relaxed state.

There's only one type of mistake in chess: overestimating your opponent.
Everything else is an unfortunate accident.
— Savielly Tartakower

It's good when your brakes are bust, and you fly forward on the wings of self-confidence and recklessness. But this only happens with kids, and not all kids at that. As you age, you become more sensible — and start to fear facing opponents with higher ratings and titles. Even strong grandmasters are sometimes overawed by their higher-rated opponents.

This fear cannot be cured, but you can weaken it. I personally benefited from my coach's advice:

Do not overestimate your opponent — everyone plays badly anyway!

Early in this book, I already told you: *everyone fears everyone*! It's similar here. If you remember that your opponents are also humans, with their own emotions, anxieties, doubts and bad, often unconvincing play, it becomes much easier for you. They'll look smaller in your eyes, and there's a chance that your fear will almost completely evaporate. (As I already said, neuro-linguistic programming practitioners combat fear by diminishing the *image* of the fear. Therefore, my coach's phrase is just superb.)

As an example, I'll show you my recent game from the Serbian Women's Team Championship. I want to dissect it thoroughly. To explain what reality is and how differently it can be seen. (Akira Kurosawa's legendary movie *Rashomon* is about the same thing: four witnesses of a crime saw it completely differently, as though they witnessed four completely separate events.)

I was playing on second board, and after nine games I had an incredible plus score – I had basically destroyed everyone. In the last round, we faced the weakest team, which had already been relegated from the First League to the Second. I played a low-rated woman; she only plays once a year, but was a good player some years ago.

Game 23
K. Brankov (1887) – M. Manakova (2250)
1st Serbian Women's League, Vrnjacka Banja 2021
Sicilian Defense

1.e4 c5 2.♘f3 e6 3.b3 a6 4.♗b2 ♘c6 5.d4 cxd4 6.♘xd4 ♛c7 (6...♛f6 was better) **7.♘c3 ♘f6 8.♘f3 ♗c5 9.h3.**

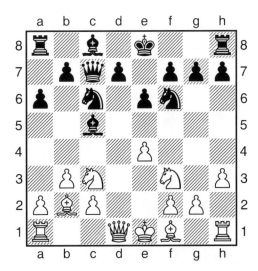

What a stupid move, I thought. How should I punish it? You can't play like that – first b3, now h3! I sit and think how to punish her. And then I realize that I simply can't, it's a normal move. I need to make a decision, but I can't, I lack willpower. And then I realize in horror that my brain has stopped working!

I'm not new to this, I know what to do in such cases. I found a distraction, gave my body a shake, ate a chocolate. Then I looked at the board – and I still can't think of anything! SOS! For the whole tournament, *whole damn tournament*, my head worked like a Swiss watch, saw everything, understood everything, but now it has just stopped from overheating. And it did that when I faced the weakest opponent on my board! What should I do?! Help! Heeeeeeeelp!!!

9...d5?

Instead of making this crazy move, I could simply have continued 9...b5, in the spirit of the Sicilian, and black's position is wonderful!

My opponent thought for a long time. And I looked at my last move and told myself: that's it, I'm screwed. She'll just capture the pawn twice now, and in torture and suffering I'll have to search for some nonexistent compensation. And, since my head isn't working, this is tantamount to losing outright.

Why am I showing you this game? Because my opponent trusted *my* calculations and totally bought the bluff. Compared to her, I was a monster – with a much higher rating, a much higher title, much better performance both in this championship and recent tournaments. In other words, *everything* tells her that I'm in great form, and if I sacrifice material, I have calculated it until the end. Even though in actuality I was experiencing an off-day, and my head was completely empty, with my brain refusing to work.

10.exd5 exd5 11.♗d3?! (Of course, the pawn could be safely captured: 11.♘xd5 ♘xd5 12.♕xd5 ♕e7+ 13.♗e2 ♘b4 14.♕d2 ♗f5 15.0-0, and black is much worse.) **11...0-0 12.0-0**

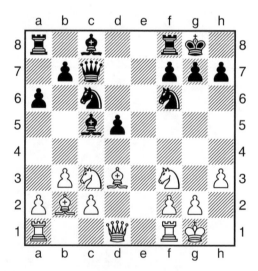

Well, while we are at it, I might as well go all-in. **12...♗xh3?!?!** The sacrifice is incorrect and very bad, but if my opponent treats me with such trust and respect, why shouldn't I exploit that? **13.♘g5??** Had she played 13.♘xd5! with the subsequent trade on f6 and capture on h3, I would have been in very big trouble. Now, however, black wins: **13...♘g4!!** The only defense, 14.♘f3, is met with 14...♕g3!! and mate next move.

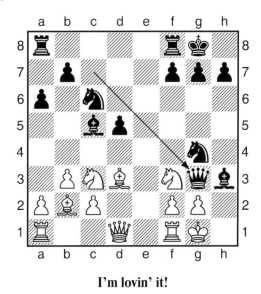

I'm lovin' it!

Kristina Brankov preferred a more prosaic finale, however: **14.♕xg4 ♗xg4 15.♘xd5 ♕d8. 0–1.**

Don't trust titled players

> Having a spine, not trembling and not groveling before the powers that be, is a rare but rather enviable quality. Why should you tremble, anyway? Today he's soaring beyond the clouds, and tomorrow, he's sitting behind bars. And you... "Go down your own road, find your own way."

Another great example of overestimating your opponent, this time by me, happened in a game against a strong grandmaster at an open tournament in Croatia.

For the entire game, Marin Bosiocic had treated me like a worm: he didn't sit at the board much, replied to my moves immediately, pressed me and acted very unhappily – like, *why is this game still continuing?.. the position was absolutely won even before the first move was made.* Basically, he used his entire box of tricks to put psychological pressure on a weaker opponent.

I'm a tough old bird: I resisted his ploys as well as I could, but at some point, after the time control, I realized that I was out of energy. In addition to being weaker as a chess player, I was also losing to him psychologically. My position was worse, I was down a pawn, but I was still wriggling somehow.

And then came a moment that justified my long and stubborn resistance. I had to use that opportunity, but I was already out of spiritual strength. I gave up inside: I believed that my opponent was strong and had no weaknesses. And, what's even more upsetting, I firmly believed that he would get some karmic punishment for such "awful" behavior — it could and should have happened!.. But it didn't — there was a late endgame on the board already... and I completely lost heart.

But punishment *does* follow in such situations. And it would have followed in this game too, if I had just retained a bit more composure and patience. I still rue this moment today.

Game 24
M. Bosiocic (2552) – M. Manakova (2288)
Split open, 2015

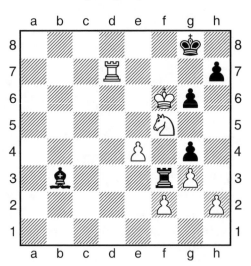

White has just blundered with 44.♘d6-f5??
Now it's black to move. How could I have drawn?

Wow! After black's rook check on f3, white could simply have put his king on g5 and maintained a won position! But my opponent spent no more than 15 seconds on every move, and here, he blundered badly.

How can black draw? White threatens to give checkmate, so the knight cannot be captured. The move is not that hard.

Why, why have I stopped believing in myself?! I made another move with my hand, **44...h5?? 45.♔xg6** and I resigned.

> *I would have drawn with the wonderful move 44...♗h8! Now white's pinned knight is hanging, and 45.♖d8+ is met with 45...♔g8!! I win a piece, although the position is of course drawn.*

Well that sucked!

An unsure player loses because of their indecisiveness, and the self-confident, on the contrary, because of underestimating their opponent's ability.
— Mark Dvoretsky

Use your advantages when you play against someone titled

> They risk losing their reputation and their place in the sun, but your hands are completely untied. Freedom is your big advantage.

Have you just been paired with a titled opponent? Rub your hands and go have some fun. Remember: it's harder for them. They need to win, whereas you can be satisfied with any result — nobody expects a draw from you, let alone a win. Surprise people on whose opinions you still depend. Yourself, for instance.

Still, you need to know some rules for facing titled players.

→ If you're in time trouble, you lose.
→ If your position is passive, you lose.
→ Watch your emotions with great vigilance — they're bubbling over, dude!
→ Do not weaken your king's position without necessity. Except in case you decide to attack.
→ Do not weaken your position in general. Except in case you decide to create chaos on the board.
→ Your appearance and your every move should radiate confidence at the very least, and preferably aggression.

Of course, all these rules are important in every game. But the thing is, if you violate even a *single* rule here, you likely won't be able to save the game.

Except for the last one. Sometimes it's useful to play possum (as I already said, this is the favorite ploy used by woman players). In that case, your opponent's high self-confidence may become too excessive: they get completely reckless, turning off their sense of danger. And that's the best time to catch them in your carefully prepared web!

By the way, don't forget to prepare the web.

Ignore your opponent's antics - they may be suffering

We are so engrossed in ourselves that we associate any behavior by others with our own person. But people simply live and do their thing, without caring about you one iota. *Nobody's on nobody's side.* So relax. If you can't resolve the problem at all, look at it from another side (from another person's viewpoint, for instance), and it will stop being a problem.

Never think that your opponent is disturbing you on purpose. Perhaps they actually are, but it's better not to think about it. Because if they are disturbing you on purpose, then their goal is to get into your head. Why indulge them, then? So, don't think about it.

I have a longstanding rival who is always terribly nervous when she plays me: she constantly chews gum, squirms on her chair, trembles, and shakes the table. When time trouble comes, everything escalates: the table starts sliding around, she keeps half swallowing her gum and regurgitating it again in her mouth, and her scoresheet turns into an unintelligible scrawl. She only behaves like that with me, she's much calmer against other opponents.

I have a sharp sense of empathy, so it's hard for me not to join her in her madness. And I always thought that she was doing that on purpose because I am the one who reacts: I also become nervous, make blunders in great positions and then lose. I asked my coach about that. He answered calmly, "Why do you think she does it on purpose? It's more likely that playing you is very hard for her, she simply cannot psychologically withstand you as an opponent."

Everything was so simple! I relaxed after that: she was simply afraid of me, it was hard for *her*, and I'm so cool it turns out.

And recently, when I realized all that, I beat her easily. You see how simple it is?! Change your attitude to the problem, look at it from a different angle, in the other person's shoes, and it will stop being a problem.

I repeat: never think that your opponent is doing anything on purpose. This will help you to stop wasting your energy. It's better to replace your paranoid thoughts with other, normal ones. Tell yourself: oh, my poor opponent... It's so hard for them! I'll try to exploit that ☺.

Cheating suspicions shouldn't make you paranoid

> There are some bad things going on in this world, but if your psyche is healthy, you can react to them in a healthy way. Take care of your mental health, folks!

When you suspect your opponents of cheating so often that it turns into paranoia, this is very bad. You might end up in a nuthouse at this rate. Cheating should be combated on the level of FIDE, chess federations and tournament organizers. If you chase your opponent during games, rummaging through toilets and listening to the sounds in the adjacent stalls, you *might* hear something and find something, but this will surely be a sign that you are unhinged.

Of course, if you know that such "investigations" of your opponent stimulate you and give you an adrenaline rush, then it's OK (actually, disregard, that's not OK, that's BS. Keeping your concentration is much more important than a cannibalistic paranoid attitude).

Honestly, I have become madly suspicious myself in the last few years. At big tournaments, when you're especially nervous, I suspect every single opponent who plays well! I check the game with a computer: hot damn, she played first-line engine moves for the entire game! How was that possible? She must have cheated, I am right, yes, yes! But as soon as you start thinking rationally rather than emotionally, you quickly find an explanation: ever since the opening, she dragged you into "her own waters". She has analyzed these positions with her coach, so she knows the main structures, plans and ideas. And she doesn't blunder because, well, anyone who has reached at least WFM level doesn't blunder. Finally, she finished you off with first-line moves because even a beginner would find these moves here!

I realize all that, but I can't do the things I love if I feel discomfort. And I can't coldly suspect my opponent of cheating and continue playing the game emotionlessly at the same time.

However, there are players who risk disrupting their concentration and report their suspicions to arbiters during the game, asking them to check their opponent for devices. The arbiters do check, and sometimes it turns out that yes, that player cheated. To take such a drastic step – filing a complaint during the game – you need to have a tough personality and lack emotion (guys like that don't accuse every opponent — they only complain when their suspicions are absolutely justified). Such players are so cool — I can't do that. Thanks to them, we can clear the chess world of evil.

But sometimes even those guys make a mistake — and, of course, this leads to major scandals.

Celebrating Boris Postovsky's 80th birthday, Central Chess Club, Moscow, 2017

Lifehacks During the Game

During the game, a chess player faces a lot of **non-chess** problems that nobody ever told them about and that are not described in any chess handbook. The most they can do is to glean some individual practical tips from various books, bit by bit.

And they also have their coach, of course. If you ask your coach a concrete question, they might have an answer. But if they are not a pro player, never took part in continental or world-level competitions, it will be hard for them to come up with good advice.

In this chapter, I discuss the most common questions and answer them, using both my own experience and that of my friends and colleagues — famous chess players and coaches.

Don't be bored when it's your opponent's turn to move, do something!

> Spend your "waiting time" in as beneficial a way as possible. Everyone gets mad while they wait. But it's OK for me. Because I don't waste a single minute of my waiting time.

You may as well watch others play, coz there's bugger all else to do during games...
— Alexander Grischuk

I was always hyperactive and couldn't sit still while my opponent was thinking. I could force myself to remain at the board, but I couldn't figure out what I was supposed to be thinking about if I'd already thought for long enough before making my own move! As I watched other players, I always asked myself what on Earth they were thinking about when they stared at the board during their opponent's move! I tried to do that as well. The brain starts calculating lines and simply gets tired. Roaming around the hall is better than this...

Only when I reached middle age did I learn the answer. First of all, chess players conserve energy: running sucks away your energy, your concentration is lowered, too. Secondly, they certainly don't calculate any lines when they remain at the table! They do many other useful chess things that don't involve line calculation.

So, what *are* those useful chess things? They:

→ Look at the position from the outside, globally;

→ Study the properties of the pieces on their squares, search for weak points, determine the weakest pieces;

→ Think about which pieces should be traded and which should be kept on the board;

→ Search for ideas. Often, the most unexpected and best ideas come when they are in the following state: relaxed, careless, looking at the position with a wide, encompassing glance, not burdened with the necessity of making a choice, and time is not a pressing concern;

→ Evaluate the position: determine the advantages and disadvantages, both their own and their opponent's.

→ Verbalize (!) the subsequent plan and search for interesting plans for the opponent.

Without calculating any lines!!!

See how much work there is to do! Why roam around then, dear? You only need to roam around if you feel the need to exercise. If your energy is stale and your sight has got diluted, or if your brain requires rest and a restart.

When your head is tired, play with your hand

> Too much boffinry prevents things from happening naturally. Trust your intuition more, it's much cleverer than what you think is your mind.

A well-known lifehack. When you realize that you're tired and can't think straight anymore, play with your hand. If your head turns off, turn your unconscious on, it won't fail you. If you're out of gas, leave your car and walk. There will certainly be some adventures, but you'll still reach your destination.

After the time scramble, finish off your opponent with your confidence

When everyone is tired, the person with confidence and energy emerges as the leader. Everybody obediently follows that person because they lack energy to resist or create anything. (By the way, that's why sects use an important technique: their members are driven to physical exhaustion to the point where their mind becomes completely malleable.)

I've got a psychological problem — and I'm not the only one. I already told you about it earlier, and now I'll give you some advice.

After 40 moves, i.e. about three-and-a-half hours of play, my confidence evaporates even if I have a won position. There had been little time left before control, and therefore I had to play confidently, without reflecting, without thinking of anything else, without suffering. But now I have passed time control, suddenly I feel pressure from the importance of the result: it's important to hold on to the win and to achieve it. Yet the most important element — *my gamer spirit* — has gone. So, I go into hibernation mode, thinking "deeply" and unnecessarily. When your head is tired, this "deep" thinking is most likely erroneous.

So, here's my advice.

Remember: *both* you and your opponent have the same problem — you are both exhausted. The one who better fakes a second wind will score an important psychological victory (the actual second wind usually comes later, but for now, fake it).

So that player should be *you*. You need to pretend that the time scramble has not exhausted you, but rather recharged you, made you stronger and more confident. Your energy can quickly knock down a tired opponent. Finish them off with your confidence. And to play such a role successfully despite being tired yourself, you should adopt a *gamer attitude*. Imagine that you're playing against your pal at home (but don't bang out the moves like you do in blitz, think normally). This attitude should help you. Force yourself to diminish the importance of this game's result.

Concerning the moves themselves — no pink ribbons or rainbow-colored unicorns, your play should be firm and ruthless.

Record the game neatly - this will help you better control your internal state

Control of your handwriting = control of your mental state

Perhaps this is not as important for tidy and collected people. People like me, on the other hand, constantly have to come up with ways of forcing ourselves to be organized. Neatly recording the game is one such way.

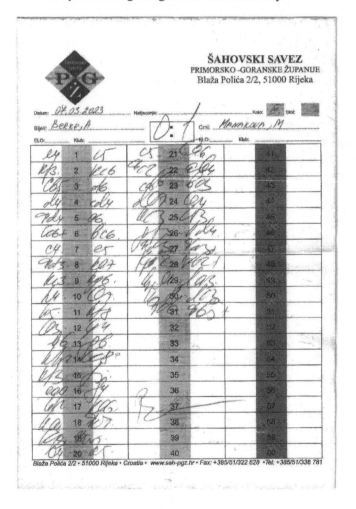

If I don't control my handwriting, then here's what happens.

I felt more or less normal during the first moves, but then it all went downhill. This is reflected in the deterioration of the handwriting. I did win the game after all, though. I didn't want to show a lost game — it's my book, anyway, not someone else's. What if someone actually gets the idea to look through the game on the board?..

But I get much better results when I control my handwriting. When I write mindfully, neatly, sometimes even with full notation. I organize myself through writing. And this actually works!

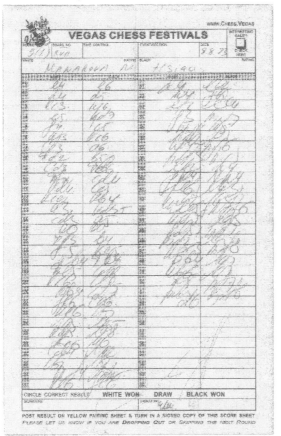

Here, I found a scoresheet with my neatest handwriting.

On the next page you will find scoresheets of players with really neat handwriting for comparison. Ludmila Belavenets vs. Olga Rubtsova and Alla Kushnir vs. Tatiana Zatulovskaya.

By the way, Fischer's handwriting was also far from ideal:

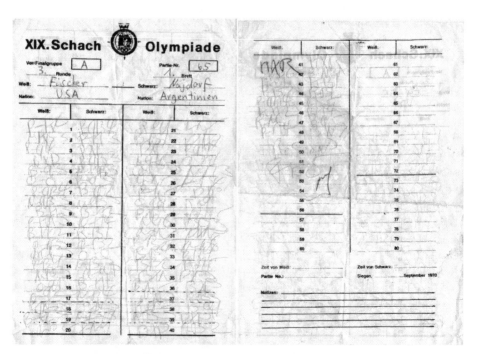

Source: photo by Michael L. Kaufman, https://en.m.wikipedia.org/wiki/File:Fischer_Score_Card.jpg

And if you are currently in the coveted state of a "chess trance", you won't even think about your handwriting, you won't care. Fischer probably played in that state.

Don't forget to snack during the game

> To avoid being as physically exhausted as an average sect member, you should remember to eat normally and sleep well — it's your source of energy.

In my time, I got to work with many teams — from the Moscow team, which featured legendary players in the late 1970s, to the Russian national team. I always brought a 3-liter Chinese flask with me, and all players knew that they would get the necessary tea at the right time. It's also good to eat 2–3 pieces of chocolate after 2–2.5 hours of the game; I recommend 70% dark chocolate, it supports your energy very well. Chess players should understand that nobody can help you during the game, you are one-on-one with your opponent and should help yourself. It's also useful to wash your face with cold water occasionally during the game, perhaps once per hour.
— Boris Postovsky

Stress and active mental work greatly increase the demand for oxygen and glucose in the brain. Everyone knows that chocolate contains tons of glucose. But fewer know that it also contains caffeine, which dilates the brain blood vessels for a short while, providing additional inflow of oxygen and nutrients, above all glucose. All chess players snack on chocolate, it really saves us. I eat one or two pieces when I sense that my head is getting tired — about two hours after the beginning, and I always eat some after the first control, especially if there was a time scramble. At that point, I sometimes allow myself to drink a cup of coffee (black or green tea is a good substitute for kids), even though I must admit that I sometimes sip coffee for the whole duration of my game. I'm a big girl now, I can do that.

Of course, you lose a lot of energy in time trouble, but if you start munching fruits, nuts, chocolates and coffee with cookies immediately afterwards, you relax far too much! Asceticism during the game helps keep your body mobilized, so don't go overboard with snacks.

Every grandmaster finds their own way: they watch themselves, experiment, determine by trial and error which foods increase their energy and which decrease it. For instance, Alexander Kotov ate ten sandwiches per game and gained weight after every game. Vladimir Simagin, on the other hand, did not

eat any sandwiches and lost three kilograms per game. Lev Polugaevsky lost even more, but nobody knew how much exactly. And so, there was a running joke: after a tournament, Polugaevsky becomes Chetvertgaevsky.[1]

I "stole" one lifehack from Valentina Gunina, it's just beautiful. Eat a banana about 1.5−2 hours into the game. Bananas are full of calories, but light at the same time. Your head becomes as fresh as a cucumber after that. Or as a banana.

Some words on drinking. You have to drink water during the game. For instance, our beloved Carlsen drinks a lot of plain water. Sometimes I brew my own tea with honey at home, but many settle for the tea provided by tournament organizers. Botvinnik brought sweet tea with lemon to the game and drank it on the third hour. The body spends a lot of water and glucose, and Botvinnik had both of these in his flask. Still, gastroenterologists say that nothing can replace pure water.

At first, I took black currant with lemon to the games, my wife squeezed the juice herself. Then I started drinking coffee. For a time, I would eat chocolate during play, I think it's good. Here's what I noticed about myself: if I gain weight during a tournament, then I played poorly, and if I come back from the game and don't feel tired, then it's also bad. If I'm exhausted, on the other hand, it's

---

[1]   The prefix "polu-" means "half-" in Russian, and "chetvert-" means "quarter". So, "Half-Gaevsky" turned into "Quarter-Gaevsky" — *Translator*

all right. After the game against Capablanca in Amsterdam, I literally couldn't
get up from my chair.
  — Mikhail Botvinnik

Let's summarize the information on energy resources. Your brain requires
three elements to function properly during the game: **oxygen, water** and **glucose**.
Thus, you have to drink water and snack on glucose-rich foods. In addition to
glucose, your body requires energy, which can be replenished with chocolate,
bananas, dried fruits and nuts.

Concerning oxygen — it might be useful to stand at an open window and
take some quick breaths, and to check your breathing during the game. Many
experienced coaches and sports doctors recommend being mindful of your
breathing and train it at home together with your overall fitness.

Should you run to the toilet in time trouble?

> You should always run to the toilet. Or sometimes walk. However
> you can.

This question is similar to "should you use the bathroom before departure?"
You want to drink, but you can't drink too much, because if you get into time
trouble, you'll be torn apart by the dilemma: should you run to the toilet or
not? Even if you are a champion runner, you'll still lose several minutes. That
is, if you get lucky, and there isn't a queue to use the toilet: now of all times,
everyone, *everyone* wants to pee before time trouble! And this is understandable:
anyone would want to get rid of this problem beforehand and then concentrate
only on the game.

Alas, this doesn't work. You can visit the bathroom as many times as you want
before time trouble, but when you have a minute left on the clock for ten moves,
your body will surely betray you and demand that you relieve yourself right away.

And you're lucky if this happens before the first time control. At the end
of the game, when you're out of time and playing on increment, you might sit
there for literally an hour, unable to get away from the board at all. And this
is brutal! Any pro has encountered such a situation at least once, you may ask
anyone. Thankfully, Red state blocks out any physiological processes that are
not essential for survival, but still, even in this case, potty emergencies happen!
So, what should you do? Should you go away from the board and lose time
when you *simply have to* pee?

I still don't know the right answer. Sometimes it becomes so unbearable that
your head refuses to think — what's the use in continuing the game in such

cases? But how can you go if you only have a few minutes of precious time for 20 moves? Here's the rule I follow: I go (do what you must, and come what may) ☺. Of course, I don't go if I only have a minute on the clock. There's no chance of making it back in time.

But the best thing to do is to avoid the root cause earlier: you should drink, but not too much. And if you don't want to drink too much during play, you shouldn't eat too much at lunch. And the food shouldn't be too salty/spicy/fatty/fried. See how it's all connected? As you grow up and accumulate experience, you find the balance that's right for you. And you also suddenly start believing all those healthy eating theories.

Speaking of toilets... I remember a particular incident. A while ago I played in a big Russian open tournament. There was only one toilet for everyone, and it was always occupied. I went to the arbiters' bathroom. Everything went well until I tried to leave the room. The door had a peculiarity: it closed very well, but couldn't open. The arbiters knew about that and never closed it fully, but I, on the other hand, stepped into a simple trap, stupidly and incompetently, during my own time trouble! What could I now do? Mobile phones were not allowed, so I started to scream and bang loudly on the door. Of course, people rushed to my rescue, someone brought a crowbar and broke down the door. They laughed and wished me luck... I won that game.

During the game, light neck exercises are useful because your neck can easily become a bottleneck for energy

During intense mental work, your neck and shoulders get strained. Strain disrupts the free flow of energy. And if the energy isn't flowing freely, you'll make wrong decisions.

When I made video reports from tournaments, I noticed a lot of things that you never notice when sitting at the board. For instance, chess players regularly rub their necks, especially when time trouble approaches. Not their heads, which are ostensibly their "working instruments", but necks. Silly filmmakers don't know that, and if they make a chess film without consulting real chess players, then their chess-playing protagonist always rubs his head before making a move. Chess players never rub their heads! Well, they do, but very rarely. They rub their necks much more often.

Cervical spine: your neck and the trapezius muscle

In the East, the neck is called the bridge between the body and the mind. The neck contains the spinal cord, 32 muscles, 4 main arteries and 8 big nerves, along

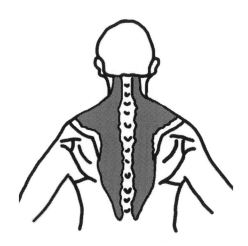

Trapezius muscle

with lots of smaller ones. The neck is an important bridge that connects the head with the whole body, sending signals to it and receiving feedback. During a chess game, the muscles in the body are tense and overloaded – not simply because the player sits in the same position for a long time, but chiefly because of the emotional strain.

The trapezius muscle (part of the back of the neck that goes from the shoulder blade to the lower occipital bone and cervical vertebrae) is also overloaded. The trapezius muscle is the nearest muscle to the neck and second-nearest muscle to the head, and its state is also very important for the thinking processes.

Reasons for the trapezius muscle becoming overloaded:
- Physical or emotional tension;
- When the shoulders remain lifted for too long (usually when the person is tense or cold, also when the table height does not match the chair height);
- When the shoulders are turned forward (this concerns people with a hunched posture, i.e. 99.9% of all chess players).

Actually, if you don't take care of your body, and especially your spine (if you don't relieve the tension after the game, don't restore the muscles after the tournament, don't do sport, yoga or at least morning exercises), you can easily get something like osteochondrosis, radicular pain, chronic headaches and other wonderful stuff like that. But we have another, more pressing question: can you relieve the tension *during* the game, at least partially?

Yes, you can, and professional players do that.

First of all, let's get back to the unconscious rubbing of the neck. Your body is actually much smarter than you are, and it knows exactly what to do. If the muscles are too tense, the body sends a message to the brain: do a micromassage. Thanks to such a massage, neck muscles relax a bit, and this allows more blood to flow to them.

Further, some chess players don't just rub their necks – they make deliberate small turns and rotations of their head. These turns and rotations are the simplest possible exercises that don't even require conscious control. This means that they don't decrease the player's concentration.

When you have more time at your disposal (when your opponent is clearly in hybernation mode), you can do some more complex exercises. Or you can even go away from the table and do some mini-gymnastics.

Play in your most comfortable clothes

> As you approach the second half of your life, your clothing priorities stabilize: natural materials, loose and comfortable fit, texture that's pleasant to touch.

Of course, you want to play in what's most comfortable for you. This was always the case. However, FIDE had introduced a dress code for the biggest competitions recently, with strict limitations.

You can't wear shorts, flip-flops, miniskirts, blouses with low necklines, jeans, T-shirts or even trainers. Basically, not much is allowed. And the poor Chosen Few cannot even wear bright clothes!

Oh, poker players have it so easy! They can express their individuality as they want. Every player has their own look, their own gimmick, everyone is special. This guy wears mirror shades, that guy comes in a cowboy hat with a gun, this girl looks like a dominatrix in a leather coat, and that girl is dressed in sexy Marilyn Monroe style... I'm always for freedom of expression, therefore, I like this policy more. In chess, however, we are forced to follow business dress code. And a bit of Sharia code, too: no bare shoulders, no bare knees, no bare toes.

There's another reason why I'm unhappy with the new dress code: chess players are under as much strain as in any other sports. They get exhausted after six hours of play. Formal shoes, suit and tie – is this really sports attire? How can you withstand the incredible strain if you're used to wearing T-shirts, jeans and trainers normally, but you can't wear them here? Or maybe you're overheating and want your body to breathe more, but you can't do that, either? You can only wear long-sleeve shirts, no T-shirts allowed!

That's why many chess players hate the new dress code with a passion. The competitive factor is very important! You should wear clothes that are comfortable for you, both for your body and spirit. Both your body and spirit should feel free and happy. The energy should flow freely throughout your body: so, no fasteners, no close-fitting materials, no belts, no bands.

My personal opinion on the dress code: yes, there should be one, but there should be only one requirement: the clothes should be clean. That's all.

Do we really need to formalize the cleanness requirement? Unfortunately, we do. Because there are a lot of schlimazels (weirdos, as I explained earlier) in our sport. It doesn't even occur to them that they should sometimes change and wash clothes, let alone iron them. The only thing that exists for them is chess, there's no place for other things or thoughts in their heads.

Clothing style

> Clothing style defines your look – and, therefore, your mood and feeling. Choose the look that's necessary for concrete circumstances – it will help you to behave accordingly and to get into "character".

Now let's disregard the previous diatribe on the lack of freedom to wear whatever we want and discuss actual clothing style.

Psychologists have long proved that what we wear defines our mood and energy. For instance, a female chess player may wear trousers not simply because

they're more comfortable. Trousers give her a masculine energy necessary for a combative mood. And if she decides to wear a long, pretty skirt instead, she's doomed — she'll definitely lose. I always do.

Strict clothing and strict hairstyle discipline you and make your thought process more solid and organized. An eccentric appearance will affect your play as well: creative flights and fantasies, unpredictability. At tournaments that don't have a strict dress code yet, you can use the following trick: your clothes should match the style you want to play in the particular game.

All of the above doesn't concern men as much. They simply wear what fell on them from the closet, like in life.

There's also a science called color psychology, which studies the effect of colors on people. If you want your opponent to be more aggressive towards you, wear red, if you want them to be more respectful, wear black, to make them more relaxed, wear white, light pink or light blue... I was interested in that for a while and even experimented with my clothes. But I soon got bored of it.

Acting Tricks Deployed
by Chess Players

Chess players can be divided into two groups: the first group is obviously acting, making faces and hamming it up, in other words, they act badly. The second group sends subtle signals to their opponents, not "acting" at all and certainly not overacting.

Kids and amateurs overact and do that openly and eagerly. You cannot talk to your opponent in chess, but you can still interact with nonverbal signals, such as your pose, manners and mimics. And so, they deliberately act out: "Oh, I blundered so terribly!", "Oh, my position is sooo bad!", "See what a cool move I made, you are so losing right now!", "When are you going to resign, chump?", "Damn, I'm running late, make your move now!"

The second group of players, **masters and average-level grandmasters**, also do that, but subtly. Because they know that if they overact, their opponent will immediately become suspicious. But if they only drop a hint – sigh, lean back on their chair, throw a demonstratively indifferent aside glance... Well, any chess player who has reached International Master level becomes a good actor. And how does a good actor act if they are a real pro? Correct, they don't "act", they actually "live it out". The same thing happens with strong chess players: acting becomes a part of their personality, they don't act on purpose.

Top chess players, even though they have already reached nirvana and risen above all the vanity of the mortal world, also engage in acting sometimes. But rarely, because of "I know you know I know". They know each other too well, have played hundreds of games with each other, have spent countless hours analyzing together – and some of them even go to parties together, take walks together, meet girls together, play football or tennis together. They know each other so well that they see each other right through.

Moreover, you should also remember that they are so adept at scanning their opponents that no theatrics will work against them. And if a person is especially adept at reading others and seeing through lies and psychological tricks, they usually think that they themselves are easy to read as well. So they normally avoid acting tricks.

And, as I already said, moves expose a player's thoughts and feelings as nothing else does. These guys don't just read the "message" perfectly – they become true masters in this. If they do engage in theatrics, they usually do it for the spectators and journalists, not their opponents. Some chess players, such as Carlsen, Kasparov, Nakamura, Grischuk and Niemann, are clearly good actors in their own right. They always want to create a show. They can't help but make such a boring thing as chess more fun with their fiery behavior. They make funny faces, engage in hilarious antics and provoking comments – and gladly share all that with the world.

Acting ruses against a weak opponent

> Remember the main rule of acting: you shouldn't "act", you should "live it out".

Marin Bosiocic, whom we met a bit earlier in Game 24, was not the only player who squashed me like a worm with his contemptuous attitude. Many masters and grandmasters do the same, and not only with me.

Here's a list of typical tricks for a game against a much lower-rated player:

→ The moves are made offhandedly, as though they are forcing themselves: like, I want to go home, what am I doing here with this amateur?

→ Pose: leaning back on the chair. (You have probably seen a photo of Carlsen reclining on his chair in his match against Caruana.)

→ Getting up after every move and watching the other games.

→ Talking to friends while the opponent is thinking, and doing that openly so that the opponent sees it (this is a dirty trick; if you see anything of that sort, notify the arbiter immediately! Talking to anyone during the game is prohibited!).

→ Playing the opening at lightning speed, never thinking for more than half a minute. Playing the whole game quickly, not thinking for more than a minute.

→ Looking at their watch, like, "when is this finally going to end?!" (Sighing sometimes.)

All these tricks greatly affect the poor opponent: they are already much weaker in chess, but there's also *all this*!

The theatrical nature of pretty woman players

> Never believe a woman

Notice that I didn't even say "women's acting". This would be a tautology, like "oily oil". Women act with their every breath, especially pretty women. When I taught chess in elementary school, I was amazed by pretty girls, still kids, using acting tricks to get their way. Nature is incredible!

Woman chess players are no exception. For instance, before the introduction of a dress code, pretty woman players would accentuate their sexiness with clothes that prevented their male opponents from concentrating on the game. A distraction tactic, if you will. Pure physiology. And some women used that successfully.

There's a famous woman grandmaster with a delicious bust. Many male chess players have complained about her behavior. As long as she has a worse position in the opening, she acts like a shrinking violet. But as soon as her opponent lets their guard down, she strikes a blow and gets a better position. She immediately sits up, puts her ample breasts on the table and finishes off her opponent in great style. This cannot be countered.

I heard a story about another beautiful woman player from her coach. He said that she once brought four huge suitcases to the tournament. "I was thinking: good girl, she has taken her books and *Chess Informants* with her (the story took place in the Soviet Union, before the computer era). I helped her carry those suitcases to her room. Can you imagine?! Two suitcases were filled with shoes and sandals! Two others were filled with clothes. And not a single — you wouldn't believe it! — not a single chess book!"

Various acting tricks

> Body language is a strong communication weapon. People are like open books for you.

Despite six years of acting on stage, despite taking part in movies, TV shows, projects and stage plays, I shy away from using acting tricks. That's because I scan people very well, and I think that others see me as well as I see them, so there's no sense in pretending. But perhaps you will make use of the simplest and most useful tricks, so here's a small list.

→ If you sacrifice a piece for attack and want it to be captured, don't show your confidence. On the contrary, slouch and clutch your head with your hands, as though you're in deep thought.

→ If you blunder, pretend that you have everything under control and walk away from the table. Rapid breathing will perfidiously betray you, so if you want to suffer, do it as far from your opponent as possible.

→ If you see a good move for your opponent, again, walk away from the table. Chess players' thoughts are very "loud", and your opponent might "overhear" that move in your head. Thoughts become much quieter a few meters away. It's even better to take a walk around the hall and forget about this move altogether — in this case, there's nothing to be overheard.

Breathing can be very telling. Sometimes your opponent holds his breath, and you see that something happened that he doesn't want to give away. Or he becomes quiet, or too fussy. After a time, you become perceptive of such things and can better recognize them.
— *Viswanathan Anand*

Study body language. There are a lot of books on the subject, and neuro-linguistic programming works are especially useful in this regard. But simply reading books is not enough, you have to do exercises given in them: don't limit yourself to the theory. If you spend a couple of months practicing it, you'll learn to read body language automatically, including eye movements. This, by the way, is useful in ordinary life too, not only in chess.

The Rules of Chess

Professionals know everything I'll say in this chapter. Not only know, they know it as well as their ABCs. Anyone who reaches master level in our sport strictly adheres to the rules of the game and requires the same strict adherence from others. Professionals also know how, when and from whom to demand punishment for violation of the rules.

Demand that your opponent adhere to the rules of the game

> The most horrible people are those who change the rules during the game. Avoid them like the plague. They are bullies with no principles, so to Hell with them. Find ways to steer clear of them.

Adhere to the rules religiously and never ever let your opponent break them. Everyone knows cases when even world champions and other top players have touched their piece, but then moved a different one or even taken their move back. Their violations were filmed or seen by eyewitnesses, they were caught red-handed, but, for some reason, their opponents did not react as harshly as they were entitled to. But opponents are the *only* people who have the right to react.

Those who have taken moves back likely weren't bad or dishonest people; it's just that their will to win is so great, their energy pushes them forward so strongly, that any "accidents" or "misunderstandings" simply cannot happen to them, that's impossible! If their opponent reacts — well, that's that, but if they don't — the game continues.

Judit Polgar was taken aback in her famous game against Garry Kasparov when he momentarily let go of his knight, but then grabbed it again and moved it to another square. Camera footage shows how she was privately resentful and sighed a bit, but ultimately she simply continued playing. Levon Aronian, on the other hand, firmly demanded that Hikaru Nakamura make a move with his king that he touched. Nakamura only shrugged: like, what king? I don't have any king! Levon then turned beet red at such audacity and insisted that he *had* to move the king. Ultimately, Hikaru had to locate the king on the board and move it, and he resigned shortly afterwards.

By the way, take note: chess fans forgave both Kasparov and Nakamura for these "misunderstandings", they are still fan favorites; dear Judit, on the other hand, got a big fat dislike for her softness. Many years have passed, but she's still widely criticized in comments. (To be fair, she's a fan favorite, too.)

Why, then, do chess players become so baffled when their opponent violates the rules? First of all, out of respect. I'm afraid to name the world champion (this would be tantamount to sacrilege, because he has such a high moral image in the history of chess and is so beloved by everyone), but my coach told me that he saw with his own eyes how he took a move back in his game. He moved a piece, let go of it, then put it back, sat and thought for a while, and moved a different piece. There were lots of eyewitnesses, some of whom were ready to testify, but his opponent got so confused that he didn't call the arbiter at all. "*Who am I and who is he? I am a trembling creature, and he has the right!* He is so great that I'm probably imagining things, let's play on!"

Another explanation is that you lose your self-control when faced with brute strength and rudeness. There are people who simply cannot resist brute force.

In such cases, I always remember a quote from my theater role, from H. Leivick's play The Golem. *I played Rabbi Maharal, a character based on the famous Prague rabbi of the same name. According to the legend, he was both a respected guru and a great alchemist. He knew the secrets of all the world, of Heaven and Hell, he created an animate slave out of clay, the Golem, and breathed life into him... And this great man suddenly comes to a very pessimistic conclusion at the end of the play: "Now I realize that I'm powerless against fists!" Against ordinary physical strength.*

Examples of correct and incorrect reaction

> You should not be overly kind to those who deliberately hurt you, now or in the past, otherwise they will get a taste for doing so. But if they genuinely beg for forgiveness then you should sincerely forgive them. Or at least try to. At a minimum, so as not to carry a heavy burden around with you. Not forgiving is bad for your health.

If your opponent suddenly starts playing Subbuteo with chess pieces during a tournament game, stop the clock and call the arbiter without hesitation. It's better to look embarrassed than to be hit on the head with a bishop.

I'll show you a couple of examples from my own career — examples of **incorrect** reactions during the game. I repeat: what I did in both cases was **wrong**, don't do that!

I played against a famous grandmaster, the strongest player in his country. He had a dubious, even poor position for the whole game, and when he finally extricated himself, he offered me a draw. I had a low rating, miles less than his, I was a nobody in his eyes, but he still thought that he was worse and that it was time to salvage what he could (earlier in the game, I would have definitely refused because my position was very good). I said that I would think about it. I'm sitting and thinking, my last minute on the clock is ticking, and he is also sitting and thinking – on my time. And then he saw that he had some winning chances – they were tiny, but they existed. I finally said that I agreed and extended my hand. And he replied, "No, I changed my mind."

There were witnesses: spectators as well as grandmasters playing on adjacent boards. Everyone heard and saw everything, and they were just stunned. And I was astonished by such rudeness and audacity. It simply knocked me out. I was speechless and lost my ability to resist. Still, I got the bit between my teeth and continued to play for some reason. I ultimately managed to draw about 20 moves later. I was as mad as a dog after the game, mostly at myself, of course. He came up to me and tried to apologize. Well, OK, I said, what can we do now... Now we're friends on social media, he sent me a friend request himself and likes my posts; all in all, I accepted his apologies and forgave him. However, what should I have forgiven here? I was at fault.

Some chess players want to win so desperately that they shamelessly exploit your softness or lack of knowledge of the rules. Recently, a player whom I know well "smudged" one of the moves between moves 30 and 39 in my time trouble (she does that all the time against inexperienced opponents, and it actually works, but why do that against me, of all people?). "Smudging" is a trick: you write down your move on the scoresheet very close to the previous one, so that when I make my 40th move and look at your scoresheet in the heat of the battle, I have doubts that I really made 40 moves and hastily make the 41st move. This is a dirty and common trick. You can immediately call the arbiter and demand to check the clarity of her game score, or you can simply continue playing, knowing that your score is genuine, and hers is false.

And here's another incident, with most foul play.

I played at Luzhniki Hall, Moscow, at the Blitz World Championship against a woman grandmaster. Many chess players, especially young ones, have a bad habit in blitz: they make a move, press the clock and immediately adjust that piece, make their next move, press the clock and adjust the piece again, and again and again. This is harmless in a classical game, but in blitz, every millisecond is important. As soon as your opponent makes their move, your brain immediately revs up to think about the reply – and it does so at ludicrous speed. You start thinking, and then their hand appears in front of your snout and adjusts a piece. Your brain goes blank for a couple of seconds, and you struggle to return to your recently launched thought process.

According to the rules, adjusting pieces on your opponent's time is not allowed, but for such guys and gals, it's simply their style. I realized that when I played blitz over the board against my student who previously only took online lessons. A good, sweet guy, but he adjusts his pieces literally on every move. I commented on that once, then twice, and then I said strictly, "If you adjust your pieces one more time, I won't play with you anymore!" And I saw him actually struggling to stop himself from adjusting them, spending time and energy on that... And then I got it: he's used to it! It's his style. A nasty, ugly style that he developed while working with his previous coach.

That WGM used the same tactic: she moved her piece and then adjusted it, then moved again and adjusted again, then moved – oops! – the pieces fell on my time, oops! – she did it again! "Oh, sorry!" "Oh, sorry again!" And what I did then was, of course, unworthy of any professional player – I behaved like a total amateur. I usually tell my younger opponents in an angry tone, "Careful!", or "Adjust on your own time!", and this is often enough. But here – oh, here this wouldn't work at all. There's a saber-toothed tigress sitting opposite you, and whatever you say would be water off a duck's back. Ultimately I got so angry that I simply started to give away my pieces left and right despite having a won position! Of course, I lost. After the game, she said to me, "I am so sorry!" Get lost! You played like that for the whole game, not just a couple of moves, she's sorry, yeah, right. All in all, I didn't forgive her, it seems.

To survive among pro players, you have to be a pro yourself – you should have "competitive anger" and the desire to destroy your opponent. And if they play dirty, you should curb that immediately and ruthlessly. This is, of course, not about me. I can berate them after the game, but little else. Small consolation for a zero in the table!

And here's the million-dollar question: what was I supposed to do? How should I have reacted?

I posed that question to several strong full grandmasters with whom I shared a tea in the lounge shortly afterwards. They replied, "Masha, what were you thinking of? You behaved like a little girl! Here's what you do: stop the clock, call the arbiter, complain about your opponent breaching the rules and ask the arbiter to watch your game. That's all."

Well, I did know that! Moreover, I had faced such behavior many times! But I lacked the composure to stop and resolve the conflict – I just continued on ahead, like a headless chicken.

Remember: if your opponent violates the rules, do not interact with them! Forget about it! You simply stop the clock and call the arbiter. The arbiter comes over, and you explain your concerns to them. Let your opponent take the rap for their own behavior. Why on Earth should this become your problem at all?! You came to play chess according to the rules of the game! You shouldn't suffer because of *their* dirty play!

By the way, FIDE introduced a new rule for arbiters in 2021: the arbiter now has the right to intervene even without a player making a claim if they see that the game is clearly not being played according to the fair play rules. Actually, they don't just have a right: they are obliged to do that. If they didn't do it when they should have done so, and there were cameras and witnesses, you should file a protest immediately after the game. Later, it will be useless to demand anything.

In July 2023, FIDE introduced VAR – Video Assistant Referee. There will be cameras watching the players all the time. In a conflict situation, the arbiter may use VAR to resolve it. So, even though morals in society have declined, technology still prevents processes from collapsing. VAR is expected to be used at all important competitions, like in other sports.

By the way, after the introduction of VAR in football, the rate of correct referee decisions increased from 82 to 94 percent.

And now, here's an example of a **correct** reaction. It's what you **should** do!

This happened at the European Women's Championship. The games are in progress, there is silence in the hall, and then suddenly we hear the sounds of a squabble at the leading boards. An arbiter is running towards them. What has happened? Alina Kashlinskaya's professional conduct is what "happened".

Her opponent, a young player, put a flask and a bowl of nuts on her table just like home and started eating chocolate, loudly rustling the tinfoil wrapping and coughing intermittently. All this was done on Alina's time. She sits there and rustles, and chews, and coughs, and chews, and coughs, and rustles. Alina, without saying a word to her opponent, stops the clock and calls the arbiter. She tells the arbiter that her opponent is disturbing her by spreading her food on the table and rustling.

The arbiter reprimanded the girl – and I hope that she learned a valuable lesson that day, and other chess players won't suffer from her foul play. (Eating a chocolate loudly at the table is a common dirty trick. When I intend to enjoy a sumptuous feast during a game, I take all the food out of my bag and walk as far from my opponent as possible to avoid disturbing them.) Impunity only leads to repeat crimes.

You should not "forgive" those who want to hurt you (you can do that later, if they sincerely repent). Forget about "nobility" and "chivalry". Chess is a game with strict rules, and nobody should violate them.

Of course, when mistakes are made *unintentionally*, in friendly tournaments or by people who would *never* break the rules on purpose, I usually forgive them. A phone goes off in your opponent's pocket during the first few moves – you do realize that this was an accident? Or when an elderly player touches the wrong piece in a completely drawn position, I usually forgive them, unless it's a team tournament. There's a certain Justice in the world, and I try to live by it.

Concerning cheating – well, I always advocated for the harshest possible punishment: a total ban from chess for life. But we'll discuss cheating later.

> *I remember a Candidate Master wiping his nose with his hands, and then touching the pieces. What would you do against him?*
> *#fromtheinterwebz*

In controversial situations, stop the clock and simultaneously raise your hand to call the arbiter

> Resolve conflicts in a civilized way. Humans would have wiped each other out back in the Stone Age if they hadn't come up with rules of conflict resolution in time.

Many inexperienced chess players make a mistake: they confront their opponent, call the arbiter, yell and quarrel, try to prove something – and do all that on their own time. Hilarious! Nobody will tell you, "Hey, dude, don't you want to stop the clock? You're wasting your time." Even the arbiter, if they aren't very professional, might forget to stop your clock.

I saw an incident at a rapid tournament with my own eyes: nobody bothered to stop the clock, they argued and argued, the "plaintiff" ultimately won the argument, and when they continued the game, he only had a few seconds left on the clock. He lost on time despite having a completely won position.

Conflicts and quarrels with

your opponent should not happen when your clock is ticking! You have the right to stop the clock to resolve a conflict. But please, as you press the clock button, immediately raise your hand to show your intention to call the arbiter, otherwise you may lose by forfeit (stopping the clock can be interpreted as resignation).

Stop the clock, raise your hand, call the arbiter (usually with a yell, but this is not necessary): this is the pro player's algorithm in case of any rule violation.

As a tournament participant, you have the right...

> Successful people care greatly about living in comfort, where and how they eat, what they wear, who surrounds them. Still, don't overdo this, please. Because these are not the most important things in the world, obviously.

...to silence, good lighting, a comfortable temperature and ventilation in the hall. Everything else is up to your tolerance and relationship with the organizers. Bobby Fischer was as fastidious as a primadonna and demanded ideal conditions: sound-proof glass for the playing hall and a chair without listening devices. When you become a star like Fischer, you can be as demanding

At a tournament in Eilat, 2012

too, but for now, try not to notice the organizers' shortcomings — believe me, they're trying their best to do good for the participants. Not simply out of kindness of their hearts, but because this is required by the FIDE rules: they should conform to the tournament stipulations.

Moreover, if you obsess too much about the bad sides of the organizers, this will not end well — you'll waste your precious mental energy. I don't like this, I don't like that, the light is too dim, it's too hot, or too cold, or too stuffy, or too loud... If you are thinking about all this, it means that you're out of playing form. *Stop it!*

By the way, the young generation pays almost no heed to such "trifling" matters as playing conditions. All they want is to push wood.

Conclusion. Non-chess players only see the result in the table. Smith defeated Jones because he was stronger, and that's all. They can't possibly imagine the *entire* backstory of that result! The struggle of personalities and nerves, digestive problems, sleepless nights, psychological pressure, dirty, ungentlemanly play, coughing for the whole game, the munching of chocolates, everyone suspecting everyone else of cheating, real cheating — suggestions from coaches and chess engines, lack of proper lighting or ventilation in the hall, disrespectful and unprofessional behavior by arbiters, et cetera, et cetera. As in every area of sport — or show business — the spectators only see the facade, the pretty pictures. "I wish you were aware from what stray matter / Springs poetry to prosper without shame!..."[1]

---

[1]   A quote from a poem by Anna Akhmatova — *Translator*

Losing

Any professional player will agree with Tal's words that a loss is a microdeath. No words of consolation help, no advice works. Only time will heal. One evening is usually enough to recover from a loss. But some losses are so heavy that they leave a wound for your entire life.

A person's recovery time depends on their stress resistance (which can be trained, by the way). But no matter how tough you are, God forbid you from winding up in the same situation as David Bronstein.

He was essentially one move away from winning the world championship in his match against Botvinnik.

One. Freaking. Move.

Bronstein couldn't fully recover from that shock his entire life. Of course, he was still cheerful and charming on the outside, but the shock still haunted

him like a black cloud. His friends confirmed that. For instance, Valery Ivanov, who was friends with Bronstein in the last years of his life, recalled: "Not long before his death, David stood at the window. Sad and glum, he was leaning on the window frame: 'Ah, why didn't I make that move back then...'"

By the way, I remember David. He once read a lecture for us in the Pioneers House on Stopani. That's how ancient I am! A dinosaur.

You simply need to survive this evening

> A loss is a small death. But there's no moving forward without losses. Gold must be tried by fire.

Fischer once lost to me, got upset and started crying. There's nothing bad in that, I also sometimes cried after losing. So, if you cry, that's normal.
— *Boris Spassky*

I play fair and I play to win. If I lose, I take my medicine.
— *Bobby Fischer*

Canonical law confirms that the papal scribes of the Vatican are allowed to play chess... If a fight occurs during the game, and one of the players kills the other, then this should be treated as involuntary manslaughter with mitigating circumstances. For chess is the wisest of the games known to man, but in no other game does a loss entail such grievous frustrations, and thus, if the loser loses control of himself, he should be treated with utmost leniency.
— *Alessandro Salvio, 16th century*

A player should possess composure and not overturn the chessboard if he loses.
— *Romain Rolland*

Many players flock from chess into poker now. They're crazy! They don't knock pieces off the board, they beat you up with a candelabra!
— *Ashot Nadanian*

After an upsetting loss in an important game, I once wrote to my Serbian friend:

That's it, I quit chess.

And he's just an ordinary man, not a chess player. And he gives a perfectly normal reply:

This is a sport like any other sport. Sometimes you win, sometimes you lose, sometimes you get injured, but you can always perform better and go forward. You're simply nervous now.

Who? Me? Nervous?! You don't get it. I'm not nervous...

...I'm dying.

These normies don't get anything!

Or here's another episode that happened recently.

I complained to a famous grandmaster during the European team championship that I lost two games in a row. Then I asked him, "What would you do in my place? How would you play afterwards?"

"If I lost two in a row," he said, "you might as well send me to a looney bin."

It's interesting to watch how chess players cope with losses according to their personality. Someone withdraws completely: they need to be alone, and woe betide anyone who approaches them. Someone else starts pestering his fellow players at dinner, literally everyone, telling them about their loss in all excruciating details. This person shares their suffering with everyone else and feels better afterwards. Others still use different ways to cope, from alcohol and sex to strenuous exercise.

I'll give you some ideas, thoughts and quotes that will help you survive that evening (the ideas are numbered). At least they did help me. And I'll start with those that make you look at losses as important positive events, a part of your Path.

When small kids turn up at chess school, we tell their parents that chess will teach their children to lose. This is true. And we teach the same ideas to the kids themselves: "You can only learn something from a loss," "If you don't lose, you won't win." If a toddler never falls, they'll never know what height is. Funnily enough, as we grow up and become pro players, we forget about these simple formulas for some reason. Even though it would be useful to remember them sometimes.

*1. Morozevich (in a private conversation): "How should you recover from a loss? You simply need to look at the game as a **part of a great path**, as one of its stages."*

2. Robert Kiyosaki, author of the bestseller Rich Dad Poor Dad*: "Everyone tries to avoid setbacks, but I hope to suffer from them because they will make me **even smarter**.*

*With setbacks, we **push the boundaries.** Very rich people, investors, live on neutral emotions. They are neutral and patient. Because they understand that bad luck is always **a part of good luck**. People who avoid bad luck avoid good luck as well.*

*My rich dad reacted in this way when I lost my millions: 'You **haven't lost enough** yet.'*

I open up my mind, *I ask people for advice, synthesize it all and develop my own solution. If I lose, it's not a matter of life and death. If I make a mistake, I don't deny it. I apologize: this is my fault. I admit it and* **move forward.** *"*

3. *Winston Churchill: "He who makes mistakes that can be used as lessons earlier than others gets a* **great advantage.** *"*

Jose Raul Capablanca: "You can learn **much more** *from a lost game than from a won game. You should lose hundreds of games before you become a good player."*

Bruce Lee: "The pain will go away as soon as it **teaches you a lesson.** *"*

4. *Alexander Gelman: "My observations show that if a chess player plays on a certain level, then, no matter how many games they lose, they will* **start winning again** *at some point to get back to that level."*

5. *Mike Tyson: "When a man gets up after falling, it's not physics, it's* **character.** *"*

6. *Kateryna Lagno: "If you lost,* **forget about it**! *Tomorrow brings a new game! If you can't forget, then don't play in tournaments."*

7. *Jose Raul Capablanca: "If you get checkmated, don't be upset. There are hundreds of lost games* **still ahead** *of you."*

8. *There's a theory saying that every chess player has a* **certain number of losses** *allotted to them in their life. So, if you lost now, then this counter has decreased. You'll lose one game fewer now* ☺.

9. *Thomas Edison: "I never failed. I simply found 10,000 ways that* **do not work.** *"*

10. *Michael Jordan: "In my career, I missed over* **9,000** *throws and lost almost* **300** *games.* **26** *times the team entrusted the final winning throw to me, and I missed. I lost* **again, and again and again.** *That's why I succeeded."*

11. *Only the first ten years of losing are hard. Then you* **get used to it.** *(A paraphrased proverb.)*

12. **All will be well.**

A magical phrase that I heard said very confidently by Alexei Shirov. He said it to me when I performed poorly at a tournament. After that, I miraculously started to win everything. During the games, I remembered his phrase and told myself, "I don't know how well all will be, but Shirov knows for sure, he was so confident!" And then I won.

And, as a bonus, a lifehack known to all chess players and recently voiced by Carlsen. If you perform poorly, play several online games — right there, during the tournament, in the evening. Play against weaker players. When you defeat them, you feel more confident and at ease.

If you can't come up with an excuse for losing you're not a real man

> When you are filled with emotions after losing, you can accuse the world as a whole and every single human being personally. But after you calm down, you should tell yourself clearly what your mistake was and what you have to do to avoid repeating it.

You are not a chess player if you don't say after losing that you had a won position.
— *Ilya Ilf*

The computer is the only opponent who doesn't come up with excuses after losing to me.
— *Bobby Fischer*

This is a peculiar feature of the human mind — seeking out reasons for a setback anywhere and everywhere but in yourself. Only later, when the emotions subside, will a clever person ask themselves: what went wrong? What was *their* mistake, which of *their shortcomings* led to that mistake? And then they work on correcting these shortcomings. Chess teaches that person to follow this algorithm in everyday life as well. It teaches the skill of *correcting your mistakes*.

He who does not possess this skill cannot progress well in life.

The better you understand the nature of your mistakes, the higher the chances of progressing more quickly... When you blunder next time, analyze that blunder. Ask yourself the following questions: "Why did I react as I did? What did I underestimate, where did my emotions get the better of me? What would I change if there was a chance to repeat everything all over again? What can I tell myself next time to think more clearly?"
— *Garry Kasparov*

However, there's obviously a lot of adrenaline coursing through any chess player's veins, even the most clever and experienced, immediately after a loss, and they're very emotional. And you remember what happens to a person who is guided by their emotions, right? Correct, judgement gets turned off, only instincts and habits are at work.

The most common instincts and habits of a chess player who loses a game:
— Demonstrating that they are not at fault (excuses);

— Demonstrating that others are at fault (the opponent, the organizers, the arbiter, the spectators, ill fate);

— Demonstrating that they were a good boy/girl (and had a won game).

Such instincts are sometimes bundled together.

The phrases most often heard after a loss: "But I was winning!", "How could I spoil an absolutely won position?" Sometimes, when I win a game and then carry out a post-mortem with my opponent, I make a terrible mistake and ask in a very innocent tone something along these lines: "Would you be so kind and magnanimous as to forgive me asking where exactly your position was won?! *Where*?! You were totally lost for the whole game, you moron! Show me, freaking show me a position where you were at least marginally better!!" (Well, I don't say *everything* out loud, most of this remains in my thoughts, but that's not the point.)

God forbid you from actually saying anything like that! (You can think it as much as you want.) Your opponent is now completely deaf to any reason, and all your requests, however tactful, to be reasonable will only irritate them — at best. In the end, what's better — to be right or to be happy?.. ☺. So, just keep silent and don't say anything.

Nicholas Breton, a 16-17th century English poet, recommended avoiding mocking a weaker player: it may turn out that he is far more skillful with a sword than with chess pieces. He ended his instructions with wise advice: *"And therefore be modest, just checkmate him and be on your way."*

Chess players' excuses are similar to those of compulsive gamblers. They always tell you that they played brilliantly, won a lot and were superb in general. But, for some reason, the gambler goes home on foot because they don't even have enough money left to pay for a taxi.

My dad, who was my first chess teacher and a big and loyal fan, used to ask me how I played. And as soon as I said, "The game was absolutely won!", he would cut me off: "Mashka, yuck, I can't stand listening to you! Don't even continue, it's obvious. I know how you played. I can't bear your endless excuses anymore! I simply asked about the result."

That was quite sobering.

List of excuses for losing. Choose any that you like!

Know that your excuses for defeat are not original. Come up with something new.

And now let's look at a list of the **most popular excuses**. You can print them out and choose any that you like after every loss when someone asks you how you played:

– I lost because I had a headache for the whole day.

– I lost because I had a cold/flu/sore throat/runny nose.

– The playing hall was unbearably noisy.

– It's so dark! It was impossible to play! I could barely see the board!

– I left my lucky pen at home.

– Why can't you offer draws before move 30? I wanted to offer a draw, but couldn't last until move 30, and therefore I lost.

– Several people approached me before the game. Every one of them patted me on the shoulder and said, "Come on, old boy, you can do it!" The nerve of some people! I lost because of them.

– I'm not accustomed to starting the game at four (three, five) p.m. Everywhere else, they start at three (five, four) p.m.

– Two games per day is brutal.

– This is the last time I'm playing with these regulations!

– My opponent chewed gum for the whole game. He/she knew that this prevents me from thinking!

– My opponent ran around constantly. After making a move, he/she would get up and move away. This massively prevented me from thinking clearly!

– I didn't get any sleep.

– Time trouble is to blame. I played very well.

– I had a totally won position for the whole game, I guarantee that! I simply blundered.

– Hot damn, my opponent was an absolute patzer... How could I lose to this idiot?!

– He/she visited the bathroom frequently, it's suspicious – it's likely he/she hid a mobile device there.

– He/she made first-line moves for the whole game – surely he/she cheated!

– Have you seen his/her coach (captain, mom, wife, husband, second)? They constantly stood at the board!

And now here's a lifehack for you. Come home, calm down and tell yourself the following: **"I lost because I..."**

And then continue this phrase. Be honest.

There are all sorts of reasons for losing in chess: a personal flaw (indecisiveness, softness, excessive anger or recklessness), a lack of knowledge (of the opening or important endgame positions), underdeveloped skills (poor prophylactic thinking, poor time control), incorrect energy allocation, slow calculation, etc. This will be the real constructive work on your growth! You draw your conclusions, and try not to repeat your mistakes (of course, you'll repeat them a hundred more times, but then maybe you'll figure everything out the 101st time). As you thoroughly analyze the game at home, after the tournament, you should write down these conclusions in a special notebook or computer document.

If your friend lost

> If your friend lost at something, think of them as though they're temporarily dying. Do not aggravate the injury, be as tactful as possible, leave if they want, stay if they need – they're your friend, after all! Actually, be like that with all people.

1. Be tactful with your friend (or any other player) after the game. If they aren't glowing with joy, aren't jumping around and laughing like crazy, it's better not to ask them how they played. You can easily find the result online – and if you do ask, you risk becoming a "negative anchor" (something or someone they associate with bad luck).

Moreover, it's simply not pretty. If you do need to learn the result ASAP, and the person doesn't look like they're dying from grief, ask the question very delicately, discreetly and without emotion.

For instance, "So, did you blow it? Your position looked like dog poo for the whole game."

2. Try not to bother a player who has lost for about the first 1–2 hours after the game. Most chess players desperately need this amount of me time. The only exception is when they turn to you themselves.

3. If the losing friend starts passionately recounting long lines, don't stop them with phrases such as "Listen, bro, I don't know what you're talking about, I played my own game and haven't seen yours at all!", or "I don't see the position in my mind anymore."

If you really want to ease your friend's pain after their loss, simply don't say anything and pretend to listen. *Every* chess player is sure that all other people in the world should be as interested in their game as they were, that they also should see all the lines and know all about the course of the struggle. The thought that you simply don't know anything doesn't even occur to them. Don't disappoint them, let them pour their heart out to you.

The Tournament

Professional deformation

Any profession causes a deformation characteristic of the relevant area of expertise. "A specialist is similar to a gumboil: his fullness is one-sided." (Kozma Prutkov). You cannot do anything about it, simply tolerate it and do not fight everyone who points out your "deficiency". This person is right.

...A very important factor is physical fitness, the store of energy, the ability to act on the same high level for the duration of the tournament.
— Evgeny Bareev

Chess professionals are sick people. They get to a tournament — and they don't give a damn where they are, what the country is called, what history it has, what it's proud of, which people live there and what they are interested in. Their schedule is fully subordinated to a single goal — to winning. They don't study the locality, and all their explorations of a given country are limited to a half-mile radius around the hotel. They walk on flat, well-lit roads in small groups, or if someone walks alone, they wear headphones.

The most they can do is go for a sightseeing trip on a rest day. They try not to visit opening and closing ceremonies if possible, they simply aren't interested in that. For this reason, organizers have started adding special clauses to the players' contracts that make turning up to closing ceremonies compulsory, on pain of a big fine. Because, uh, well. A lot of bucks were invested in that event, and they need at least some spectators.

I remember once playing in the open section of the European championship in Israel. The championship organizer, a big chess fan and then chairman of the Israeli Chess Federation, Moshe Slav, wanted to host the most unforgettable closing ceremony in the history of European championships. He invited famous stars: singers, circus performers, bands, and even the world-famous mentalist Lior Suchard. You can only imagine how much money he spent on all that, especially Suchard.

Moshe was not a novice in the chess world, but he didn't understand a simple thing: chess players do not need all that! They waited until the award ceremony, then ripped off their medals while still on stage and immediately walked away. Some players did stay to see Suchard's performance, but then they left, too. The second part of the show was only watched by arbiters, organizers and a handful of tournament spectators.

So, here's my advice for organizers: don't try too hard. You're dealing with sportspeople, even worse, with chess players, for god's sake! They suffer from serious professional deformation: there are only black and white squares in their heads, and everything that's colored and not checkered is simply not interesting for them. Minimize your spend on grand ceremonies, ask the officials and sponsors to keep their speeches short, quickly take some photos for your PR team and the press – and the players will only be thankful for that.

P.S. Of course, some players do stay for opening and closing ceremonies out of respect and gratitude to organizers. There are also some unique players who actually love watching shows. But they are clearly a minority. Most players have to be coerced into attending grand ceremonies with a stick.

The right tournament regimen

> If your body is accustomed to certain hours of working and resting, this simplifies its existence and helps produce more energy. But I'm totally convinced that these "certain hours" are different for every person. And this opinion of mine differs from that held by 99 percent of doctors and psychologists, who say that you need to go to sleep before midnight and get up early.

The more professional a chess player is, the better their regimen. The usual daily schedule for grandmasters is as follows:

Before the game: breakfast, preparation for today's opponent, lying down doing nothing, a small walk.

After the game: dinner, walking, doing nothing, talking to friends or browsing social media, preparing for the next opponent.

Some also like a small amount of exercise: running or swimming in the morning, some light swimming in the evening, but only if this doesn't overexert them.

This regimen has been tried and tested by many generations of chess players; it helps you play at peak efficiency. When mixed and women's tournaments are held at the same venue, there will be, of course, more interaction in the evening, but not a lot more.

While the first half of the day is usually similar for all players, they find different ways to relieve stress in the evening. They mostly congregate in small groups: analyzing games, playing blitz, laughing, flirting or going for group walks around the hotel. Introverts usually plunge into social media or play online. (What do they play? Chess, of course, what else?!) Everyone tries to go to sleep at a normal time to get to breakfast in time. However, some players never make it to breakfast, because they are used to getting up late.

The Soviet chess school patriarch Mikhail Botvinnik recommended avoiding sex before games, but his explanation was rather strange: "Because you lose phosphorus and accumulate tiredness." (I thought that this was the other way around: making love relaxes you completely, and, through relaxation, your energy deposits are revealed. But I'm simply quoting here. Anyway, we considered this question near the beginning of the book.) Mikhail Moiseevich also recommended not going to concerts or other entertainment events "not listed in the regulations" and to go to sleep early.

Immediately before the game, all players – literally all – avoid tension! They prepare for the game, and then make it as comfortable as possible for their body and soul (remember that a good mood is the most important thing).

Reading is thought to strain your eyes. Some light meditative activity, however, is permitted. (Remember Valentina Gunina and her embroidery.)

I've been doing morning exercises for more than seventy years. I never smoked except for a couple of months in my youth, never drank alcohol, always ate 1½ hours before the game and then lied down, but did not sleep, because if you lie down, nobody bothers you with pointless conversations.
– Mikhail Botvinnik

The sixth world champion usually walked to games: a 30- or 40-minute walk before the game was exceptionally beneficial in his opinion.

Go to the game alone or with a person you are comfortable with. Avoid uncomfortable interactions, run away from energy vampires, save your energy. The road to the tournament hall is the proverbial "green mile": you'll play in the same mood that you get from walking it.

All in all, playing in tournaments is a job for most players. Unlike some scientific conference or seminar, when delegates can barely wait for their trip to finally escape from their daily routine, from their husbands, wives and children, and to engage in debauchery.

Here's a recent example from my own life. At a European team championship, I wrote to another player and agreed to meet him for a coffee, a walk and a chat. We agreed to do that at the start of the tournament, but we never found the time to actually do it in ten whole days. In the morning, we prepared, stretched our legs and set the mood for the game. In the evening, we participated in team meetings to maintain the team spirit, and then rested from our games. Of course, if we reeeeeally wanted to meet up, we would have found some time. But you'd need a reeeeeally good reason for that – for instance, to fall in love. Or you are longtime friends. Or you are willing to sacrifice something for the sake of a pleasant conversation (this usually happens at less important tournaments). Otherwise, it's only work, work and more work.

Eating before games

> Before doing something important, try to experiment as little as possible with your body (unless you want to explore it further). Eat what you are used to eating, sleep when you are used to sleeping, do what you enjoy.

Now that I have told you about the horrors of potty emergencies, of exhaustion during games, of blood sugar crashes, it will be easy for you to understand what food you should eat before the game.

1. Make yourself happy with your favorite food. (By the way, I think that I don't need to explain to you that the most beneficial things are always those that are done with a *desire*.)

2. Nothing too salty, too spicy or too fatty – they will make you want to drink.

3. No food with a dubious use-by date/smell/composition – this might further aggravate your overstressed digestive system that suffers from your nervousness. If you have even the smallest doubt about the quality of your food, don't eat it but throw it away with no regrets.

4. Some players need protein during the game, others need carbs. Listen to your own body's needs and don't listen to anyone else's advice. Practice shows that there are no one-size-fits-all norms and rules.

5. Give yourself at least an hour to digest food. Going into battle with a full stomach is very, very wrong.

And don't forget: it's "we eat to live", not "we live to eat". Do not overeat, do not drink too much, but don't go hungry either – normality and balance provide positive results and a good mood. Try not to "over-" or "under-" anything. Go for the Middle Way.[1]

Catch the wave!

> You are on a lucky streak? Woo-hoo! Hold the wheel tightly and pile up your winnings! This period might end as abruptly as it begins, so try to squeeze as much as you can from it. Don't sleep for half the day, don't watch TV serials, act!

---

[1] One of the most important concepts in many religions: Buddhism, Judaism, Confucianism, Christianity, etc.

Successful people know this feeling of riding the wave. You join the flow of events that carry you to success through such incredible luck on every step that you inevitably ask yourself, is this really happening?!

Chess players also experience "waves", both in their careers and individual tournaments. The person flies on the wings of success, literally sweeping away everyone on their path, nothing can stop them, luck is always on their side. History knows the games that are created in this mood — they are listed among the treasures of chess culture. Or, at the very least, get published in "My Best Games" books.

Here's how it looks from the inside: you simply *know* that you're going to win a certain tournament, nothing to discuss. Other players know that too — or, at least, it seems that way to you. You look at the other players as you play your game and think, "Extras! You're all a bunch of extras! You are playing, but you don't know that the result is already decided. I am the winner." Then you win one game after another and know for sure that you're going to win the decisive game as well. Often, you subconsciously avoid going for an equal endgame (without any chances to win) and get a worse (or even lost), but playable position instead, because you are sure that luck will favor you. And it does.

Sometimes you ride that wave of luck for several tournaments in a row, and your rating goes through the roof as a result. This usually happens at a young age, when you feel that you can take on the whole world and win, and you don't fear losing.

It's important to exploit this wave of luck as much as possible and not lose opportunities: play as much as you can, take risks, bluff while you are at it — everything will work. Be happy, fly, collect your winnings as much as possible, because this streak is eventually going to end. *This too shall pass.*

At the beginning of the book, we discussed how to control your luck. Here, we're not talking about simple luck: we're talking about an entire chain of lucky events that don't depend on you. Can you create such a chain yourself? Or is it not man-made?

I don't know if you can create this chain, but I do know a pattern. Here's when the wave of luck comes to you:
— I feel so good that I don't give a damn about the result!
— I feel so bad that I don't give a damn about the result!
— I don't give a damn about the result. I just play and enjoy myself!

Clearly, luck comes your way when you are not concerned with the result. Or, as my teacher Boris Yukhananov would call it, you are "unbiased". In such cases, nature takes its course, together with its faithful helper — intuition.

And sometimes it happens that a player gets lucky because they play chess better than all their opponents. Such things happen too, can you imagine?

If you don't play well at a tournament, give yourself a shock

> Pinch yourself in your "sleep", do something unpleasant or even painful to wake yourself up. One of the protagonists of *A Nightmare on Elm Street* did exactly that. Life does the same thing to us if we fall asleep behind the wheel.

I had to explain something to him and get him out of the crisis, because a depressed state gets aggravated if you don't try to escape it. If you have reached that stage and started to nosedive, something needs to be done quickly to save you. This should be done by your psychologist, or doctor, or physiotherapist, or team captain.
— *Boris Postovsky*

The tournament isn't going well? You seem to be doing everything right, you are playing decent chess, but suffer from horribly bad luck and everything is going wrong? There's a technique to counter that: shock your body to get it mobilized. Take a hike to the mountains, jump into an ice hole... Choose a shocking activity that is not harmful to the body, and preferably beneficial. Because some players just go on a bender for the rest of their life. Devise your own way to reboot your system, to rouse both your body and mind.

If you have a good and experienced coach with you at the tournament, they will recommend some things to do. Mark Dvoretsky, for instance, forced Sergey Dolmatov to ski for dozens of miles, while Boris Postovsky demanded that his team members dive into the water. Fabiano Caruana's coach poured ice water on him before the St. Louis 2014 super-tournament. After that, Fabiano couldn't help but show an incredible 7/7 start and obtain what at the time was the amazing Elo of 2844.

After the third or fourth round, I gathered the whole team and told them, "Guys, you are playing badly and you don't swim in the sea — why did you come here at all?" They stared at me in bewilderment, trying to understand what I was talking about.

It's not recommended to swim before the game because this takes away your strength; thus, chess players usually swim in the sea in the early morning or late at night, so that the coach doesn't see them. I say, "Let's try to change something." Everyone asked, "What?" "As soon as the game ends, we go and swim in the sea to strengthen our bodies at least a little. I won't take 'no' for an answer."
— Boris Postovsky

The reverse is also true: if everything is going well at the tournament, do not burden your body with unexpected stress. It will be much better to maintain a regular rhythm and tempo.

Use your rest day wisely

Can you rest properly? No? Turn off your cell phone, lie on the bed and don't talk with anybody. Just vegetate for a bit, walk around your room. Modern people have forgotten how to relax, that's why society is so psychotic. Orthodox Jews, on the other hand, have Shabbat, which is good for the body. They just rest for a twenty-four hour slot in a week, without TV, smartphones or any other technology. This is an official holiday in Israel, when working is prohibited by law. After compulsory rest, you can't help but get to work with renewed energy at full throttle.

And so, the long-awaited rest day arrives! OK, let's plan. First of all, you want to go on all sightseeing trips provided by the organizers, secondly, you want to go to all the discos, thirdly, you want to take a walk with your friends and visit the places *you* want to visit rather than the places the organizers are offering, fourthly, you need to rest and catch up on your sleep, fifthly, you want to swim in the pool or in the sea (whatever is available), sixthly, you want to sunbathe, seventhly, you need to prepare for the next game, eighthly, you just have to turn on the chess engine and see how you should have replied to 45.♘e4 in the third round...

It only recently occurred to me to check the stats for the games I played after rest days, and... the horror! The horror! I've been losing every game! The reason was my desire to do every single thing I planned, to embrace the boundless. As a result, the day designated as a "rest day" turned into a Hellishly intense "work day".

I had a 5/5 score at the 2012 Olympiad in Turkey against strong opponents. In the evening before the rest day, I went to a disco and danced till I dropped. I noticed that all women's teams were at the disco, except for Russia and China. I learned that their captains had forbidden them from having fun. Such sadists they are, I think, tyrannizing people like that for the sake of results (I still think that way, by the way). On the next day, the rest day, I walked among the streets of Istanbul until late evening, hung out with friends whom I hadn't seen for a long time, and got completely exhausted. I lost my subsequent games, one after another, and finished the tournament with a small plus.

But what was I supposed to do?! When will I come here again? When will I be able to look at the city and its locals? Now, though, I have worked out a "quota" for myself: on a rest day, I only go on a small sightseeing trip (unfortunately, all such trips take half a day, but I give myself permission to do that). Afterwards, I swim in the pool for a bit and then go and lie in my bed. In the evening, I prepare for my games as usual.

You should remember the most important thing: you are a professional player and you came here to do your job. And the rest day is for resting, not for gutting yourself in your attempts to "do everything you want".

That's how professional deformation comes about – here's a case study for you. You simply don't have the time or energy to discover a new country. And this happens at every tournament. There comes a time when you become completely deaf and blind to any new experiences – chess, only chess and nothing but chess.

But you can stay for one day after the tournament, can't you? Of course you can, but almost nobody uses this option. After the tournament, everyone is so exhausted both physically and mentally that the only thing they want is to go home.

Don't neglect your body during the tournament

In intense, stressful times, your body enters a state of "martial law": it mobilizes and does not send pain signals if something is not right. You will only get sick afterwards, when it's all over. Thus, here's a piece of advice for you: try to take care of your body at least a little bit in such moments.

This asana is perfect for normalizing blood pressure, stimulating the thyroid

and relaxing after an intense working day

A healthy body is an important component of a chess player's success. You simply cannot withstand 5–6 hours of total mobilization if you're in bad physical shape. Here's when your body can fail you:

→ Towards the end of the game, especially in endgames, when you simply run out of energy;

→ In the middlegame, when you have to "maintain the tension";

→ Between the 30th and 40th moves, when positions are complicated and you panic because of approaching time trouble;

→ In important, stressful rounds;

→ Towards the end of the tournament, when you can't withstand the long distance (9 or 11 rounds).

When this happens, your brain works more slowly, and its work quality is lower ("a healthy body makes a healthy spirit", therefore, an unhealthy body makes an unhealthy spirit). Further, you risk falling ill during the tournament – and that's it, *finita la commedia*.

Playing with any illness, even a runny nose, is impossible. A common cold is the chess player's worst enemy. When I saw that, I immediately sent him (his pupil – M. M.) to the doctor and got him a bye for one round. Therefore, you have to wash your feet with cold water and take showers.
– Boris Postovsky

Maybe in old times, leading chess players did look like classic "gentlemen" in tuxedos, smoking cigars and occasionally engaging in cricket or croquet. But towards the middle of the 20th century people realized that decent fitness was necessary. In modern times, grandmasters enjoy football, tennis, basketball, volleyball, table tennis, running, the gym, yoga, or weightlifting. And they don't simply pursue them as hobbies, they reach a high enough level, actually taking part in competitions and marathons. Not being able to play some sport is almost unbecoming of a modern chess player, and drinking and smoking are simply taboo for many. There are, of course, some shining exceptions, but these exceptions only confirm the rule.

Therefore, in addition to chess preparation, a professional chess player dedicates a lot of time to physical preparation. Exercise is necessary and should be regular.

But only between tournaments. During them, you don't have time for sport or any other kind of strenuous exercise. Thus, you are recommended to do a light morning workout at tournaments: it charges you with energy for the whole day and helps your body to maintain top form when under heavy stress and sitting in the same pose for 5–6 hours.

We all know that you won't do any morning workouts (personally, I only do it rarely), but can you at least make yourself leave the hotel and take a little walk?

Ingenious exercises for life

> All emotional tensions get stuck in the upper spine, neck and shoulders, and the consequences of sitting for long periods get stuck in the lower spine, lower back and the sacrum. Do something about that. You can't live with the tension. Energy doesn't course around your entire body, it gets stuck in these nodes. Your well-being, self-perception, thinking processes and life progress depend on this simple thing that you definitely can control. Don't be lazy, do something. A straight back and a straight head looking straight ahead is a distinguishing feature of someone who's satisfied with life.

I once felt pain in my heart. I went to the clinic and took some tests — everything was in the green, no problems with the heart at all. For some reason, I was referred to a manual therapist. And she enlightened me: my spine was at fault. Spinal problems affect internal organs: they start aching, as though there's something wrong with them.

The upper spine affects the upper body's organs, while the lower spine affects the lower body. And so, this wonderful woman prescribed me some simple therapeutic exercises. All the pain just vanished. And then I added my favorite yoga asanas to these exercises, and I've been regularly doing this workout for about twenty years. The full workout that I devised for myself lasts about three hours. I do it once or twice a week. The simple therapeutic workout (see the table) lasts for an hour. I strongly recommend it. Everyone is envious of my energy, so I am sharing some secrets with you.

Here's the 1-hour program, consisting of simple and brilliant exercises.

Back and Pelvis Exercises	Straighten your back and tense your stomach and back muscles. Hold for 7—10 seconds. Repeat 10 times.
Elbow Plank	Raise yourself on your elbows as high as possible without lifting your hips from the floor. Hold for 7—10 seconds. Repeat 10 times.
Back Muscle Stretch	Bend your chest towards the floor as low as possible. Hold for 7—10 seconds. Repeat 10 times.
One Leg to the Chest	Bend your knee and pull your leg towards your chest. Hold for 7—10 seconds. Repeat 10 times.
Knees to the Chest	Bend both knees and pull your legs towards your chest. Hold for 7—10 seconds. Repeat 10 times.

Angry Cat	Pull your chin down and arch your back, stretching your stomach muscles. Hold for 7–10 seconds. Repeat 10 times.
Back Extension (Press Up: Sphinx Position)	Position: lying on your stomach, on extended arms, without lifting your hips from the floor. Relax your lower back and glutes. Hold for 7–10 seconds. Repeat 10 times.
Three Points of Support I	Extend your hand forward without bending your neck. Keep your back straight. Hold for 7–10 seconds. Repeat 10 times.
Three Points of Support II	Extend your leg back, parallel with the floor. Keep your back and neck straight. Hold for 7–10 seconds. Repeat 10 times.
Lower Back Twists	Position: lying on your back, hold your legs together and bend the knees. Alternate turning your knees to each side. Hold for 7–10 seconds. Repeat 10 times for each side.
Two Points of Support	Extend your leg and the opposite arm at once, stretching the stomach muscles. Hold for 7–10 seconds. Repeat 10 times for each side.
For Stomach Muscles I	Position: lying on your back, clasp your hands on your chest. Lift your head and shoulders off the floor. Hold for 7–10 seconds. Repeat 10 times.

For Stomach Muscles II 	Position: lying on your back, cross your arms on your chest. Lift your head and shoulders off the floor and turn them to the side. Hold for 7–10 seconds. Repeat 10 times for each side.

Two useful formulas

> After sitting in one place for 40 minutes, you should take a short break to do some small exercises. Don't accumulate grudges, anger or envy inside yourself. They all build up in your organs.

The First Formula

To understand how to maintain decent fitness both at home and at tournaments, remember this formula:

You can do anything that is not the following four things:

1. Lying

2. Sitting

3. Standing

4. Eating

If you practice this constantly, you won't have any trouble with your physical body — its volume, weight, wear and tear.

I found this advice online. It's completely useless, but it sounds nice.

The Second Formula, which actually works

My manual therapist shared it with me when I was a teenager.

You're a chess player, and it's strictly prohibited for you to sit in one place for more than 40 minutes! Get up, do some light exercises, walk around the room... and sit down again.

Back troubles are the greatest scourge of *all* chess players, it's basically their occupational disease. I've never met a chess player with a healthy back, all their spines are curved and twisted in all possible ways. And sitting in one place for long is not the only reason. We know that the spine accumulates emotions and stress. In other sports, without leaving your workplace you can scream, swear, jump for a bit, fall over, even turn yourself inside out — spectators, organizers, journalists and PR teams just love all those raw emotions.

But you cannot scream in chess. You should sit silently like a clam. All your emotions accumulate in your back. Cramps, knots, curvatures... If you have a massage therapist with you at the tournament, it's great. But if... but since you do not have one, please do not neglect your back's health and do things you can do: exercises, walks, therapeutic workouts, some light yoga. At least so that you withstand the stress over the long distance and don't falter at the finishing stage of the tournament.

> *It happens sometimes that a player gives his all in the struggle, then leaves the hall and literally collapses, his legs can't support him. For instance, Alexander Beliavsky always played like that. He fought with such intensity in every game that he could barely stand on his feet after games — and he's a very sporty, fit and strong man.*
> *— Boris Postovsky*

Recovery after a difficult tournament is a separate topic. You just lie down for a week or two, then you slowly recover your human abilities. I recently overheard Serbian grandmaster Sinisa Drazic advising his pupil: "You should be able to recover quickly between tournaments. If you can't, you should not become a chess professional."

Stress relief after the game

> Learn healthy methods of stress relief. You want to do something beneficial for yourself, right? It's not recovery if you do something you need to recover *from* afterwards.

As I already said, everyone has their own ways to recover. One player just won and plays some blitz with their friends in a good mood, another lost and went to his room to comment on political posts, the third goes into the shower for an hour and then hides under the blanket; this rowdy group went to a cafe to share a pizza, another group goes for a walk around the hotel, and some hurry to the casino... Everyone has experienced huge stress, and they won't be able to get to sleep if they don't relieve that stress. And if you don't get enough sleep, you won't think straight the next day (in very rare cases, sleep deprivation can be beneficial for "intuitive" play, but it's best not to go there so simply try to play "intuitively" even when you have had a good sleep).

Boris Postovsky: "I remember our greats — Stein, Korchnoi, others — often played dominoes after the game. They'd play for a couple of hours, with jokes and banter, then forget about chess for a bit and fall asleep easily.

You should walk as much as you can in the evenings, so that your mental strain transforms into physical strain. In this case, he (the player — M. M.) will simply fall into bed and sleep well. Don't try to get him to sleep as soon as possible: it's hard to fall asleep, moves and lines are still swirling in his head, together with doubts – 'What if I play this, or I play that...?' How can you sleep in such a state?

I'll reveal a little secret. I have worked as Kramnik's second numerous times, he goes to sleep very late – it's his regimen: he goes to sleep late and gets up late. He always takes a warm bath before going to sleep. It's also effective. And if you also add some salt and medicinal herbs, it's just amazing!

When another ward of Postovsky, Nana Alexandria, lost sleep and appetite because of nervous strain in her match against Irina Levitina, they went skiing together on a rest day and he forced her to ski for several hours. She stuffed herself in the restaurant afterwards, and then slept like a log the next day. Until lunch. The stress was relieved, she won the game, and everything went well.

There are, however, stories without a happy end as well. For instance, Ian Nepomniachtchi couldn't sleep properly towards the end of his world championship match against Ding Liren. He took sleeping pills with him as a countermeasure. And – believe it or not – at the most important moment, before the tie break, the pills disappeared from the hotel room. Well, at least Ian said that in the interview. He couldn't sleep well before the all-important game, and so he didn't win the world championship.

How to fall asleep when it's impossible?

You are sure that you are sufficiently tired, and so you lie on your bed to recharge your batteries, but cannot fall asleep?

OK, here are some tips:

1) I don't believe you. Go and get properly tired first.

2) Go to bed with the intention to sleep.

3) Having an established sleep ritual helps. This is the most important tip of all.

4) The second-biggest tip is to clean yourself of negative emotions.

5) The third most important tip: clean your brain of any thoughts whatsoever.

6) Regulate your breathing.

7) Don't try to force yourself to sleep. If you spend ages trying to get to sleep, fall asleep later instead.

8) Just lie there with your eyes closed – it also kind of helps you recover. Forgive yourself this weakness today.

Sleeping trouble at a tournament is a serious problem for many chess players. You constantly think of the game you had that day, the lost opportunities, and the

opening in the next round. Some chess players cannot sleep well for the whole tournament! With time, everyone devises a certain array of actions that help them fall asleep. Here's my set — maybe it can help you as well?

1) You cannot go to sleep because you are too excited. Therefore, you should first **relax**: take a shower, or take a walk, or find a good distraction, or exhaust all your emotions in conversations, or burn some calories with exercise. Pet cats also really help you to relax.

2) **Rituals** help very much. If you already have an established sleep ritual, it will be much easier for you. Your body has anchored to the fact that a certain chain of actions leads to shutdown, and so, when you repeat these actions, it shuts down automatically.

3) If you go to bed, you should have the **intention to sleep**! Don't think about the day as you lie on your side, don't plan for tomorrow, don't hold an imaginary conversation with other people — just sleep! If you're falling into anything but sleep, then get up, get dressed, drink a mint tea and go back to bed when you intend to sleep. Bed is for sleeping!

4) **Regulating your breathing.** The simplest and quickest way to fall asleep if nothing above works.

5) You can't fall asleep because your head is full of thoughts. Yes, you did go to bed with a clear intention to sleep, but thoughts swarm inside you like bed bugs and don't let you sleep. There are various ways to **empty your head completely or supplant the thoughts that worry you with other thoughts, which are absolutely not important for you.**

→ Meditation: practice meditation that turns thoughts off.

→ Audio and video: choose a recording or video that lulls you to sleep the quickest: long boring audiobooks (such as *War and Peace*... oh, how appropriate!), or spiritual practitioners such as Sadhguru, Osho, Castaneda, Zeland (these texts are usually read in a pleasant, monotonous, hypnotic voice). You might also try listening to some smart but emotionless political experts and journalists. This last method always works on me.

→ Switching your mind to dumb, automatic action. For instance, try the classic counting sheep: first you count to one hundred, then back to one (visualizing each one). You might also try counting every third sheep: one hundred sheep, ninety-seven sheep, ninety-four sheep, ninety-one sheep... There will come a moment when your brain becomes so irritated with this crap that it runs away from you and into sleep!

6) Can't sleep even though you do have the intention of doing so (unlike in point (3) above)? To Hell with it! Get up, get dressed, take a walk around the home, browse social media, go to sleep **later**. You'll fall asleep more quickly after that, even if you sleep less. If your sleeping time is divisible by 1.5 hours (1.5, 3, 4.5, 6, 7.5), it's fine, you'll feel that you slept well! The body "recharges" every 1.5 hours. (This is nonsense, of course, but I read about it back when I was a schoolgirl, and I believe in it so religiously that it actually works for me.)

7) Still can't sleep? Then ditch your attempts to fall asleep, just forgive yourself, lie down and relax. This **state of rest**, without falling asleep, is also useful. Practise simple meditation for gradual relaxation of every body part (it's important to concentrate diligently on each body part; this concentration will automatically drive away the swarm of thoughts that bother you). This yoga exercise is called Shavasana, every yoga session ends with it. This rest is also beneficial for your body. And maybe you'll manage to catch some hours of sleep as you rest. For a stress-filled tournament, this might be more than enough.

8) It's believed that you should not go to sleep with negative thoughts. Because even if you fall asleep easily, your brain will process negative information all night long, which is clearly not beneficial for your health. Therefore, spend a couple of minutes on forgiving **others** (for the bad things they've done to you today), but also ask for forgiveness for your bad deeds. Whom to ask? Yourself, God, the Universe – I don't know, whatever works for you. Your thoughts definitely enter some Universal Information Field. But even if they don't... you'll quickly fall asleep and have a good, restful sleep.

Oh yeah, also, don't forget to express your **gratitude** for the day. Even if the day was actually awful, you're still alive (as proof of that, you are playing in a tournament and currently trying to fall asleep) and therefore in a better state than those who are not alive.

Do not seriously analyze games during tournaments

> While you're at peak mobilization, you should not spend time reflecting on yourself, your mistakes, how to correct them or future plans. As long as you are in "combat mode", this work will not be deep enough. And it may even harm you: you are mobilized and all set on achieving a result, whereas "self-improvement" may overly relax you.

Just a little while ago, coaches were dead set against you analyzing your games with a computer during the tournament. The player, they said, should first get back home, analyze everything by themselves, and only then check everything out with the silicon friend. In our time, however, coaches have finally stopped demanding the impossible. The player goes back to their room after the game, and there's no power in this world that can stop them from turning the engine on. No person with that amount of willpower exists.

But you still *can* do one thing — avoid serious analysis with long lines. Quickly look through the game, find the answer to the main question — where did the evaluation (the logic of the game's course) change, satisfy your curiosity, because it won't leave you alone for the whole evening. And then — either suffer and calm down, or cheerfully prepare for the next opponent. You'll analyze this game seriously after you get back home.

Journalists, photo reporters, interviewers, fans...

> Enthusiastic fans, journalists, and photo reporters satisfy your ego and vanity, but block rational self-assessment at the same time. If you get carried away with your fame and forget about your goals and self-improvement, your "celebrity disease" can slow down or even kill your creativity, take away the breath of true life. Just remember that. Let your inner voice whisper this reminder to you in a key moment — when there'll be nobody around to tell you honestly what an asshole you really are and how much all your so-called masterpieces suck. You may already lose all your real friends at that point.

Chess has lately made great forays into the digital world. Pro and amateur players don't just play each other online: they take part in tournaments, simuls, solve puzzles (both on their own and puzzle rush), study chess, analyze games together, watch their idols play online, listen to commentators... in other words, they do everything that was done in the real world, but online. Yes, I forgot to mention that they also play bughouse, suicide chess and other fun chess-like games. And thousands of spectators can watch that.

The situation with over-the-board chess is sadder. Spectators are not allowed to enter the playing hall — except for big events, where they are allowed to sit in specially designated areas, watching the games on monitors and listening to the commentary. The main reason for these measures was not the noise in the playing hall, but rather the possibility of cheating — every spectator can now turn on their mobile phone and suggest a move to the players with secret gestures and signs.

By the way, all games played on digital boards (in other words, the vast majority of international tournament games) in every part of the world can now be watched online for free through apps and sites, complete with computer analysis.

Elite grandmaster tournaments have their own rules and regulations for media activity. Journalists can take pictures and videos of players at the start of the games, and then they take part in press conferences after the games. Chess players are obliged to appear at these pressers because they signed a contract with a corresponding clause before the tournament.

At these pressers, journos ask the grandmasters questions such as why they put their knight on h3 instead of e6, and what they are planning to do in the evening. Everything is decorous and innocent, but incredibly boring, and so, if not for that stupid contract, no player would show up there. Instead, they would do what they always did in the past after the game: go back to their room and take a shower, or go to dinner, or take a walk.

If a player doesn't appear at the press conference, they have to pay a fine. Some players who are especially upset after losing choose this option. If the player is in an especially good mood, however, they can answer some muckraker's question about their secret plans in the King's Indian with some unexpected witticism, amusing the public. In this case, the said witticism becomes the biggest news item in the chess world, and the reporters get to write about something more than chess moves in their reports.

I remember the times when grandmasters played on stage, and the spectators sat in the hall, applauded beautiful wins and then ran up to their idols to get an autograph. I also remember the times when chess tables were surrounded by throngs of fans, and this did not disturb anybody.

That was a preamble. The real question is, should we chess players talk to journalists and fans during the tournament or not? On the one hand, all this distracts us, numbs our thinking, sometimes it's even annoying or makes us angry. On the other hand, if we don't talk with anyone period, the sponsors might think that we are not interesting to anybody, there's no sense in advertising anything at chess tournaments and, accordingly, no sense in giving us money. As a result, everyone will suffer.

Therefore, I choose balance. What stops you from making people – spectators, fans, journalists – happy after your game and talking to them a bit, posing for a few photos and giving autographs? Forget your haughty manners, who needs that? Chess *as a whole* will benefit from your open, friendly, maybe even somewhat flamboyant behavior. This won't hurt you even if you lost. *Hey, prima donna!*

Before the game, on the other hand, you should not waste energy on interacting with the outside world. That said, when sponsors and organizers drag you to photo shoots with them 15 minutes before the game, can you really protest? They are your sponsors! You have to do it, and you know it. (You can't expect them to understand that chess players should not be disturbed in the last hour before the game.)

Therefore, don't whine and do something good for chess, come on!

Communication and social media

> Uh, do whatever you want!

Humans are social animals, so they cannot live without communication. It's literally necessary for your well-being — and especially for a positive mood and success at the tournament. Even introverted introverts need to talk to people. However, as the joke goes, there's a small detail. We are surrounded by different people. Interacting with some people makes us comfortable, happy and energetic, but there are also people who sap your energy and spoil your mood, and any time you spend with them feels incredibly wasted. So, how can you avoid making mistakes here? Of course, those who go to tournaments with their coaches, seconds or parents are lucky. You already have established relationships with them. With rare exceptions, talking with such people is comfortable, calming and predictable.

However, if you have only recently started working with your coach, it's better not to take risks. I had negative experiences in this regard. With parents too, it's not always rosy. I had a pupil with a strict father: he didn't just force his son to study chess, he even physically abused him if the boy made small chess-related mistakes (even though the pop himself played awfully). His mother was too afraid to interfere. And, as luck would have it, the boy almost always traveled to tournaments with his father. The kid told me, "When my mom goes with me, I always play well!" A desperate cry of the soul... I recently met his mom by chance. She said that he quit chess a couple of years ago and doesn't regret it.

Therefore, if a loved one or, even better, a trusted coach travels to the tournament with you, this is great! The problem of finding a source of positive interaction solves itself (as Dovlatov wrote, "I prefer to be alone, but with someone nearby"). You feel good both **before** the game (they charge you with positive energy) and **after** it (they console you or share your happiness).

It's harder for others. They need to find a person they like. Everyone usually has a chess-playing buddy at tournaments, or even several. In this case, you can hang out together. Sometimes you meet a player at a tournament, and they become a good friend to talk to (this has happened to me several times, and I have achieved great results thanks to that).

However, on the game day, chess players prefer to spend time either alone or with a close friend, to conserve energy. Another reason to avoid interaction before the game is that you may inadvertently join their list of "those who bring bad luck".

It's good if you can accurately determine if a person is a good fit. But it often happens that you chat, and chat, and then feel that something's wrong, but it's too awkward to just walk away. It's not that easy to escape. You finish your walk, then you get back to your room, look at the clock and see: the game is starting soon, and you feel like a squeezed lemon. Your head is swollen, your mood is awful, there's darkness before your eyes.

If you don't manage to recover before the game, you may lose it, and this would be the price of your experience.

Look at pregnant women, pay attention to how and with whom they interact. It looks like they are completely focused on themselves, only interacting with the outside world with their outer shell. It looks like they're trying to protect themselves and do that completely naturally. They are not concerned with such trifle matters as "it's awkward to refuse", "I don't know what to say", "I don't want to, but I have to." All their energy is turned inwards.

You should do the same. Fully concentrate on the game ahead, which should be "born" healthy and beautiful.

Also, you should avoid toxic people. How can you detect them? They don't like to laugh and don't tolerate any criticism of themselves; they always discuss other people. And they only say bad things about other people, either directly or indirectly ("indirectly" means things like "She lived in the provinces, and then hooked up with a strong grandmaster and now goes to all the tournaments with him...", or "He ingratiated himself with the federation president, and now all kinds of doors are open for him"). Of course, all people are more or less prone to envy and gossip. But toxic people thrive on it. And you suffer because of them! The Talmud wise men teach: **"Malicious speech about a third party kills three people. It kills the one who speaks malicious speech, and the one who accepts the malicious speech when he hears it, and the one about whom the malicious speech is said."**

I recently took a flight together with a grandmaster. The flight was brief, and this was the only thing that saved me. For two hours, he talked non-stop about various male and female chess players, gave them descriptions, reinforced those descriptions with anecdotes from their life, and then almost invariably came to a conclusion: "He/she is absolutely crazy." At the start of the flight, I didn't sense danger and tried to parry his accusations somehow, to defend the other people, but after about ten minutes I was completely drained of energy, and all I could do was nod my head stupidly to avoid any clarifying questions (what's worse, he spoke English, and I couldn't comprehend about 30 percent of what he said). Only God knows how I survived this flight. That's how you drain a person of life without even touching them.

There's also another class of energy drainers: those people who are always unhappy and constantly complain about their life, the weather, tournament conditions, opponents, their spouse, men or women in general, chess officials, the country, the government, the Freemason conspiracy, the reptiloids (yes, the very same ones that contacted Kirsan – some people don't like them, you see).

If your search for someone pleasant to talk to has failed completely (or *you* are the one nobody wants to talk to), then jump on social media. That's a good thing if you don't go overboard and don't develop an addiction (although social media addiction is a veeeery common affliction of our times).

Once on social media, spew out all the bile accumulated inside you, virtually beat the virtual ass of your virtual friend, and you'll feel better. Or, on the contrary, go there to have some harmless fun: kittens and puppies, funny memes, videos – just scroll through them for half an hour, and you'll feel so gooood! And, what's really cool, you can express your unsolicited opinion anywhere you want, and there will be no consequences. Smashing!

I still don't know if you should read messages from people you barely know or don't know at all during the tournament. On the one hand, there may be fans who write, "Go Masha, we're with you!" On the other hand, there may be people who say something like "Maria, you disappointed me!", or "Why do you play 1.d2-d4?! Everyone knows that 1.e2-e4 is much better!" The contact is not much more than a beginner, but they still feel the need to spit or fart out nonsense not only in social media, but also in direct messages on Messenger or WhatsApp. Though I can believe that they are a genuinely good person, and they genuinely think that they are doing you, a grandmaster, a big favor by recommending that you move the king's pawn on the first move instead of the queen's pawn.

Therefore, I always tell myself that during the tournament I shouldn't read messages from social media friends whom I don't know personally, but then I always forget my own admonitions. Curiosity is pressing on you, and you know that you shouldn't go to games under pressure. However, if I do read the message, curiosity gets replaced by a spoiled mood, and you don't know what's actually worse. So, I'll use this opportunity to address my dear fans: Please!!! Do buzz off with your advice and consolation during a tournament! If I want consolation or some positive vibes before the game, I know whom to call or write to. And you only do harm! Or, at the very least, try to learn to distinguish good from bad. For instance, short messages consisting solely of joyful exclamations and small motivating phrases will do. I'll accept that. But if I lose, leave me alone!!! I'm already suffering more than enough without being bothered by you.

Thanks for your understanding.

Harmful Lifehacks

Harmful tournament conditions

> Never. Fall. Into poverty.
> Oh, I'm sorry, I should have said it like this:
> Always. Have. Money.
> Poverty deprives you of freedom of choice and pushes you to accept "unsavory" offers.
> All life coaches tell you how to get rid of the poor man's mentality, how to attain a rich man's mentality, how to be financially literate, how to do this, how to do that... I have only one piece of advice: get your lazy ass of the couch, pull away from the phone, pull away from the TV and go and work! And preferably work for yourself, not for others.
>
> "The only way to get rich with a book on how to get rich is to write such a book."
> (Christopher Buckley)

Here is a story from my own life. An organizer I was familiar with invited me to a tournament held in a country that I had wanted to visit for a long time, and offered luxurious conditions. I replied, "Of course I agree!" He: "But there's one condition. We have two norm-seekers there, and you must lose to them. I said no, I never throw games. Well, OK, he says, draw with them both, then. I agreed because there's nothing wrong with draws, and I can return the organizer's favor in that way. OK then.

I played in the tournament, took the lead, everything was okey-dokey, and then it was my turn to play those candidates. I asked the organizer who called me: so, we play a quick prearranged draw tomorrow, and that's that? And he replied, "No, you can't do that. You should play the game as though it's a real game, but it must end in a draw." That was the trap I stepped in. I didn't know how disgusting this trap really was at the time, I only found out during the game.

I come to the game and I see that my opponent is so wound-up as though this is the last game in his life. I even got scared: what if he doesn't agree to the draw? There's no guarantee! We played the game completely seriously, with all the nerves, tension and time trouble... After the time scramble, I got a huge advantage and saw his expression sour. The worst thing is that you actually play the game, you put in a real effort, but you realize that this is all fake! No matter how much you huff and puff, your opponent won't lose. This feeling of disgust made my stomach churn for the whole game.

Only when my position had become completely won did my opponent finally offer a draw.

That's what I'd gotten myself into. Of course, I drew some conclusions:

1. Never descend to such a level where you seriously have to consider unsavory offers.

2. Discuss all conditions with the organizer beforehand, to prevent any mutual grievances.

3. My personality is such that even prearranged draws (a common practice in chess, especially between men – women engage in it less often) make me physically sick. (Lately, however, I have also started playing prearranged draws – in the last rounds, to guarantee a prizewinning place. That's how pragmatic I have become. I think that this is progress, because I am specially working on my skill of rational decision-making both in chess and life.)

4. Try to avoid organizers who might, even theoretically, ask you to lose or draw on purpose. Both in life and chess, try to engage only with people who have a good reputation.

Buying a point or a title? My pleasure (in other people's leisure)

> Take care of your honor from childhood

If you are reading this book, and you're not a chess player at all, someone uninitiated, then let me tell you a secret: in my sport, buying and selling points, titles and entire tournaments is commonplace. Chess players know of these things, but for some reason, openly talking about such tournaments is considered as bad taste as actually playing in them. Still, I'll tell you about them, albeit without naming any names.

There are certain organizers of fake tournaments who sell titles and ratings left, right and center. The cat quickly gets out of the bag, and the rumors about their tournaments spread around the whole chess world. And if these organizers later try to hold an "honest" round-robin tournament, normal chess players try to avoid such people to uphold their reputation.

Nevertheless, their business is rather popular. They sell their services to those who have money and want to obtain a certain title, but lack the talent – or they simply don't want to work on chess too much, but they need a title or some rating gain.

I know a woman player who realized that she would never obtain the WGM title in the normal way (to become a WGM, you have to dedicate half your life to chess, and she didn't do that). But she desperately wanted to become one! She wanted to increase the prices for her chess lessons and other activities. And so, she bought a couple of norms. There are also cases when some player wants to quit professional chess but hasn't reached their set goal yet. They simply "purchase" that achievement with money.

Let's refer to the title-monger's customer as the Main Norm-Seeker. The organizer quickly cobbles together a tournament with the necessary line-up: several titled players, one or two highly rated guys, and some extras. The tournament should comply with the FIDE standards to ensure that the paying customer gets their title.

The Main Norm-Seeker pays a hefty sum to the organizer for the "result": like, this is not my job, but yours. You should assemble the line-up and arrange the necessary losses. The Norm-Seeker plays in the tournament and scores the needed points: they defeat the weaker players on their own, arrange some draws, and everything else is settled by the organizer.

There were some hilarious cases when these tournaments *did not even take place*! They were played on paper, all the necessary documents were filed, but no games actually happened. Or, alternatively, the tournament "partially" takes place: some participants never arrive at all, but on paper, they did arrive and played their games. All the paperwork was done, complete with written scoresheets, but the games themselves were composed.

Some organizers are too lazy to actually invent games, so they scour the databases for some rare games of old masters and try to pass them off as games from their fake tournaments. If a chess historian accidentally recognizes such a game, they scream at the top of their voice, "How dare they! It's the game Duz-Khotimirsky – Alapin from the 49th round of the San Marino tournament! Monsters! They should burn in Hell for that!"

Here's another story: a businessman "purchased" master titles for himself and his driver. He answered the criticism with, "I'll make my dog an IM too if want to."

By the way, he was almost serious. Recently, chess society took note of a player who participated in several of those fake tournaments. Nobody knew him, he was a total stranger. But his name was rather unusual. Something vaguely like Garfield Murkenstein, or Tom Jerryman, I don't remember exactly. And so, they started investigating.

It turned out that the organizer of fake tournaments simply invented a list of players. Some real players had already agreed to be on this list, while some others allegedly didn't know that they were on the list... But when our organizer ran out of ideas, he added the name of his favorite cat to the list. It went down in history, so to say. This wondrous animal played in several tournaments and, thanks to his owner, got quite a ratings boost. FIDE didn't even care — they simply ran the calculations as usual.

Honest tournaments

I hasten to add that most round-robin tournaments are held by the same formula — but without a Main Norm-Seeker and buying/selling points. Organizers earn their money from norm-seekers' entry fees, while the players live in hotels that are largely empty in off-season. Sometimes the tournaments are sponsored by local authorities or philanthropists — in this case, the tournament expenses are minimal, and the organizers can even earn something.

Some organizers say that they don't earn anything but a good reputation. I want to believe them. They indeed have a great reputation, they do a most useful favor for chess players: some of them get an opportunity to earn a norm, others can earn some money as a prize or appearance fee and hone their skills. And thanks to them, new stars appear in the chess sky — future grandmasters and champions. One such organizer was Maxim Shusharin from Chelyabinsk, who unfortunately died recently. He did a lot of good things for chess players, he was beloved and respected. May he rest in peace.

The moral of the story

Should you buy points and titles? I personally have no doubt: you may become a ten-time world champion, the greatest of the greats, the worthiest of the worthy, but if you ever bought a title, you'll never wash off that stain with anything — neither soap, nor bleach, nor sulfuric acid. Chess players keep silent about you, but everyone knows, believe me. Life is long, and you will have to live with it till you die. Do not go this way, play normal, honest chess. And you'll get your title eventually.

Or you won't. Then it wasn't to be. But I think that your reputation is more important.

Other funny things that happen in chess: prearranged games, thrown games, score manipulations

> Be a Warrior of Light

When I, an honest, naive, straightforward and very simple Soviet girl, arrived in a European country in 1993 to play in a rapid tournament, I was astonished! Only six or seven rounds were played honestly, and then the leaders stopped playing their games – they simply prearranged them! They mostly prearrange draws, but sometimes they would throw games to each other.

Another common phenomenon is the "safety net" method. The game is played honestly, but the winner, if they manage to win a prize, gives a part of their prize money to the losers. And so sometimes it happens that a player gets a big prize, but after all those "safety net" payments only a paltry sum remains, barely enough to buy a ticket home. Like in the old Soviet cartoon *The Italian Job*.[1] Yes, such things happen, too.

Here's what can also happen (or rather used to happen – such things are dangerous now): the player sees that their next opponent is seeking a norm (for instance, they need a draw to earn their IM norm, or even losing is enough provided the game actually takes place – they need a certain number of rounds and a certain average rating of opponents). And so, our villain protagonist, who has nothing to play for in the tournament, goes to their opponent's room the night before the game and says: pay me to play you, otherwise I'll no-show the game, and it won't count for your norm.

What should you do? You can't do anything, and you can say goodbye to your norm if you don't pay. However, arbiters strongly recommend filing a complaint in that situation. In this case, your opponent may be 1) disqualified from the tournament; 2) added to the database of "crooks". Thankfully, this has become possible with the advent of computers and the Internet: many chess federations have such databases, and the arbiters know what to expect from whom.

And another thing. A group of strong players from one country comes to a tournament. They have an agreement: they manipulate their results in some way, and then divide the prize money between themselves. How do they manipulate the results? One player can purposely lose to another, for instance. Or one "conspirator" loses to some player in the middle of the table because this loss improves the Buchholz coefficient[2] of another "conspirator" (in cases when Buchholz is used as a tie-breaker). In this way, they invade the tournament like a

---

[1]   A parody animated short made in 1978 that has no relation to the 1969 movie of the same name. The cartoon's plot involves a jobless drunkard whose wife tells him that he's so useless he can't even rob a bank to provide for his family. The man borrows money from his neighbors, openly saying that he is going to rob a bank. Soon, everyone in the town knows that he wants to rob a bank and encourages him. His friends eventually bring him to the bank, the bank workers also recognize him and give him a large sum of money. He is chased by all his creditors, returns all the money to them and ends up with empty pockets again. Then his wife reappears with a rolling pin... – *Translator*

[2]   The Buchholz coefficient is used as a tie-breaker in Swiss tournaments. It's the sum of the points scored by all opponents of a given player.

horde of locusts and win some good prizes with their manipulations. During the games, of course, they constantly talk to each other, annoying their opponents in this way, too.

But wait, there's more! A chess player can purposefully lower their rating for a whole year to take part in the C- or D-group of a big open tournament and easily win against players with actual low ratings. However, there are so many players using this smart tactic (called sandbagging) now that they actually compete with each other for the top 10 prizes (which are mostly tiny, lol).

There have also been cases when a player simply changed their legal name and passport. Then, under the new name, they played in tournaments as an amateur and won all the amateur prizes (there are usually prizes such as best performance by a player rated under 2000, under 1800, etc., at big events). Not long ago, an arbiter in India caught such a fraudster because he recognized his face ☺.

And recently, an even funnier story happened. Organizers of the 2023 Kenya Open championship promised big prizes for women. And so, one male player, a certain Stanley Omondi, donned a niqab, registered under a woman's name and started scoring wins. Which, of course, surprised and angered other participants. They complained to the arbiters who decided to remove his niqab. Under it, they found a person with a beard, mustache, and all the other male attributes. His punishment was a three-year ban. Meanwhile, the whole chess world got a laugh out of it and humorous headlines appeared in the newspapers.

Cheating in chess

Cheating is a felony

Using engine help in chess is akin to doping, but actually much worse. Because you simply cannot fight it at the board. Imagine a rookie runner taking performance-enhancing drugs and then taking part in a world championship race together with the world's greatest runners. He will lose, even with doping. But in chess, a near beginner can completely destroy the strongest grandmaster in the world if he plays with the help of a chess engine. Do you comprehend the scale of the disaster?! I am forced to talk and write about the problems of cheating in chess, as are many others. Because I love sport, because I want everyone to play in equal conditions, so that the strongest wins – not the one who has the best engine.
– Alexander Galkin

Lichess once held a championship of some Bavarian district. The level was low, there were no prizes, they basically played for nothing. And yet, two cheaters were caught. And you're asking me now why I don't play online.
— *Mikhail Prusikin*

I cannot defeat these devilish programs, which, sadly, will eventually kill my beloved chess.
— *Lajos Portisch*

A computer once beat me in chess, but it was no match for me at kick boxing.
— *Emo Philips*

Cheating involves getting outside help, and it has existed for as long as chess itself. In the era of mammoths and dinosaurs, moves were suggested by spectators and fans who stood around the table of two masters, watching them play. When it became too troublesome to calm the especially loud "tipsters" down, a rule was adopted that obliged everyone to keep silent during the game.

In the times of the Soviet chess school, hints were delivered by coaches and captains, mostly by secret signs. And now, people get help from engines – chess programs that play much better and faster than even our beloved Magnus Carlsen. A super-strong engine can be hidden in a mobile phone, the phone is hidden behind the toilet, and the toilet under a pile of toilet paper. That's how they usually do it. Oh, sorry, you hide the phone under the paper, and the paper under the toilet. Um, no. The paper under the phone, and the phone in the toilet... no, wrong again. Well, the exact technology is not important, but you got the idea. The most important lifehack of this book.

Now, mobile phones are banned, together with all other electronic devices. Everyone is thoroughly searched as they enter the tournament hall, even a fly won't get in undetected. But, of course, the world does not stand still – cheaters always find ways to circumvent any newly-introduced restrictions.

You have likely heard about a huge scandal that arose when Hans Niemann defeated Magnus Carlsen in a game, and the then world champion withdrew from the tournament, dropping cryptic hints that the winner cheated. How could Niemann have cheated? Someone suggested that he hid a vibrating device deep in his body that transmitted moves just like Morse code. Niemann responded to the allegations by claiming that he could play naked because he had nothing to hide.

Actually, he said lots of things in reply, but this particular sentence stuck in my mind. The grandmasters separated into two camps: some supported Carlsen, while others criticized him for attacking a young and promising player. They used this example to claim that you can now attack anybody you like if they play well against you. Indeed, in recent times that's what has been happening — everybody criticizes everybody else. The result is that the chess atmosphere has been infected with paranoia.

Chess players hate cheating with a passion, because the vast majority of pro players were brought up on the principles of fair play. The smallest suspicion of cheating by their opponent makes them incredibly angry. They implore officials to combat it, and organizers to tighten the anti-cheating measures. They sign petitions, file complaints and statements, they spread rumors about suspicious players... in other words, they do all they can. However, since human morals have dropped through the floor in recent times and are finding creative new ways to get to a new low, the number of fraudulent chess players is growing every day.

Some years ago, I published a video where my committee (the Women's Committee of the Russian Chess Federation, which I headed for several years) held an open conference on cheating. After this video, a famous chess programmer (who is rumored to be a super cheater who organizes this complicated process at the highest level) called me. He said something along these lines: "Masha, dear, you're discussing ways of jamming electromagnetic waves: metal detector checks, banning watches, pens and headgear, checking legs for wires, etc. You can't even imagine, you look like you are helpless children! There are other waves *(I forget which ones he named — M. M.)* that you don't even think about, and these are precisely the waves that are most actively used for cheating in recent years!" I don't know whether to believe him, but I decided not to make his opinion public and give him free publicity. Let him search for customers on his own.

By the way, in respect of high-level customers. Some especially paranoid players believe that cheating also exists at the very top. They say that this is something beyond mere "toilet cheating" — it's organized by a criminal group at the level of governments. Huge money is involved, everything is covered up, you cannot prove anything definitively, and so you can only either believe in this "conspiracy" or not.

The current FIDE President Arkady Dvorkovich, when asked if elite chess players cheat, said that he never doubted the honesty of elite players, because "reputation is their greatest asset", and this looks like the truth. Well, if you don't believe in the conspiracy theory...

The question to Dvorkovich did not appear out of the blue. As I already mentioned, during the worldwide COVID lockdown, people flocked to online chess *en masse*, from top grandmasters to untitled amateurs. Leading chess portals, such as lichess.org, chess.com and others, started to use strict cheating detection measures, checking if the players made too many engine first-line moves.

And, believe it or not, they caught several cheaters per day. Can you imagine? Logic dictates that those were precisely the players who would have cheated in over-the-board tournaments as well if there were no threats of harsh punishment.

Interestingly, they used engine help even in tournaments with a prize fund of \$5–10, even in tournaments with no prize at all. The player simply can't help but cheat, they're sick, what do you want from them? There are a lot of kleptomaniacs in the world, after all. And, by the way, kleptomania is a true mental illness: the person simply can't help but steal!

> *A rich amateur recently defeated Anand in an online simul and then boasted how smartly he used an engine to win. Very funny indeed.*

How can you cheat online? It all began with the simplest possible method: your friend sits beside you at your computer and suggests you strong moves. Then there were special programs, such as Chess Killer, which suggest moves for you or even make them for you. Site admins started to actively detect and ban players who used these programs. Other programs have been developed since, such as "Chess Cheat Bot for Blitz and Bullet"[1] and others. They can be used with any engines, and they can play in various styles, including "human style".

You can insist as much as you like on installing two dozen cameras in the room of an online tournament participant, so that you can view them from every possible angle. The player can even decorate themselves with cameras to look like a Christmas tree. But if a cheating program is installed on their computer, and the player uses it smartly, it's very hard to combat it. Chess players even came up with the term "smart cheating" to describe this phenomenon.

---

[1] Superfast chess where players get less than 2 minutes for the whole game (the most popular control is 1 minute per game).

And to top it off, here are some posts from an open chat where cheaters freely discuss the best ways of using the Chess Killer app: the pros, the contras, the pitfalls. And this was written way back in 2008! In the subsequent 16 years, the "science of cheating" has taken huge strides!

T374, weak club player:
"I'll share my experience of using [Chess] Killer 1.71 (with the Rybka 3 engine). I managed to obtain a 2980 rating on Playchess in two weeks. My user name was ELDER MASTER. They banned me afterwards, but, of course, I still play there under another user name ☺."

Kevin, resident:
"Of course you can do that if you're careful. If you adhere to the 'smart cheater's rules', as I call them: do not gain a lot of rating points in a short time; sometimes play without an engine and even lose on purpose; do not open any other windows during play; set a small lag for the engine, so that it doesn't spend exactly the same amount of time on all moves; rename the file from 'internet chess killer.exe' to 'winamp.exe', for instance, and, of course, rename the engine file too (from 'Fruit' to 'tb gen', for example); use a relatively weak engine such as the old Fruit; occasionally move your mouse so that others don't see "Inactive" status; try not to play against grandmasters – there are too many spectators who may suspect something; do not play against Germans, because they don't like Russians in general and accuse every Russian opponent of every sin they can come up with; try mostly to play with pawn-rank opponents (this lowers the probability that they have a serial number and can send the game to an administrator for analysis, and, in addition, they aren't likely to file a complaint with such a low rank); occasionally send applause and nice evaluations to players and notify them, be polite in the chat, give your opponents rematches and sometimes lose to them so that they continue playing; do not use engine opening books (such as Hiarcs 12.1), otherwise the program will make moves instantly, which doesn't exactly look like human play; play diverse openings, without repeating yourself much, and even use novelties, because it's sometimes useful to surprise your opponent in bullet; you can also make the opening moves yourself and then switch the engine to autoplay and just sit there, drink tea and watch the battle unfold; you can (and probably should) install a virtual machine, which is almost ideal for a professional cheater, and launch [Chess] Killer from it. That's about all. I may have forgotten something, but not much. Experiment and play! Good luck!"

Therefore, the main question of the last few decades is "Will chess die because of cheating?" Online chess certainly will, but over-the-board tournaments will survive for a while if serious anti-cheating measures are taken. However, serious anti-cheating measures require serious money investments, and the organizers of small opens and round-robins just won't be able to afford them. By the way, many players ask: why can't we just install jamming equipment in the playing hall? I asked the same question to people in the know. It turns out that jammers are banned by law in most countries. Because you can accidentally jam the signals outside the playing hall, in some adjacent building, and if someone has a heart attack in that building and won't be able to call the ambulance, the tourney organizers will be blamed for their death.

Besides, the clumsy, unwieldy FIDE machine simply can't keep up with technical progress. Tell me, just tell me how you can catch a person who receives computer help through smart contact lenses that were invented recently? They are put directly into your eyes, and nobody but you sees what information you receive on them. By the way, manufacturers of these lenses announced that they will soon be available on the open market.

There is also some talk about implanting a chip under a player's skin to receive outside help. But this is only a rumor as of now. Of course, organizers with their obsolete metal detectors won't be able to find either lenses or chips.

That's all, folks. Chess is doomed.

Let me finish at that.

Acting in a musical at the Gnesins Russian Academy of Music, Moscow, playing the role of an orchestra conductor, 2011. Photo by Y. Manakova

Made in United States
Orlando, FL
04 July 2024

48599117R00159